UNDERSTANDING TELEVISION TEXTS

Dedicated to Helen, and to my parents

UNDERSTANDING TELEVISION TEXTS

Phil Wickham

Publisher's Note

The moving image is an integral part of our daily lives, representing an increasing share of our cultural activity. New generations of students know the moving image more intimately and more intensely than their predecessors, but are not always well served in relating this experience to the academic study of film and television.

'Understanding the Moving Image' is a series of short texts designed to orient the student new to the formal study of screen media. Each book introduces an important topic or theme within the subject. All the books are written at an accessible level, with no assumption of prior academic knowledge, by authors with teaching experience and a passion for their subject.

The series represents the BFI's commitment to making the appreciation and enjoyment of film and television and other screen media accessible to wider audiences. In particular it is useful for the following readers:

- Students of film and media studies at post-16 level;
- Course leaders and teachers of film and media studies in schools, colleges and universities (first year);
- The general reader wanting an accessible introduction to the topic.

In *Understanding Television Texts*, Phil Wickham explores, in an interesting and insightful way, a popular and fascinating topic. We hope you enjoy reading this book and that it helps you as you get to grips with the subject and develop your study of it. If you have any comments please do get in touch by emailing publishing@bfi.org.uk.

With thanks to Stacey Abbott, for her help in the development of this book.

First published in 2007 by the
British Film Institute,
21 Stephen Street,
London W1T 1LN.

There is more to discover about film and television through the BFI. Our world-renowned archive, cinemas, festivals, films, publications and learning resources are here to inspire you.
<www.bfi.org.uk>

Typeset by: Fakenham Photosetting Limited, Fakenham, Norfolk
Cover design: Paul Wright
Cover images: James Gandolfini as Tony Soprano in *The Sopranos* (1999–2007, David Chase, HBO); Kirsty Young as newsreader on *Five News* (Channel 5 Television/Independent Television News (ITN)/ Sky News)

Printed in the UK by The Cromwell Press, Trowbridge, Wiltshire

British Library Cataloguing-in Publication Data

A catalogue record for this book is available from the British Library

ISBN 978–1–84457–172–7 (paperback)
ISBN 978–1–84457–171–0 (hardback)

Preface

Television has been a big part of my life. I grew up watching it in the 1970s and 1980s, and what I saw and enjoyed then has helped dictate my tastes and opinions in later life. Some shows made me laugh, some made me excited and some made me want to know more about the world outside our living room. As an adult I've been lucky enough to get work involving television, for many years as an Information Officer and now as a TV curator at the BFI, and to write and teach on the subject.

I think that TV is fascinating and important because of the way we interact with programmes as viewers and because of the breadth, and sometimes the depth, of its content and what it says about us as individuals and as a society. TV is so firmly established as a fixture in our everyday lives that it is very easy to take it for granted, to think of it as somehow trivial, or to believe that we know all there is to know simply by watching it. This is far from the case – television is a complicated medium and needs careful analysis. Its concepts are complex ones and demand a high level of reflexivity; we need to be aware of our position in relation to what we are watching.

This book sets out to start you thinking about this process and to

A Level modules

For A/AS students the book is an appropriate resource for a number of different modules:

WJEC
– Modern Media Forms
– Media Representation and Reception
– Investigating Media Texts
– Changing Media Studies
– Text and Context

AQA
– Texts and Contexts in the Media
– Comparative Critical Analysis
– Reading the Media (AS)
– Textual Topics in Contemporary Media (AS)

OCR
– Textual Analysis
– Critical Research Study
– Media Issues and Debates.

consider the role of TV in all our lives. I hope that it will be of interest to anyone who watches television. We all engage with TV texts and need to understand them. However, of course, most of you will be studying, or teaching, television in some kind of formal setting. The book acts as an introduction to thinking about television texts by considering the questions the medium raises and providing some historical and critical contexts that might help to build answers to them. It is aimed principally at first-year undergraduates studying the number of 'Introduction to TV' courses that are happily blossoming across campuses in Britain, and at A/AS Level students tackling media studies.

Many thanks go to Stacey Abbott, Wendy Earle and Caren Willig, and to readers who have helped in shaping the book. Also thanks to Steve Bryant for his support, and to my parents, Helen Hanson, Moira Mooney and Bryony Dixon for keeping me cheerful.

Contents

3: **TV fiction**   89
    Theoretical considerations   90
    Characters and performance   91
    Narrative structures   107
    Authorship   118

4: **TV fact**   125
    Factual entertainment   127
    News   146
    Current affairs   160

    Conclusion   164
    Bibliography   167
    Index   172

Introduction: Thinking about TV

This is a book about television – how we watch it and the nature of what we watch. There are many ways to think about television: it can be looked at as a reflection of society, or as a personal activity, a site of technological change, or as a mass communications industry. Inevitably these approaches will influence the discussions in these pages. However, the primary focus will be the qualities of the programmes themselves and our interaction with them.

There is a tendency when studying television to approach it as one amorphous mass affecting its audience. Yet while we can see that TV as a whole is a phenomenon that has transformed culture and society over the last fifty years, our experience tells us that it is far from the brainwashing machine turning out an indistinguishable stream of moronic pap that is sometimes still alleged. We know that programmes are different from each other in all sorts of ways. They are different in style, different in approach, different in what they are trying to do and how they are trying to talk to us, the viewers. We also know that we respond to them in different ways: some make us laugh, some move us, some excite us, some make us think – others of course can bore or infuriate us.

These differences in approach and response will be considered and analysed in relation to particular shows. We need to understand the contexts that create programmes and how they come about. Likewise we need to think about how we are influenced when we watch them – what makes the consumption of a TV programme different to our experience of reading books or seeing films or paintings. Far from becoming morons, we are actively making judgments about programmes all the time: whether we want to carry on watching, whether we care about the characters, and we are thinking about what might happen next.

Most of all we are wondering whether we think the television we are watching is any good or not. Evaluation is seen as a treacherous area of critical engagement but, while there are certainly pitfalls to be avoided, we need to recognise that, as Charlotte Brunsdon puts it, 'we make judgments all the time. Let's talk about it'

(Brunsdon, 1990: 31). To understand television texts we cannot detach ourselves completely from them. This is nothing to be afraid of – we are bound to feel that some programmes really are better than others. What we must do is make sure that any critical judgments are informed ones, that we query every assumption and interrogate every aspect of the text. Television programmes offer up particular kinds of meanings, whether conscious or unconscious, that can be 'read' and we bring meanings to the programmes as well. It is this search for meaning that makes television so interesting and enjoyable.

This book is called *Understanding Television Texts*. The term 'texts' is sometimes considered an academic pretension, used when 'programme' or 'show' would do just as well. I use those words too, but 'text' can be a useful term. A 'text' is the object of study; in television this can be a programme, a series, an episode, a clip, an advert or a promotional link. We can read meaning into all these forms just like we can in a book or a film.

How the book works

This book includes many different textual examples. They illustrate the diversity of the televisual experience, and in some cases scenes will be examined in detail, exploring how they work on us as viewers. While context is extremely important we cannot lose sight of how a programme works as a text in itself, how it encourages us to feel or think, and the contribution of the scene, the moment, the piece of dialogue or the camera position to the whole.

The book is primarily based on the experience of television in Britain, although the importance of American TV is reflected in a discussion of the different structures and approach to the medium in the US. Reference is also made to some American programmes, and case studies and textual examples drawn from them, but these are all shows that are in one way or another part of the television landscape in the UK.

Other television industries have tended to take the lead from British or American broadcasting models and English-language material has held a vice-like grip in terms of international impact. There are a few exceptions: occasionally shows like *Heimat* (Germany, ARD 1984, 1992, 2004) and *The Kingdom* (Denmark, Zentropa/DR 1994) have garnered critical praise across the world; and Brazilian soaps and Japanese animation are forms that have achieved global popularity with particular audiences and markets. While various domestic markets may produce other interesting works in international terms TV is a western, English-speaking medium.

The book is structured in two main parts. The first part will put the 'text' into context by looking at production and the industry and examining how TV programmes are affected by the way they are made and the structures and organisations that create them. The second part looks at ourselves as viewers and how the circumstances in which we watch affect texts and our understanding of them. These circumstances are changing very rapidly and the future may be very different from the television environment we have been used to up till now. Each piece of new technology can change our approach to watching the small screen (indeed it could now be a vast or a minute screen).

The second half looks more directly at the programmes themselves and is divided into 'TV Fiction' and 'TV Fact'. 'TV Fiction' considers how we respond emotionally to characters and the performance of their portrayal. Our understanding of the different fictional forms and their creation alters our perspective on the action unfolding in front of us and we need to make sense of that process. 'TV Fact' considers our relationship with reality when we are watching television. This is a key question, not just in 'reality television' but also in documentary and news. Can we believe what we are seeing? How is it being mediated? How do these texts make us feel about the people and situations that they portray? What do we enjoy about them?

'Factual' has often been thought of as a synonym for true, but contemporary debate from all shades of opinion no longer accepts this to be so. We need to consider the facts presented in news bulletins and current affairs programmes and discuss how they are contested. To this end a full day of news broadcasting is analysed and the creation of the news agenda discussed.

Debates about texts and their contexts are an important area of study. They form what is known critically as a 'discourse' about programmes that locates them within a social framework. Anyone can contribute to this discourse, even if they do not watch the programme. This was the case in January 2007 with *Celebrity Big Brother* (Endemol/C4), where media, public and even political attention became fixated on the alleged bullying of Shilpa Shetty in the *Big Brother* house and the social, racial and personal implications of these events.

Studying TV

Although the book tries to cover a fair amount of ground in thinking about how we look at TV programmes, clearly it cannot hope to be comprehensive. It aims to be a stepping-stone to more defined, critical works and will give you the equipment to venture further into areas of television study. With the help of some references to TV theorists and their work, you should be in a position to begin to understand the terms on which those critical debates are conducted.

Television studies as a critical activity has taken very different forms. It has been influenced by an eclectic range of other academic disciplines, all of which shine a light onto the medium and can create a greater understanding of it. These include history, sociology, ethnography, literary studies and, of course, film studies. Initially the focus was on the effects of TV on those who consumed it. As the medium has matured, studies have tended to concentrate either on the texts themselves (using approaches from literature or film such as structuralism) or on context. 'Context' can be either the audience that watches TV (which remains a rich area of study, bringing in modes of working from social sciences) or the production or institutional background. Clearly text and audience cannot exist without each other, and the tension between them is a fascinating site of enquiry. Much scholarly work in TV (Hall, 1980; Morley, 1980; Fiske, 1987; Ellis, 2000; Lury, 2005) has focused on this, exploring the extent to which we as viewers can make meaning.

The BFI publications *Tele-Visions* (Creeber, 2006) and *The Television Genre Book* (Creeber, 2006) are a logical next step, as they include more details on critical debate. While I will refer to aspects of TV history, and in some places will enter into detailed case studies on aspects of the televisual past, a chronological and detailed overview can be found in *The Television History Book*. To delve further into understanding the questions about audiences and aesthetics I raise, John Ellis's classic studies *Visible Fictions* (1982) and *Seeing Things* (2000) are still very useful, while Karen Lury's *Interpreting Television* (2005) is an essential tool in understanding in general terms how television affects us, and is particularly good on the impact of technology. See the Bibliography for more details.

Most of all, this book should make you think and then question those thoughts. It aims to make us reflexive about our reactions to what we see on screen. To help this process, at various points in the text, as in other titles in this series, there are inset boxes. Some of these will ask you to think about TV as a form, or about your own experience as a viewer. These are headed 'Think about . . .' Others will give further information on critical thinking or on relevant history, without interrupting the flow of the main discussion.

How is TV different?

When we try to make meaning from TV programmes, one question we need to ask is what makes them distinctive to television. How are they television texts as opposed to books, plays or films? These distinctions will be examined in detail, because they work on our understanding of what the text is, or could be. Our responses are guided by a number of external factors but also by aspects of the text itself, not to mention our own individual experiences and predilections. They are also influenced by the nature of the medium, by what Charlotte Brunsdon calls the 'specificity' of TV (Brunsdon, 2004: 230).

One useful way to understand this 'specificity' is to think about the ways in which studying TV is different to studying other cultural forms. Theatre can have the same 'live' qualities as TV, but having living and breathing actors in front of you encourages a very different relationship with the audience. Radio also 'broadcasts' and shares some of TV's forms but is not a visual experience.

Film is the nearest obvious relation to television; they are often lumped together as a subject of study and clearly have similar elements, as both are moving-image platforms frequently based around some form of narrative. However, there are also many differences between the experiences of TV and cinema. You may have studied film before and it is important to recognise that understandings and assumptions about TV programmes need to be different.

As we will see, there are differences in the production process – although there has been considerable crossover of companies, finance and personnel. We must also be aware of a difference of scale and volume, because we are likely to see vastly more TV programmes than films.

Rather than particular billed performances that we choose to attend, TV texts form one continuous stream of product, which we can tap into at any time –what critics Raymond Williams (1974: 90) and later John Ellis (1982: 117) characterise as 'flow'. 'Flow' is an integral part of the experience of TV: programmes made up of related items (or sequences) lead into other programmes and textual matter, and our perception is influenced by our encounters with this mass of material feeding off each other. Williams suggests that 'flow' is 'not the published sequence of programme items but this sequence transformed by the inclusion of another kind of sequence, so that these sequences together compose the real flow' (Williams, 1974: 90).

Similarly most of the films we see will be formally constructed in the same way – linear narratives with goal-orientated protagonists that conclude with some form of closure. They will also be almost always fiction, in which actors playing constructed characters and a story that we understand is not real are the focal points of interest. In contrast television delivers a myriad of forms and experiences. Some of these are fictional but others offer actuality or presentation or interpretation of fact. Many programmes do not provide any type of closure but remain open-ended. There are all sorts of radically different genres, from news to reality shows to drama to sitcom, that offer us different meanings and pleasures and need to be understood on their own terms.

The language of film shares many aspects with the language of television. In both, different camera angles are selected and the *mise en scène* (i.e. what is put in front of the camera) is framed to produce particular effects. Texts are edited to deliver meaning to viewers more clearly. Soundtracks complement visual images and help to convey information.

However, there are also considerable aesthetic differences that derive from the small screen and the industrial organisation of TV (the studio environment and its three-camera set-up for example – see Chapter 3). Codes and conventions develop from the audience's

> Film and TV aesthetics
> David Bordwell and Kristin Thompson's seminal *Film Art* (1979) outlines very clearly how the look and sound of a film is constructed. In contrast, TV aesthetics have often been undervalued critically, but in recent years their importance has been recognised. John T. Caldwell's *Televisuality* (1995) explores an increasing complexity in the look and sound of TV, as does *Interpreting Television* (Lury, 2005), and there is an excellent guide to how TV language forms the text in *Tele-Visions* (Creeber, 2006: 38–41).

experiences of the programmes they are watching, that diverge from those they experience at the cinema.

The most obvious difference between film and television is in how TV is consumed. Instead of sitting in a darkened, neutral space set aside only for this kind of engagement, separate from our surroundings, we are in our own environment, with much more control over the medium. We can also change our minds about what we watch. In a cinema we can't suddenly berate the projectionist and ask for *The Matrix* instead of *Shrek*. From the mid-1950s when a mass audience developed, TV has offered choice, albeit initially between just two channels but latterly many more. Chapter 2 will show how the way we watch is vital to understanding television, and technological developments mean that choice is now becoming almost limitless.

The notion that there are film 'texts' – particular works that will bear analysis through their intrinsic qualities – is now well established. *Citizen Kane* (Orson Welles, 1941), *Blade Runner* (Ridley Scott, 1981), *Aliens* (James Cameron, 1986), *Fight Club* (David Fincher 1999) and many others are firmly ensconced in the curriculum and it is accepted that these films have more to offer as objects of study than just as examples of popular taste or symptoms of social behaviour. When we look at these films we might take some account of production process or reception but we will also look at theme, character, narrative and our own emotional responses to what we see on screen. I would argue that we should do exactly the same with TV shows – indeed we make those kinds of judgments and have those kinds of thoughts all the time we are watching. However, received critical option tends to suggest that TV is more transient and banal. Mamoun Hassan proclaimed in the early 1980s that 'television is at its best dealing with concepts, explaining and describing . . . cinema is at its best when it concerns itself with the ineffable, with that which cannot be expressed' (Hassan, Sight and Sound, 1984). He is implying that TV can only aspire to be informative, not to be poetic or 'ineffable' art.

After much debate, film is now firmly established as a medium that can be considered as art. Television as a serious subject of study is still developing, but surely television can be art, if what art does is pose questions about the way we live and the nature of human existence. Like the best films, the best TV programmes can offer insight. Even programmes that are not the best, or do not attempt to affect us deeply, can still tell us much about our world. It is these texts that we will attempt to uncover and decipher, first by looking at the context in which they are created and brought to us.

1 Contexts

This book stresses the importance of the text itself – the meanings we see in TV programmes and our responses to them. It argues that TV texts are complex works of art that comment on how we live and how we feel. Clearly, however, they do not come fully formed from nowhere. To understand a text we have to comprehend both the context in which it is created and that in which it is received. We need to ask how the context affects our experience of the text and the meanings we find there. This section of the book looks at the construction of TV texts by analysing the context of TV production and then looking at audiences and consumption.

1. Production

This chapter examines the following issues:

- *How the different structures involved in television production work and how they might affect what we watch.*
- *Who makes the programmes, both collectively and individually.*
- *The effect of competition and how it creates a certain kind of business environment that dictates the way programmes get made and seen, how this operates on both commercial and public service channels and how they are distinctive.*
- *How the television business offers up its products for 'sale' to the viewer through branding and the schedule. Deconstructing one day's schedule for British TV in detail can reveal how production, consumption and TV business interconnect and influence each other.*

Case studies will be used to clarify how organisations and structures affect what we view.

Television programmes are not dreamt up by artists in garrets; rather they are conceived by a large and powerful industry, demand the labour of many people and need considerable financial investment. They are transactions within a business that is subject to forces of economic change and has a number of interconnected functions – production, distribution and transmission. This business is made up of competing companies. Competition for customers (viewers, subscribers or advertisers) creates a dynamic commercial environment. This has been the case in most territories throughout the medium's history, even if, as in Britain and many other countries, there has been a large broadcaster supported by, or representing, the state. The intensity of this competition has increased significantly in the last ten to fifteen years as technological and regulatory change has dismantled some existing structures and offered different delivery systems and programme choices. One outcome of this change has been that a medium formerly based on the national is increasingly becoming transnational, building businesses across boundaries rather than being confined by them.

Theories of production

Critics have always alleged that the nature of production influences the texts that are produced. As early as the 1950s the Marxist thinkers of the Frankfurt School (German émigrés based in the US such as Adorno or Horkheimer) saw television as a form of mass production selling a cultural view of the world that reduced people and ideas to the lowest common denominator. As a 'mass medium' that aims to appeal to the majority, and is accessible to all, television has often been considered a kind of 'opium of the people' (as Marx described religion) turning people into gibbering fools, slumped on their sofas in front of an indistinguishable flickering mass of unchallenging but insidious images. Throughout its history TV has been accused of corrupting people, or at least inhibiting their thought, and there is concern that children watch too much, and that it is detrimental to their development. Pressure groups like White Dot blame television for all kinds of problems (for example, 'Child obesity! Why is no one blaming television?') and encourage people to 'live' by getting rid of their sets (<www.whitedot.org>).

This view of television – encapsulated through its once popular moniker of the 'idiot box' – has proved enduring for critics of both left and right. Lately, reality shows like *Big Brother* (Endemol/C4 2000–) have been the focus of this kind of criticism, with claims that TV is a malign, moronic social force. It is important to remember, however, that such allegations have always dogged the medium. A similar debate took place over the variety shows of the 1950s. Television's place in the home and the extent of its potential influence have ensured that it is often demonised for its social and cultural role – you will be familiar with the charge of 'dumbing down', but many earlier critics considered TV intrinsically 'dumb' and dangerous in the first place.

Equally the reach of TV means that it is seen as politically culpable in a way that film, which demands that viewers make an active choice to leave the house and go somewhere else, is not. This has expressed itself in occasional panics about sexual or violent content, or of a more generalised moral breakdown through influenced behaviour (as discussed in Chapter 2). It also means that TV is contested as a mouthpiece for political groups. Needless to say this can work both ways. There has been a long-held view by the right in both the USA and UK that individuals with a liberal-left agenda or a dubious moral worldview control TV, and indeed the entertainment industry as a whole (see <www.mediawatchuk.org> for a British example).

On the left it has been argued that television sends out messages supporting the system, which, whether we like it or not, enter our consciousness, influencing the way we think. Italian Marxist Antonio Gramsci characterised this process as 'hegemony' – the way in which the masses come to accept their oppression by those in power. In the opinion of cultural theorist Stuart Hall, this happens because 'the dominance of certain formations was secured not by ideological compulsion but by cultural leadership' (Hall, 1980: 85). Like the Frankfurt School (Adorno and Horkheimer, 2001: 41–72), left-wing cultural critics such as Pierre Bourdieu (1998) and Raymond Williams (1974) have seen this hegemony as inextricably linked to the big-business structures that define the television industry. To them these structures inevitably mean that the texts they produce reinforce capitalism and social control. But what are those structures, how do they operate and how are they changing?

Production structures

Television productions are created through different organisations. The structures they go through can vary in number or complexity but in essence all productions take a similar road from idea to screen. Projects are commissioned, then shot on location or in a studio and are either transmitted live or undergo a post-production process prior to broadcast. The nature of that road has changed considerably, however, and to understand the production contexts it is important to look in detail at the type of organisation involved, the constraints and opportunities involved in the process, and delve into some developments in television history. There are different levels of structure within TV: broadcasters/networks, channels, production companies and individuals. They all interconnect and the relations between them can vary in the formation of different texts.

Broadcasters and networks

At highest level of the TV hierarchy is the broadcaster, or network, as it is referred to in the United States. This is the body, or corporation, that controls the output on a channel or group of channels. It may exist as a chartered state organisation (like the BBC), a public limited company floated on the stock exchange (such as ITV today) or a limited company. Some networks are owned by multinational corporations, not always run from the same country (for example, CBS is partly run by Japanese electronics giant Sony), and as economies become more globalised this is likely to be a common feature of media industries.

Broadcasters in the UK

For the first fifty years of television as a popular entertainment form in the UK, broadcasters controlled and defined most aspects of TV. The British Broadcasting Corporation (BBC), an amalgam of various radio companies, was made a publicly owned corporation by Royal Charter in 1927. The BBC started television broadcasts (to a limited range in London) in the 1930s and then restarted services after the war with national coverage, being sole television provider until the advent of its commercial rival Independent Television (ITV) in September 1955. Prior to the

British TV History
For detailed studies on the history of TV in Britain, both institutional and creative, look at some recent publications, including:
British Television Drama: A History – Lez Cooke
ITV Cultures – edited by Rob Turnock and Catherine Johnson
The Television History Book – edited by Michele Hilmes

launch of Channel 4 in November 1982 (see case study on page 34) the British TV industry was structured as a duopoly (a monopoly controlled by two competing organisations, essentially offering only one choice to the consumer) between the BBC, the national state broadcaster for television and radio, funded by licence-fee payments from viewers, and ITV, then a network of federated regionally based commercial companies funded by advertising and controlled by shareholders.

The regional structure of ITV, which lasted until it became one company in 2004, allowed the industry to expand outside London, creating important production centres in Manchester, Leeds and Birmingham in particular (although smaller centres such as Norwich and Carlisle also produced hit shows). However, although there were several different companies, they only competed with the BBC, not with each other, as they were the only commercial broadcasters operating in their region. Competition among these commercial companies came only in the supply of programmes for national transmission, for it was national controllers that dictated the content of most slots on ITV, which were broadcast across the different regions.

The duopoly

Under the duopoly, production was overwhelmingly operated in-house by the BBC or the ITV companies. They owned studios, post-production facilities and employed technicians, script editors, producers and directors as full-time staff. This meant that the broadcaster had, in principle at least, full control over the creative process. This had its disadvantages: ideas were vulnerable to political pressures within the organisation; it was hard for voices outside those structures to get heard; and there was only one alternative source of employment for talent who wished to work elsewhere. The perceived iniquities of the duopoly were the prime reason for the creation of Channel 4 and its very different approach to a more pluralist form of TV production, with a range of different programme providers.

However, others have pointed out, particularly with hindsight, that the duopoly did have many good effects. As Chris Dunkley suggests, the BBC and ITV could withstand, and to some extent support, each other:

> The BBC learned how to make more popular programmes to withstand ITV's onslaught on the ratings, while ITV taught itself how to win not just big audiences but the sort of prestige which had hitherto been the monopoly of the BBC. (Dunkley, 2000: 8) online reference www.bfi.org.uk/features/tv/100

Certainly the lack of intense commercial pressures had an impact on some texts. A culture developed at the BBC (notably in drama) and also at ITV (especially in documentary) that allowed creative talents to develop their skills over time and encouraged experimental ideas. It manifested itself in a willingness to screen innovative work, to allow programme-makers to develop their own voice and address and challenge the audience. This led to thought-provoking social dramas like *Cathy Come Home* (BBC 1966), experimental dramatic work (for instance, *Penda's Fen*, BBC 1974) and factual programmes that questioned the existing order and the establishment (*World in Action – Who Bombed Birmingham?*, Granada 1989). Programmes that later became huge popular hits were allowed to develop slowly and build up an audience gradually by word of mouth.

If the environment began to be challenged by Channel 4, it changed utterly following the 1990 Broadcasting Act, which started the process of deregulation in British TV.

British broadcasting today

The possibilities of satellite television were exploited by Rupert Murdoch's Sky Television, which built up a subscriber base through acquiring sports and film rights, taking over its rival, British Satellite Broadcasting, in 1990. The expansion of cable and satellite, followed by the rapid advance of digital technology, overcame the limits of the analogue spectrum and now companies can deliver a dizzying range of channels. More choice in delivery systems and service providers, as well as product, has inevitably weakened the power of the broadcaster. Until the early 1980s there were only two companies and three channels to choose from and for most of the next decade just one new competitor. Now the open marketplace created by digital makes the industry and its structures much more disparate and fluid.

The familiar identity and status of the network broadcaster competes with rivals who have moved away from the mixed schedules offering 'something for everyone'. The mixed schedule forged a bond between viewer and network and was the way in which the relationship between these two elements was understood.

1990 Broadcasting Act

In Britain the government sets up a legislative framework for broadcasting through Acts of Parliament. These are drafted as 'white papers', consultation documents that are discussed both by interested parties and by MPs in Parliament before the final legislation is ratified by a vote. The 1990 Broadcasting Act is acknowledged as the key moment in the transformation of television culture in the UK and the creation of the digital marketplace. While much less deregulatory than might have been expected from the then Conservative government, it set up the notion of the free market in television, allowing the development of media interests outside the television establishment. The main provisions of the Act were as follows:

- The Independent Television Commission (ITC) was established as regulator, but with different powers to its predecessor, the Independent Broadcasting Authority, which was technically a broadcaster too.
- The ITV franchises were to be auctioned for a ten-year licence. The main criterion was the highest cash bid, although a 'quality threshold' could also be invoked. Ultimately this led to the demise of Thames TV, one of the leading ITV companies.
- Channel 4 now had to sell its own advertising, although there was a safety-net arrangement with ITV.
- Subsidy for ITN (Independent Television News, the news provider for ITV and Channel 4) was ended.
- A 25% quota of independent productions was introduced for the BBC and ITV.

Broadcasters have had to work hard to re-engage with the viewer and invigorate that relationship in a new and very different broadcasting environment. Later this section will look at how the BBC pursued this strategy with some success, and at how Channel 4 maintains a broadcast identity. It is ITV, for decades the most successful broadcaster in the UK in terms of income and numbers of viewers, that has found this process most difficult. Pressures of competition led to the dismantling of the federal structure and the formation of one company (based primarily on the Manchester franchise, Granada). In fact to date this seems to have exposed the company to even more intense commercial pressure from its shareholders and advertisers, as well as rival channels. This has had an effect on the texts made, as the search for ratings means that programmes are quickly dropped from the ITV schedule if they do not perform (for instance, the reality show *It's Now or Never* in August 2006.)

Broadcasting in the USA

It is interesting to compare the very different broadcasting experience in the United States. Broadcasters here are known as 'networks', whose power lies in distribution and programming rather than production. The networks have a national reach through their ownership of affiliate local stations in key areas of population. It is the accumulation of these stations that gives them sufficient power in the marketplace and the network programmes the affiliate's primetime schedule. As in Britain the pattern of broadcasting was determined by radio, but no state broadcaster was established. Two of the biggest radio manufacturers, CBS and NBC, formed two of the three national networks. The newest, ABC, for many years struggled to match its competitors. From the 1950s to the 1980s the network system reached huge domestic audiences and generated additional profits from the sale of hit programmes abroad. Deregulation of ownership by the Federal Communications Commission (FCC) has now created a broadcasting environment close to a free market (although, as we will see in the next chapter, this is coupled with ferocious restrictions on the actual content of the broadcasts).

Networks have become part of the media strategy of corporate giants and are now a delivery system for other brands as much as a brand or institution in themselves. ABC is owned by Disney, while CBS (as a group owned by Japanese electronic corporation Sony) has joined forces with Viacom, owners of Paramount, and NBC is owned by General Electric. Networks are useful purchases for both hardware manufacturers and software providers, as a way to distribute and showcase their product and afford opportunities for cross-media promotion.

The newcomers to the network system are indeed Hollywood studios all: Fox, Warner Bros. and Universal/Paramount. Fox started its own network in 1990 and has quickly become a significant player in television worldwide, with landmark shows such as *The X-Files* (1993–2002) and of course *The Simpsons* (1990–). Fox, as well as being a Hollywood studio, is part of Rupert Murdoch's News Corporation empire. News Corp. owns Sky TV in the UK and the satellite service Star in the Far East, as well as many leading newspaper titles all over the world. The new networks, while still organised through local affiliate stations, are more than ever globalised concerns. The everyday life of Homer and Marge in Springfield now enters living rooms in every corner of the earth. Other Hollywood-owned networks WB and UPN proved less durable (despite hits including *Buffy the Vampire Slayer*, (1997–2003) and in 2006 they merged into the CW Television Network.

> **Think about . . .**
> . . . some long-running US shows you have watched. Consider the way that these texts are constructed and about the choices that may have been made to ensure their effectiveness with audiences. What options might have been rejected and would the programmes have been more interesting if they were less polished?

Inevitably the US networks, lacking the protection afforded broadcasters like the BBC, are vulnerable to changes in technology and in the audience. Faced with unlimited access to content from so many sources, the old commercial broadcasters operating through their affiliate stations could soon become an anachronism. However, despite this, and despite the commercial and regulatory pressures that mean networks tend to play safe, it has proved to be a staggeringly successful revenue model. As long as money is still being made, it is likely to continue.

The lucrative returns from network TV do also mean that expensive shows, expertly produced, will still be made as long as they can be sold. If you are producing and distributing television shows in the US, the Holy Grail is syndication. This means that the programme is sold to stations for non-primetime screening. They will repeat a series more or less in perpetuity, so prices are phenomenally high. This does require a large amount of material, however, and the magic number is sixty-five episodes, the lowest number eligible for syndication deals. The dream of syndication, where big profits can be made, will inevitably affect TV texts in the US. This could mean lowest-common-denominator tactics to gain an easy hit, but it could also mean rigorous quality control to ensure that each episode is perfectly constructed and full of resonance – there are plenty of examples of both in American network history.

Channels

At one time broadcasters and channels were thought to be synonymous. ITV meant the channel ITV, Channel 4 was Channel 4 and so forth. The BBC was an exception, having gained a second channel, BBC2, as far back as 1964. The multichannel era has changed this structure. There is no longer a technical impediment to the number of channels, and broadcasters like Sky have built up their business by having several clearly defined channels under their control. General entertainment channels, Sky One, Two and Three, are supported by others with specific remits (Sky Sports, Sky Movies and so on), which can be sold as elements of a package. The choice can then be extended by additional channels delivering more of the same, so

Think about . . .
Flick through the multichannels on your set-top box. Look out for the ways you think they are trying to target specific sections of the audience through their adverts, marketing and the way in which their programmes are constructed.

Sky Sports 2 might show an alternative football match, a boxing bout or cricket coverage instead of the Arsenal European match on its sister channel. While the various Sky Sports channels offer nothing but sport, different programme styles are used to present it to the viewer, including entertainment and news as well as live footage and highlights. Numerous channels (delivered by cable, satellite or set-top box) can exist either as independent entities supplying specific types of programme (Paramount Comedy, the Sci-Fi Channel) or under the umbrella of a larger brand.

Recently in the TV business this latter route has come to be seen as a commercial imperative for broadcasters – it is now considered necessary to have a 'family of channels' that can maximise a viewing audience, a strategy that terrestrial broadcasters have used as a basis for digital expansion. These channels are sometimes specific in nature (FilmFour for example) but may also appear to offer general scheduling. I say 'appear', because a closer look at their programming reveals that while they may include a variety of genres, many of these channels target a particular demographic. For instance, ITV2, BBC3 and E4 are focused on the under-thirties, while the reruns on ITV3 are aimed at an over-forty audience. In commercial terms this is important, because advertisers can confidently predict that the viewers may be disposed to buy their products because the channel fits their gender or age profile. Thus Nike or Bacardi may decide to advertise on E4 rather than ITV3 (or vice versa for Saga Holidays and life-insurance companies) as they seek to spend their advertising budgets more effectively.

Channel identity is therefore becoming more precise, while the number of channels multiplies. One channel is no longer the only way that broadcasters can reach their audience. The nature of channels beyond the analogue system is complex, however, and can depend on how the relationship with their consumers operates. Some channels rely on advertisers, some on subscribers, some on a mix of both, and some, like BBC3 and BBC4, are subsidised by the licence-fee payer. The movement as a whole, however, is away from 'broadcasting' – transmitting a schedule to appeal to the broadest section of society – towards 'narrowcasting' or appealing to 'niche' markets, whether these are defined by age, race or gender, or just by their tastes. This implicitly excludes large sectors of the potential audience by concentrating on others.

CASE STUDY – HBO

Home Box Office (HBO) is an interesting channel to consider in this context, because it has achieved both critical kudos and commercial success by going against some of these tendencies in modern television. It has built a distinctive brand of programmes and programming that distinguishes its product from other types of television – hence their advertising slogan 'It's not TV, it's HBO'. As well as examining the history and nature of HBO itself, we will explore how that is expressed in the text in one of its signature programmes, the sitcom *Curb Your Enthusiasm* (2000–).

HBO began in the early 1970s in the nascent days of cable TV in America and built up a successful business from licensing Hollywood movies and major sports matches to paying subscribers. Having built up a considerable subscription base, HBO started to invest in high-end TV drama production in the early 1990s. In the last decade it is this work – including *The Sopranos* (1999–2007), *Sex and the City* (1998–2004), *Big Love* (2005–), *Deadwood* (2004–6) and *Six Feet Under* (2001–5) – that has become synonymous with the channel. It is important to recognise how much this reputation, and this work, which includes some of the most talked about and critically esteemed TV texts of recent years, results from the nature of HBO's business. In TV, industry and art work together to create texts.

HBO does not carry commercials on air. It is owned by the Time-Warner conglomerate (which includes Hollywood studio Warner Bros.) but is only one part of their television and film empire. Profits and money for making programmes come largely from the (fairly substantial) subscription payments individual customers have to make if they want to watch the channel. Not only does this free it from the commercial pressures suffered by the networks but from its regulatory constraints too. As people are paying specifically to take its programmes, rather than encountering them unexpectedly in the home, they are not subject to the US government regulator, the FCC, and their puritanical ire. Network TV shows are not allowed to feature four-letter words, nudity or much sexual activity or excessive violence. This makes it hard for drama producers to address adult themes or offer a convincing picture of real life. A daring show that garnered plenty of regulatory trouble such as *NYPD Blue* (ABC 1994–) is still unable to depict the realistic language of New York cops and the low-life streets they inhabit.

HBO has been able to take advantage of this situation. Viewers want to see something of real life, as well as the depictions of sex and violence available in cinemas (not to mention on their local street corner). Creative talents also feel constricted by the regulations and commercial pressures of the network system. They want to use the time and space afforded by the television medium to tell complex stories and develop interesting and ambivalent characters.

As will be discussed in Chapter 3 the long-form series gives viewers plenty of time to get to know the people on screen and to create an alternate reality in which these people live their lives. Soap opera is one way of achieving this, the HBO signature style is another, melding situation, character and building up a labyrinthine structure of interconnected plotlines. All this, allied with the distinctive tone of each programme, engages a set of viewers who become avid fans.

The line 'It's not TV, it's HBO' evokes the kudos of art-house cinema (Nelson, 2006). It claims that what is shown on the channel is the opposite of the ephemeral fluff on the free channels, that instead these shows are meant to last, to be watched again and to be owned as artefacts (DVD box sets). Yet there is something irritating about this branding line, excellent though many HBO productions are. The texts that HBO produce most definitely *are* TV. That's what makes them so good. The complexity and intensity of the ideas would not work as well in any other media; it is the peculiar intimacy of TV and its role in people's lives that mean it resonates with the audience.

Curb Your Enthusiasm

What HBO really means, of course, is that it is not *network* TV, and a closer look at one of its best-known shows illustrates why this is the case. Unlike most of the HBO programmes listed above, *Curb Your Enthusiasm* is a sitcom rather than a drama. It is the creation of Larry David, a writer who is famous in network TV as the creator of *Seinfeld* (NBC 1990–8), the top-rated show of the 1990s, and who stars as himself in the show. *Curb Your Enthusiasm*, however, would never be a network show, despite David's pedigree.

The obvious reason is one of content, particularly language. Four-letter words are common in the show and indeed one episode features a fiesta of swearing containing every obscenity under the sun. There are also full and frank discussions of the characters' sexual foibles. There is more to the distinctively non-mainstream character of the show than this, however. The lines between reality and fiction are made hazy and complex. Larry David plays a version of himself, also called Larry David. Unlike the vehicles for early TV comedy stars Lucille Ball or Jack Benny, who played characters that used their personas but were not identified as the 'real' them, this is the actual Larry David who wrote *Seinfeld*, albeit portrayed in a less than flattering light. The aesthetic of the programme is also distinctly low-tech, much removed from both high-end drama gloss and the (still) norms of the US studio sitcom. There is one roving video camera tracking Larry's day and the lighting is stark and harsh. No studio audience or laugh track is in evidence, upsetting the norms of how TV comedy is still defined in the US.

Most of all the tone does not fit the network. The series is based around Larry's failure to cope with the rigid social codes of LA life. His awkwardness, selfishness, but also his honesty, bring him into conflict with almost everyone he meets, usually in the most excruciating way possible.

This humour is too uncomfortable for mainstream appeal. It develops some of the ideas David first raised in *Seinfeld* but takes them much further. David acknowledges this, citing one episode involving Larry falsely claiming to be an incest survivor to get out of an embarrassing situation that would 'never have got near a network' (David interview on DVD of Season 1). Comedically it is entirely justified, but the juxtaposition of comedy and abuse, whatever the treatment or context, would be too much for the networks to risk.

Within American TV the existence of HBO allows *Curb Your Enthusiasm* to exist. The freedoms that come from being a subscription channel allow David to extend

Larry David's humour works by making the audience uncomfortable

his range and push the boundaries of situation comedy, raising complex ideas about reality, form and the individual in society in the process. Once given this freedom, the skill of the piece is such that viewers support the show, and while its audience is not large, it is loyal. Word of mouth from viewers increases the audience base and encourages a commitment to the text, so that fans buy DVD sets. HBO *is* TV, but a different type of TV that is a move away from casual consumption. The phenomenon shows that TV texts and the way they are consumed are linked to how they are produced and the channels that create them.

Production companies

Producers in the UK

The importance of the production company is a relatively recent phenomenon in Britain. There were some notable exceptions, programmes made from the 1950s to 1970s, often made by independent producers on film as co-productions with an eye to international sales. These included adventure serials like *The Adventures of Robin Hood* (ATV 1955–9) and Monty Berman's ITC productions such as *The Saint* (ITV 1962–9) and *The Champions* (ITV 1969–71). Oliver Postgate's Smallfilms also made several much-loved animations for children in this period. Largely, though, television was produced by large integrated companies that also distributed and screened the material.

2003 Communications Act
The main provisions of the Act were:

• Plans for analogue switch-off so that TV becomes entirely digital
• Establishment of OFCOM as a 'super' media regulator
• Deregulation of the laws of media ownership, allowing a single ITV company and opening up the possibility of foreign ownership, and of Rupert Murdoch's companies investing in terrestrial TV (which finally occurred in November 2006 when Sky bought a stake in ITV).
• 25% quota was renewed and production companies were allowed to retain rights and sell their formats and programmes.

However, as Channel 4 became established as a market for programmes of many different genres, a thriving independent production sector became established in the UK. Many of these companies were run by proven programme-makers, who valued the independence that allowed them the freedom and ability to exercise their own judgment.

Successive Broadcasting Acts ensured that both ITV and the BBC were also forced to open up at least 25% of the output to the independents and not just commission in-house. Since the 2003 Communications Act the landscape of production has changed once more as the plethora of smaller companies that served the early days of Channel 4 found it difficult to produce work and break even on the smaller budgets that digital channels offered. The result has been a succession of mergers creating so-called 'super indies' such as Ten Alps and talkbackthames, whose fortunes are inextricably tied to sales of their programmes and formats now that legislation has wrested rights and profits from the broadcasters.

Some companies have been floated on the stock exchange and several of them (for instance, Endemol and Tinopolis) are umbrellas for different production 'brands'. Some producers have decided that running their own production company is no longer the route to flexibility and creative control. Documentarist Denys Blakeway sold his Blakeway Productions to Ten Alps because he hated being a businessman and was not able to concentrate on making programmes (source: *Broadcast* 28 May 2004). Managing to retain the brand and creative control within a large corporation meant that the endless pressure of eking out budgets and bidding for commissions to ensure the survival of a small company was lifted.

Some production companies maintain a general slate of commissions. Increasingly, though, companies have concentrated on providing specific types of programming. This builds a reputation for future commissions and achieves an economy of scale. Optemen TV, for example, primarily makes cookery programmes, while even a giant like Endemol sticks to its successful reality and game-show formats.

Producers in the USA

By contrast, in the United States the production company has long been an important part of the television business. The rise of television in the 1950s took place at the same time as the decline of the Hollywood studios (partly due to antimonopoly laws). The networks began to mirror the role of the film studios, and production companies supplied these new distributors. Ironically, however, many of these producers were the Hollywood studios themselves, who saw TV production as a way to diversify and protect their profit margins. Thus many successful US shows have been, and continue to be, made by Hollywood giants like Paramount (*Star Trek* franchise 1967–), Universal (*The Rockford Files* 1974–80), Warner Bros. (*Friends* 1994–2004) and Fox. Increasingly programme-making involves collaboration between these studios or corporate giants and smaller companies who creatively develop the series. Thus Fox helps produce *The Simpsons* for its Fox network but the primary creative impetus comes from Matt Groening and his company, Gracie Films.

The concept of greater creative control, and also the greater likelihood of a profit for producers, was grasped early in American television. *I Love Lucy* (CBS 1951–9) was a vehicle for the talents of comedienne Lucille Ball, who played the madcap housewife Lucy, opposite her own husband, musician Desi Arnaz. The series has a huge cultural importance as one of the defining TV shows of all time, setting the template for domestic sitcom. Industrially it was immensely significant too, however. Ball and Arnaz insisted that they produce the show through their own company, Desilu Productions, in Los Angeles on film, rather than through the New York studios. This was eventually agreed, the couple gaining complete ownership of the series (and thus ultimately a massive fortune) in exchange for taking a lower fee initially and covering some costs.

With a model like Desilu, production companies unsurprisingly became an integral part of the structure of American television, although the power that derives from being the hub of creative ideas is tempered by a reliance on the networks to deliver the programmes to homes. This has been, and still is, a cut-throat business. Shows will often be cancelled after a few episodes if ratings are not high enough. Years of development, months of script work and shooting and millions of dollars can be wiped out at the drop of an email. Naturally this is a system that encourages producers to

---

The example of RDF

One of the most successful production companies in recent years has been RDF, founded in the early 1990s by businessman David Frank. Starting out as a producer of serious documentaries, often on scientific subjects, the company began to take off when former BBC producer Stephen Lambert joined as Director of Programmes in 1998. Since then its output has been a mixture of authored documentaries, such as Adam Curtis's study of consumerism, *The Century of the Self* (BBC 2002), and formatted factual programmes.

Many of these have achieved spectacular success for Channel 4, notably *Wife Swap* (2003–) and *Faking It* (2000–4). These are high-concept, flexible formats that can be easily adapted. As we have seen, following the 2003 Communications Act, companies could retain the rights to their own programmes and ideas, rather than handing them over as part of the contract with broadcasters. RDF's greatest triumph has been in pursuing this opportunity relentlessly, and in retaining control of its product. It has made American versions of its hit format shows and launched a subsidiary, RDF Rights, to make money from its creations, floated on the alternative stock market, and acquired a number of smaller production companies that have been placed under its umbrella. Frank and Lambert's success comes in part from the qualities of the texts themselves, but also from their exploitation of the new broadcasting environment. Production companies can now have a much greater degree of power and RDF have exerted its rights of ownership to improve its market position, establish itself as a 'super indie' and deal with broadcasters from a position of strength.

play safe and provide something familiar enough to elicit an instant response that keeps networks and advertisers happy. It takes a resolute network to take a decision to wait and see if audiences grow and keep commissioning production companies to take risks in the hope that a programme's worth will eventually be recognised. Fortunately NBC did just that with *Seinfeld* and *The Office – An American Workplace* (2004–).

The business and structural organisation of television influences the form that TV texts can take. They are products of their place and time and the economic demands of the media industry. It is important to recognise that they are commissioned to a specific brief set out by the channel. A show has to fill a particular time slot, complement the programmes around it and adopt a tone of voice appropriate to its environment. This will vary according to who is commissioning the text. Producers will make a different kind of programme for HBO than for a US network, and shows like RDF's *Faking It* would feel different if made for the BBC or ITV instead of Channel 4.

This is also the case if the series is sold to other territories. While some texts can translate directly across cultures with the original series being shown unaltered, it is more common for a home-grown version to be made based on the imported format. Even if the format is the same, the tone is likely to be altered through transference to another culture. *Who Wants to Be a Millionaire?* (Celador/ITV 1998–), *Big Brother* and *Survivor* (Planet 24/ITV 2001–2) are just some of the programmes that have been through this process, changing their character in different territories.

Technology and TV language

Other parts of production practice, apart from companies and organisations, matter too. Technological resources and the way these are used develop the language of television and play a very important part in how we understand the programmes we watch. The next section of this chapter examines some of these key issues.

> Think about . . .
> . . . how a particular programme (*Faking It*, or choose your own example) might be different on another channel. Would it use the same material or format? (in *Faking It*, for instance, the activity or the type of contestant might be different). The programme might be edited in a more traditional style if it was on a channel with an older demographic like ITV1, or have more educational content if it was on a licence-fee-funded channel like BBC2.

Recording

The status of television was shaped early on by its transient nature. Broadcasts could only be captured beyond their transmission if an expensive film crew was employed to shoot the performance in addition to the studio cameras, or a film camera was trained on the TV set when it was broadcast. Plays on television were often performed live and any subsequent transmission would involve simply reassembling the cast for another go (Jacobs, 2000: 83). Consequently very few studio programmes from the 1950s survive and the output remaining from this key period includes a smattering of adventure serials, filmed news reports (but not the presentation) and the occasional light entertainment show. Until the widespread availability of recording technology at the beginning of the 1960s, this transience was a major disadvantage for the medium: after all, how could you take something seriously if no trace of it remained?

From the early 1960s (twenty years before consumers began to tape programmes) broadcasters at least had the facility to keep their own programmes, although notoriously they often failed to do so.

From the late 1960s, programmes no longer had to be made or performed live, because video recording also made video editing possible. Shows could be shot out of sequence and assembled from footage by an editing team, allowing programme-makers much more creative freedom. This freedom increased further when digital editing techniques arrived in the late 1980s, offering endless possibilities for revision and freeing programme-makers from the tyranny of physically cutting videotape. It also allowed the editing process to stay under their control: as technical demands ease, so creative possibilities increase. In recent years a new editing style has developed, aided by these advances. As in film (and possibly derived from the style of MTV), the tendency now is to cut much more, creating a greater number of shorter scenes. This has greatly influenced the way we view (Nelson, 1997: 24).

Cameras and film and video

The very cameras that are used in television had an enormous influence on how programmes looked. Most programmes were made on tape or live in the studio using three or more cameras – unlike the single-camera style that predominates in cinema. These studio cameras were initially incredibly heavy and had limited mobility, spawning a relatively static look on the screen. It was unfeasible to use them outside, so any location shooting had to be done on film, which used lighter equipment. As film was not only more expensive, but under the stringent union rules of the pre-Thatcher period necessitated an entirely different camera crew, some programmes frequently had only a cursory film insert or no external shots at all.

Missing believed wiped

As recording technology developed, broadcasters could theoretically preserve their programmes for posterity. However, during the 1960s and early 1970s tape costs were astronomically high and it was deemed economic to record over programmes to reuse the tape. TV was still considered, even by some of its institutions, as a transitory medium of momentary pleasures rather than one producing lasting works of art. Thus it was entertainment programmes and drama that were often lost in favour of news and 'important' works of high art. As the importance of TV talent became widely recognised, it was realised that some milestones – Bob Dylan's appearance in a drama, *The Madhouse on Castle Street* (BBC 1963), Peter Cook and Dudley Moore's shows, episodes of *Steptoe and Son* (BBC 1962–74) and *The Likely Lads* (BBC 1964–6) – had been lost. In recent years there has been a major push to try to rediscover some of these lost gems, both by the BBC and the British Film Institute, who instituted a scheme called 'Missing Believed Wiped', seeking out copies made at the time by the crew, filmed from TV sets or acquired by collectors. This has been extremely successful and many items have been found and restored – perhaps most famously the 1970 series of *Steptoe and Son*, painstakingly made watchable again from tapes on a long-obsolete format found rotting in writer Ray Galton's basement.

At the height of the so-called 'Golden Age' in British TV drama (approximately the 1960s and 1970s), single-drama producers would green-light a small number of scripts for their slot (*Play for Today*, for example) to be made on film, with the understanding that the other commissioned plays would be made on tape (Shubik, 1975: 113). As well as lower budgets, scripts would have to be written or adapted to conform to the demands of studio shooting, with very limited outdoor scenes and a curb on any costly effects. This created a particular kind of text, often with a claustrophobic, intense feel, where the emphasis was on dialogue and close-ups of the actors. Film and video look very different – the harsh lights of the studio contrast with the grainy, more naturalistic images shot on film.

In factual television the arrival of electronic news-gathering equipment in the late 1970s revolutionised news broadcasts, allowing reports to be filed and pictures to appear within minutes rather than hours straight into the viewer's living rooms. Instead of filming the event and then processing and cutting the footage, signals containing the image could be sent to studios and edited easily. Again production technology was transforming texts, enabling them to create a much more dynamic and efficient relationship with the audience.

As camera technology has developed, particularly with the rise of digital, lightweight equipment, there is much more creative freedom to shoot whatever the story demands – even effects that would have seemed ludicrously ambitious and unachievable thirty years ago can now be computer-generated with relative ease. The studio production process has also moved on: there is usually now just a single camera and a new aesthetic has developed with this mobile, light equipment. US shows like *NYPD Blue* (20th Century Fox/C4 1993–), *ER* (NBC 1994–) and later in the UK *This Life* (World Productions/BBC 1995–7) inserted the viewer into the action through constant camera movement, creating a gripping, anxious mode of address and a range of perspectives. This style has also been used effectively in documentary. An interesting survivor of older practices is soap opera, where the sheer volume of text still makes studio set-ups practical and economic.

Reception

While production techniques and practice have influenced the way we watch, the way we watch has also influenced production. It is important to remember in the age of high-definition and plasma screens that the technical attributes of television sets were fairly limited right up until the 1990s and the quality of the image was frequently extremely poor. TV sets took a long time to warm up and then frequently offered a fuzzy image that was difficult to tune precisely, often necessitating moving an aerial around to get a watchable picture. The analogue signal depended on your position in relation to the transmitter, so that people living near large hills or buildings such as steelworks had great trouble with their reception. At times of high-pressure weather systems, those of us that grew up near the south coast got used to watching TV with French television pictures superimposed on top of the British channels.

In such circumstances, and with the pictures transmitted on small screens, an aesthetic developed that avoided complex imagery in favour of clarity. That is not to say that some programmes were not visually inventive but it was undoubtedly a consideration – texts were not being made for ten-foot screens in glorious Technicolor but for an environment where details and grandeur might be lost. Technological improvements and the digital age have created new possibilities for the role of the image within the medium. It is rather like the advent of colour television (from the late 1950s in the US and the late 1960s in the UK), which allowed a whole new approach, including creating a market for new kinds of programme that relied on colour for their appeal, such as gardening programmes or snooker.

Studio and locations

Sometimes the shapes of texts are influenced by more prosaic production factors. Locations affect our experience of the programmes, as they form the landscape that the characters inhabit. TV is a medium where space is important in the way we formulate our response, whether it be the studio interiors or the streets where the protagonists live. We recognise the street set of *Coronation Street* (ITV 1960–) or 'the square' in *EastEnders* (BBC 1985–); the office space in *The Office* (BBC 2001–3) helps us to understand the pain of thwarted lovers Tim and Dawn; the journey through New Jersey in the title sequence of *The Sopranos* establishes Tony's domain. Yet the locations we see are determined by availability and other factors. Location managers seek out appropriate housing estates and wasteland for cop dramas, and the ability to get council approval or logistical needs may favour one location over another. Sometimes decisions on actions or the look of the text will be decided by the realities of the space. Think how many times plot points in *EastEnders* have hinged on emotional moments on the bench in the square – a case of space working with the text to produce meaning. If that bench were not there (and if we didn't know it was there), then the process of revelation, recrimination and the possibility of the chance encounter would have to be rethought.

Space also means place and it is interesting to consider the settings within TV. Inevitably logistics and travel times play a part and areas further away from production centres can be rather overlooked. In news reports reactions to political developments or shocking events are likely to be gathered as close to the studio as possible to ensure quick delivery. In fiction the situation is if anything worse. As well as production convenience, writers, producers and executives are likely to live around major media centres and can be drawn to texts that reflect their lives.

In Britain this has had a long history. Many of the great sitcoms of the 1970s, for instance, were set in the suburbs of south-west London like Surbiton (*The Good Life*, BBC 1975–8), Norbiton (*The Fall and Rise of Reginald Perrin*, BBC 1976–9) and

Hampton Wick (*George and Mildred*, Thames 1976–9), locations conveniently close to TV Centre in Shepherd's Bush and to the homes of those involved.

In more recent years drama has been even more prey to a limited sense of place. Some drama is London-set (including, of course, continuing dramas like *EastEnders* and *The Bill*, talkbackThames/ITV 1984–) but broadcasters acknowledge that regional life should be depicted too. Unfortunately all British regional life seems to have become represented by Manchester, Manchester and Manchester again. The BBC's main production centre out of London is in Manchester, as is Granada TV, the primary drama supplier for the ITV network. The talent base reared by *Coronation Street* (Paul Abbott and other writers, actors and directors) and a concurrent group of comedy performers (like Caroline Aherne, Peter Kay and Steve Coogan) has formed an important creative pool and naturally they often write about their own communities. Whatever the sources, the dominant position of Manchester in British TV fiction is being endlessly perpetuated. In recent years Manchester-set shows have included: *Cracker* (Granada/ITV 1992–6), *Shameless* (Company Pictures/C4 2004–), *The Street* (BBC 2006), *Cold Feet* (Granada 1998–2001), *Queer as Folk* (Red Productions/C4 1999–2000) *Early Doors* (BBC 2003–4), *The Royle Family* (Granada/BBC 1998–2000, 2006), *Paul Calf* (BBC 1993–4), *Sorted* (BBC 2006–), *Phoenix Nights* (C4 2001–3), not to mention *Coronation Street*.

There are some exceptions, of course. *Emmerdale* (ITV 1973–) and Kay Mellor's dramas are set in Yorkshire and *Doc Martin* (ITV 2004–) uses scenic Cornwall, but some UK areas rarely feature on our screens. What was the last drama you saw set in the Midlands, East Anglia or the Welsh valleys? The less often places appear on screen the more alien they are held to be for the viewer, and something of a vicious circle develops. Long-running medical drama *Casualty* (BBC 1986–) is set in the fictional city of Holby, an obvious substitute for Bristol where it is filmed. Yet no sense of place emerges and the few Bristol accents in the show's early years were quickly excised.

Individuals

People make television. This is, of course, obvious, but it is easy to see broadcasters and TV companies as abstract entities and forget that decisions are made by individuals occupying particular positions. The actions of individuals in power can lead to an industry created in their image, where what they think of as social or professional norms become replicated. Although it might be argued that the media industry is a product of larger forces, like international capitalism, or nationalism, on a day-to-day level these and other forms of control are in the hands of the individuals who work within it.

It is vital then to think about who exactly creates programmes, and indeed who does not. In the UK, people working in television come from a relatively narrow niche of society. As commentators have often mentioned (including Greg Dyke, who as, Director-General, complained that his BBC was 'hideously white'), the representation of ethnic minorities is low. What is also true is that those working in the media are overwhelmingly middle class, and have often been educated at public school and Oxbridge, especially in influential areas like news. A survey by the Sutton Trust in 2006 found that only two of the thirty-three top news presenters in the UK had been to comprehensive school, and just three out of nineteen editors and producers – which means that more than 60% overall have attended independent schools when the national average is less than 10%.

Technical staff are still predominantly male, but increasingly in junior production and middle-management levels, television is becoming a mainly female industry. Again, though, these women are largely from middle-class backgrounds and often young; employment practices in television do not favour working mothers.

Certain dubious working practices that have become part of the industry in the UK work against widening the pool of talent in TV. It has become commonplace for companies to hire young people for months at a time on unpaid work experience. As the practice is widespread, people take these positions hoping that it will help them gain contacts and experience later down the line. Drawn by the supposed glamour of a television career, an endless stream of young people are willing to fill these functions. Often they do jobs that would otherwise be paid rather than having a 'work experience' in the proper sense. In all, 75% of freelancers have had unpaid work experience (source: *Broadcast*).

This affects the programmes in different ways. First, staff are less experienced and less likely to be motivated, as they are not being properly rewarded. Areas like research are often now delegated to work-experience placements rather than professionals on the basis that a cursory trawl on the Internet is easier than informed detective work to find a range of sources or voices. Also the number of people who can afford to work without wages is inevitably low. The system becomes more and more based around a privileged few who can be supported by family or have private incomes, and have somewhere to live while toiling on the set of the latest reality or makeover show. This is hardly a healthy situation, particularly as the people who make television become more and more removed from those who watch it.

Similarly what was once an industry with a high percentage of salaried permanent employees is now

Working in the industry
UK TV industry employment data (source: *Broadcast* – survey published in November 2006 of 1000 workers who responded to a questionnaire):

- 44% of respondents were freelance workers
- 60% of respondents found their job fairly stressful and a further 16% found it very stressful
- 38% worked ten hours a day or more
- 82% did not think the broadcast sector offered a job for life
- Only 32% of respondents were over forty years old
- 91% of respondents were white
- 53% were female
- 68.3% of junior roles were female
- 79.1% of managing director roles were male
- 71% of respondents did not have children, including 84.9% of women.

Ending exploitation?
Recently campaigns have been initiated by freelancers, runners and others at the bottom of the media ladder to rectify this situation, partly through a website called Tvwrap (<www.tvfreelancers.org.uk>). In February 2007 a set of guidelines on work experience was agreed that aimed to end the exploitation of work experience, limiting unpaid placements to one month and advising a programme of workplace development. It remains to be seen if these guidelines will be implemented across the sector, however.

overwhelmingly freelance. Freelance work offers some financial rewards and flexibility but lacks security – rights are few and far between and collective structures are very limited. Sick pay or holiday pay is rarely available – again making life very difficult for those with dependants. Unions were once very strong in British broadcasting, especially in ITV, but attacks by the Thatcher government in the 1980s and deregulation have dissipated their strength. In an ironic contrast, union membership in the American TV industry is still very high, forming one of the most organised sections of the workforce in the country.

Production practices can impact on what we see on the screen. Unhappy employees, or an inexperienced production team, or indeed one drawn from a very limited social sphere may be less likely to make complex or engaging shows. If a programme is commenting on society, it is worth thinking about the credentials of its makers in telling or understanding those stories. Certainly representations behind the camera can influence representations within the programme, and there has been extensive research on this relationship with regard to gender (through the organisation Women in Film and Television) and race.

Branding and marketing

Companies, organisations and people operate within particular structural mechanisms. In most TV cultures (and certainly in the UK and the US), this is based around competition for viewers. Broadcasters, networks, channels and producers are all jostling to maximise their audience, sometimes in terms of pure numbers, at other times in relation to a specific demographic (believed to be the core audience). The competition battle is measured in ratings, conducted through marketing and branding, and seeks the favour of advertisers and subscribers.

Branding and marketing have traditionally focussed on the channel, as much as on particular programmes. Certain programmes are heavily promoted but often this is in the context of the channel on which they are screened. What the adverts say is 'Look, we show things like this. Come to us.' The battle then is to retain viewers, ensuring they watch other programmes on the same channel. The terror of the remote control looms large in the television corporate mind (see page 56). There is now a determination not to let the viewer's attention waver for a second in case they dare to switch channels. Once credits were allowed to roll at the end of programme, but this is now considered to be 'dead time' that needs to be filled with voiceovers or trailers for the next show. Equally the spaces between shows are getting longer, even on non-commercial BBC channels. An ident will be followed by a programme trailer, before a short promo clip extolling the virtues of the corporation (and its new digital options), then another trailer or two before the next programme begins.

Corporate image

Channels used to promote a similar mixed schedule to strive for a broad appeal but there was still a differentiation between them. ITV has always cultivated a more populist, working-class image over a BBC seen as somewhat stuffy and worthy. Naturally the truth was more complex than this upmarket/downmarket characterisation implied – ITV broadcast investigative documentaries (John Pilger's films on Cambodia, for example, in the late 1970s and early 1980s) and the BBC had plenty of game shows and less than classic light entertainment. The point is that there is a common perception of what a channel is like, and at various times channels seek to reinforce or alter this understanding. Channels use programmes to change perceptions or to add to supposed strengths.

An interesting British example is Five, a channel whose (partly self-inflicted) reputation from its inception in 1997 was for downmarket, laddish programming centred, in the words of its Chief Executive of the time, Dawn Airey, on 'the 3 'f's – football, films and fucking'. While this had a certain pull, the image of a channel populated by pole dancers, Steven Seagal movies and obscure UEFA Cup qualifying games created a great deal of antipathy from some viewers and some advertisers who did not want to be associated with downmarket tastes. Over the last few years Five has tried to change its image through programming policy, while retaining its young male audience. Given limited programme budgets, much of this has been achieved by acquiring quality American crime shows like *The Shield* (fx Network 2002–) and the *CSI* franchise (CBS 2000–). However, it has also commissioned some human-interest documentaries in the *Extraordinary People* strand (2003–) that belie their rather sensationalist titles (such as *She Stole My Foetus* or *The Woman with Half a Body*) and built up a reputation for strong visual arts programmes. These documentaries, usually introduced by a young expert called Tim Marlow, are unashamedly highbrow shows that are tied in with exhibitions at major UK galleries. This gives them a cultural currency and kudos that can be transferred to the channel, and the restrained production style adds to a feeling of gravitas about the programmes that Five can use in its defence against the old 'lads' TV' stigma.

Some programmes might fit certain channels and not others. The youthful, glossy protagonists and slick visual style of US desert island survivors' tale *Lost* (ABC 2005–) suits Channel 4's identity as young, vibrant and exciting, and they marketed the series very heavily through a variety of media, until losing the third series in a bidding war with Sky. It might not suit the image other channels wish to communicate, however: at the 2005 Edinburgh TV Festival, BBC2 Controller Roly

Keating stated that he would not have bid for the series, as it was not appropriate for his channel.

In the new ultra-commercial digital marketplace, branding and marketing are seen as essential to preserving fast-diminishing viewing shares (Caldwell, 2002: 253–73). There is evidence that as programmes become 'content', available in different media and able to be consumed at the public's convenience, the idea of channels as we understand them may be superfluous. This fear is keenly felt in the TV industry: hence the notion of a 'family of channels' to maximise viewers. In such an environment the promotion of programmes/content may move away from the channel and be led by certain user groups, who will infect others with their enthusiasm for a show. Chapter 2 will show how modes of consumption are radically changing marketing.

The other consequences of the multichannel environment are channels that offer a much more restricted range of programmes. The hope is that the content works to strengthen the brand naturally, as viewers who like, say, comedy or nature documentaries will inevitably gravitate to the station to see programmes they know they will enjoy. This could be significant for our understanding of television texts, because the danger is that we may watch shows purely because we have seen them before or because they sound like programmes we have previously enjoyed. More than ever, pressure could be exerted on producers to deliver the familiar and predictable, resulting in fewer opportunities to encounter the new and the random.

Marketing campaigns

Already broadcasters have to come up with more and more ways to sell new programmes through a multitude of different platforms. Typically a campaign will now comprise several elements. A set of trailers will appear at the beginning or end of programmes that are likely to have a similar audience, or book-ending the ad breaks in a show screened on a commercial channel. There may also be an extensive poster campaign on streets or public transport that attempts to convince us of a show on the basis of an image or a quote (e.g. 'The funniest show on British TV' – Ricky Gervais for *Peep Show* (C4 2003–). Channel 4 is very fond of this approach, and niche channels like Living or Bravo have adopted it extensively, at least in London. Interestingly these digital channels emphasise the programme (frequently a US import like *The L Word*, 2004– on Living) rather than the channel. The implication is, however, that to access the content shown you need to subscribe to or watch this channel, thus it acts more like a service provider than a traditional TV station. Digital channels also try to identify themselves on screen, anticipating the confusion of the channel-hopper. An ident for the channel will appear in the top left-hand corner telling us that we are watching BBC4 or More4, and sometimes provide further schedule data – in 2006 *The Sopranos* aired on Thursday on E4 with a logo-branded bubble saying 'brand new' and on Sundays with 'another chance to see'.

The new and rapidly expanding personal technologies are increasingly being used to market programmes individually to viewers through text messages, mobile video clips and on the Internet through pop-ups or by targeting people through email lists. All this marketing and branding is interconnected and works as a whole. We might see a trailer and make a positive mental note. An on-screen pop-up or an email from an entertainment list will seek to remind us of our interest, assuring us that it is meant for people like us and providing specific information on how to access it. Frequently there are now many opportunities for accessing shows beyond one weekly transmission. There may be screenings on sister channels or streamed access for a limited period from the company's website.

Ratings

If branding and marketing are the tools of competition, the success of these strategies is measured in the ratings. Ratings are an estimate of the numbers watching a programme gathered from a sample group of the audience. Additional data can be gathered from these groups to provide information about the composition of a show's audience so channels can find out how many women watched, or how many 16–34-year-olds (an increasing preoccupation). Ratings information is regarded as crucial evidence of a programme's success and can dictate whether it has a future at all. Overnights give a verdict on this within twenty-four hours, clarified later by consolidated figures, which include those who recorded the programme and intend to watch it through timeshifting.

How ratings work

In Britain ratings are collected by a company called BARB (Broadcasters' Audience Research Board <www.barb.co.uk>) partly owned by both the BBC and independent broadcasters. BARB was set up in 1981 to bring together two rival ratings systems operated by the BBC itself (through written diaries and interviews) and an electronic system run on behalf of ITV and its advertisers by various research companies over the years. Ratings are now based on sophisticated electronic measuring devices operated by members of the public that can ascertain numbers and types of viewing. What you might find surprising is that the sample is still relatively small in terms of the numbers quoted. A panel comprises about 6,000 individuals selected to be representative of different social groups (an extensive shake-up of the panel and of collection practice in 2002 led to significant changes in the numbers reported). The numbers watching particular shows are extrapolated from this panel and multiplied to reflect the potential national audience – typically a few million viewers.

> Think about ...
> ... how you have encountered a favourite show through marketing and how you have reacted to different aspects of a campaign. How did your interest develop? from? How much did the recent marketing innovations, outlined here, affect your interest? Or were you influenced by more traditional means like newspaper articles?

Broadcasters don't only look at the total figures for a show, important though these undoubtedly are. They also consider elements in the data such as the viewer's age, gender or social class, the TVR figure (the proportion of the total population that is estimated to be watching) and crucially the per-cent share figure, which refers to the numbers watching each channel. The comparative channel shares in particular slots are one of the chief weapons in media competition, proving that rivals are being defeated and viewers retained. Controllers may expect shows to perform better in certain slots – youth shows on a Friday night, for instance – or expectations may be lower if programmes are scheduled against proven audience favourites on other channels (like *Coronation Street* or *EastEnders*).

Sometimes low numbers may be compensated for by other factors. *Ultimate Force* (ITV 2001–6), an SAS drama starring Ross Kemp, never got high numbers but it pleased advertisers looking for a male demographic they thought could otherwise only be reached by football matches. Thus, as Head of ITV Drama Nick Elliott admitted, revenue from car and beer adverts was a factor in deciding whether to recommission or not (source: *Guardian*, 6 October 2004).

Qualitative ratings

Other research work sourced by broadcasters about audience's responses includes Appreciation Index (AI) reports, which indicate how much a show's audience actually liked what it saw. Unfortunately this is not usually published and is regarded as commercially confidential but one would hope it is an important factor in deciding whether programmes are successful. Ricky Gervais has said that he would prefer *The Office* and *Extras* (BBC 2005–) to be 1 million people's favourite show rather than 10 million's fifth favourite and it is a good point. Surely understanding responses is as much about depth (the intensity of the response) as breadth (the numbers responding). In a rare public discussion of the AI index, the then BBC Controller Jane Root recommissioned Craig Cash's splendidly doleful pub sitcom *Early Doors* (BBC, 2003–4), despite only getting initial audiences of just over a million. AI studies had shown that those who watched the show, although a select band, really, really loved it (Jane Root: speech to Royal Television Society, 10 February 2004).

Falling figures

Ratings are also an interesting way of charting TV's rapid change from a mass medium to something rather different. In the 1960s and 1970s, popular shows frequently drew in over 20 million viewers in the UK (over a third of the population). This was not just acknowledged greats like *Steptoe and Son*, *Morecambe and Wise* or the big soaps and Royal occasions; it was also for long-forgotten game shows or minor sitcoms like *Miss Jones and Son* (ITV 1977–8). The fact is that numbers were very high because there were few rival attractions. Not only were there just three channels, there was not a lot else to do other than watch TV –

cinema was in decline, rival home entertainment forms were not yet widely available, the shops all shut at 5.30 and nightclubs and restaurants were few and far between. As a leisure economy developed and new channels appeared, ratings numbers began a slow decline. Only in the last two or three years has that change accelerated: a combined figure for 'other channels' than the terrestrials now have the biggest weekly share and numbers have peeled away from the mainstream broadcasters (ITV's share, for instance, has tumbled from 23.5% in 2003 to 19% in 2006. Source: BARB).

> Ratings history
> You will find details of top-rated programmes in the UK decade by decade at <http://www.bfi.org.uk/features/mostwatched/>. Examine the numbers and the types of programmes achieving high figures and think about why they have dropped in the last decade. Can you think of any other factors that might explain the decline?

There are several possible reasons (including changes in the collection of data) that may be partly responsible for the falls in figures for both channels and programmes, but the two key factors are the large take-up of digital TV through the Freeview digital box (which does not require a subscription) and the Internet's transformation from solely an information medium into an entertainment source.

The consequences have been dramatic for the industry with even proven favourites like the big soaps losing several million viewers a week. The traditional gap between figures for the programmes from the mainstream channels of the BBC and ITV and the so-called minority channels has also changed. Channel 4 now frequently gets audiences of 4–5 million, not just for *Big Brother* but also for some lifestyle programmes and quiz formats like *Deal or No Deal* (2005–) as a number of primetime shows on their mainstream rivals drop below that figure. BBC executive Ashley Highfield stated at the Edinburgh TV Festival in 2006 that in the future only an England World Cup win or a Royal wedding will gain over 10 million viewers, and given the recent numbers it is hard to argue with his forecast (except perhaps over the Royal wedding). The change has been dramatic – in 2003 twenty-seven different titles managed to clear the 10 million hurdle that now seems such an insuperable challenge.

The consequences of ratings

In the US, ratings, collected by Nielsen, are employed in an even more brutal fashion. Once the figures are in from the viewers' panel, action is taken very swiftly with new shows being frequently axed if they are not performing against rival networks. There is heavy pressure from advertisers to deliver numbers so that commercials can be sited in shows perceived as successful. This has long been the case and the emergence of a more complex environment beyond network broadcasting will only intensify this pressure. The new autumn schedule is a particularly fraught time under this Darwinian system, as few survive.

The consequences of the ratings competition on texts are considerable. At the most basic level, if programmes don't garner enough other viewers fans won't be able to watch them any more because they will be cancelled. Fans have on occasions fought for their favourite shows to continue, sometimes successfully (*Cagney and Lacey*, CBS 1982–8, *Prisoner Cell Block H*, Grundy TV 1979–87 and, *Baywatch*, NBC 1989–2001) and sometimes not (*Arrested Development*, Fox 2004–6).

The race for ratings success doesn't only affect those shows that struggle to achieve numbers. The need to maintain channel share also puts pressure on proven popular performers. When a show is clearly a hit, there is a tendency to produce others in a similar vein that can dilute its impact (for instance, the numerous panel shows that came in the wake of *Have I Got News for You?*, BBC 1990–) or to produce more of this winning formula with longer runs, more frequent series and extra episodes.

This has been the case with the top soaps in Britain, which have gone from two, to three, to four nights a week in recent years, and in the case of *Coronation Street*, frequently double episodes on one night. The plan here is to trounce rival channels by ensuring that fans have to keep watching the soap rather than the programmes provided by competitors. The ratings slide for the soaps suggests that this could be a pyrrhic victory, however. The demand for more content on the soaps puts a great deal of pressure on the production teams and on the writers, who have to produce more and more material. It might be argued that this has led to a decline in standards as the need for continued high ratings raises the dramatic stakes. Storylines become more contrived, with a reliance on more sensational 'drama' rather than the rhythms of everyday life that used to dictate the pace of the series, and less emphasis on character.

Advertising

Ratings are, of course, of particular interest to advertisers, who not only want to see their products sold to large numbers of people but also to market their wares to audiences likely to be in a position to buy. Advertising is sold for particular slots. A mass audience show like *Coronation Street* will command higher rates than less popular programmes. Adverts will also be aimed at a supposed (and indeed intensively researched) audience for particular programmes – cars and beer for football, CD releases and trainers for cult youth shows and so on. This also applies to particular times of day: daytime adverts in the UK are noticeably different from those aired at prime time, frequently targeting those with financial problems, for example, or promoting services for the retired and restless, such as Saga holidays.

Commercial channels rely on advertising revenue to survive and advertisers are, naturally, aware of this power relationship. If channels are not delivering the numbers or desirable markets for the advertisers, then the latter can exert pressure for a change of direction in management, scheduling or production. In the US this pressure has always been very clear and the influence of advertisers was evident from the start of broadcast television. In the 1950s it was common for firms to sponsor programmes, including challenging drama strands. Ford and Colgate were among the companies whose names were attached to programme titles (*Colgate Theater*, NBC 1949–58, for instance). Eventually this was seen as too blatant an intrusion of commercial over creative control and the sponsored shows disappeared, but advertisers can, and do, still call the shots. In the spring and autumn seasons when ratings for new shows are revealed, it is advertisers who primarily dictate decisions on whether a series continues or is pulled from the schedules. If advertisers are not happy with the placement of their commercials, and the return on their investment in expensive slots, then the schedule is changed to deliver audiences to products more efficiently.

In the UK the system has been rather less direct. Doubts about the American model meant that the legislation that set up ITV prohibited programme sponsorship in favour of 'spot' advertising – that is, the screening of adverts in batches between programmes and in clearly signalled breaks within them. However, in the early years of the channel there were programmes called admags, such as *Jim's Inn* (Associated Rediffusion 1957–63), in which regulars dropped into the said establishment extolling the virtues of whatever new appliance they had just purchased. The 1962 Pilkington Report into broadcasting was fiercely critical of what it saw as ITV's rampant commercialism, and new regulations banned the admags and set limits on advertisers' encroachment into programmes. The 'spot' model has been adhered to ever since.

One development that was permitted from the early 1990s, albeit within strict parameters, was some form of programme sponsorship – although this did not include an acknowledgment in the title. These are negotiated deals and usually with products seen as compatible with the show's audience: so, for instance, *Heartbeat* (Yorkshire TV/ITV 1992) and Dreams beds; Champions League football and Amstel beer; or *I'm a Celebrity . . . Get Me out of Here* (Granada/ITV 2002–) and Iceland supermarkets (advertised by a former winner of the show, Kerry Katona) . . .

The changing face of commercial TV

The advertising landscape can suddenly change, however. In late 2006 the government and OFCOM announced measures banning the advertising of junk food in programmes children were likely to see. Anticipating enforcement, and perhaps extensions of the ruling, Domino's pizzas and Cadbury's chocolate announced the end of long-running sponsorship deals with *The Simpsons* and *Coronation Street* respectively. In the same period, however, OFCOM announced that it would now be possible to sponsor new channels, so as one door closes another opens for the broadcasters. However, as industry organisations like Save Kids' TV have argued, this kind of decision – well-meaning though it might appear – has important effects, in this case making it uneconomic to produce new children's programmes on commercial channels.

Regulation of advertising
There are still heavy penalties to pay for promoting products (or seeming to do so) within programmes, as Richard Madeley and Judy Finnigan have found out to their cost. In 1994 the then regulator, the ITC, reprimanded *This Morning* for undue prominence of branded products, and in 2003 *Richard and Judy* was rapped for over-promotion of the couple's autobiography (source: ITC/OFCOM).

In the new television landscape it will be interesting to see how and to what degree advertisers exert their influence. Now that technology like personal video recorders (PVRs) allow viewers to skip over adverts if they wish, then TV's worth as a site for advertising will diminish. Commercial TV relied on a captive audience that had to watch the ads to see their favourite programmes. This is not just a problem for advertisers and the firms they represent but for the industry as a whole, because the sale of adverts was very profitable revenue-wise and allowed expensive programmes to be made, even if it carried with it the threat of compromise. It may be that in the future, advertisers will need to be involved in production in some way to get their message across.

The alternative ways of making money in television are from selling programmes to different companies and onto different formats, or, as demonstrated by HBO, to get money directly from subscribers. Or, of course, do both, as Sky does in the UK by charging a subscription fee and carrying spot advertising. Thus the channel subscribers can be addressed as a marketing group as well as being a source of direct revenue. Subscription services are still under pressure, but increasingly this comes from their shareholders. Instead of looking at the money brought in through advertisers, they look at the number of subscribers and particularly at 'churn'. 'Churn' is the difference between numbers of new subscribers and those who have declined to renew and is used as a measure of the effectiveness and success of subscription channels and their delivery systems.

Public service broadcasting

So far we have been looking mainly at commercial television and the extent to which competition and the pressures of the marketplace can affect the programmes that we watch. There is, of course, another type of television, usually known as public service broadcasting (or PSB), which has a different approach to the medium and subsequently has a very different relationship to its audience, closer in many ways but sometimes fraught and controversial. PSB does not operate as part of a free market motivated by profit; instead it embodies the idea that broadcasting is a service for the good of the people in a similar way to healthcare or state education. In Europe and many commonwealth countries PSB developed as a dominant system of TV, and only in the last decade or so has this dominance been seriously challenged.

Although versions of PSB were adopted in France, Germany, Italy, Australia and indeed in the old Soviet bloc, it originated in Britain with the BBC. The BBC enjoys a status as the 'national broadcaster', although it is supposed to be independent from the government, being controlled up to now by a board of governors (to be replaced in 2007 by an independent trust). The corporation, and thus its programmes, is funded by the licence fee. This is a payment made by all UK households who own a TV set, and is currently set at the princely sum of over £130 a year.

The existence of the licence fee has ramifications for the broadcaster and the programmes it makes. As long as it rises with inflation and stays in place, revenue for making or buying programmes is assured and reduces the pressure to produce the instant commercial successes that advertisers or shareholders require. However, as the licence fee is essentially a tax on citizens to watch TV, it acts as a constant source of controversy. Taxpayers understandably wish to make their views on the programmes known and feel they have a personal stake in their production, and government involvement and scrutiny is intense, as the political position of the state broadcaster is somewhat precarious. Ultimately the pressures can be just as great and wider-ranging as those commercial broadcasters face.

The BBC, unlike some PSB stations in Europe such as TVE in Spain, RTE in Ireland, and TF1 in France, does not take advertising. This does not mean that it is not competitive in the marketplace, however: its rivals in Britain are constantly complaining that it has an unfair advantage through its licence-fee funding and allege that its public service position is used to make commercial business decisions and perpetuate the views held by its executives as social norms (for instance, Rupert Murdoch at the Edinburgh TV Festival in 1990 and Paul Dacre, editor of the *Daily Mail* at the Cudlipp lecture in January 2007, who painted a picture of the BBC as a cosy liberal 'subsidariat'). The BBC would counter that its funding gives it special responsibilities to British society and culture. Within the British PSB model, they argue, it is vital that the BBC does not just exist, but is big, popular and powerful. For its PSB requirements to be meaningful, for it to be 'the voice of the nation' and to make challenging programmes, ground-breaking drama and comedy, as well as documentaries about the world we live in, there must be viewers. If viewers turn on to see *EastEnders, Strictly Come Dancing* (2004–) or *Doctor Who* (1963–89, 2005–) they may also watch the more obviously PSB material. However, providing well-made popular shows that people want to see can be regarded as a public service activity in itself. Equally the popularity of these programmes can be used to bring issues into the public sphere, like the domestic violence suffered by little Mo in *EastEnders*.

The BBC likes to position itself as a unifying force in British life, something that binds people together to be entertained or informed. In the face of criticism from commercial rivals (both from other TV stations and media, especially newspapers), it has sought to communicate this view directly to the public on screen and through extra-textual means such as its market-leading website. 2006 saw a programme particularly employed to stress its public service remit and capabilities – the natural history series *Planet Earth*.

CASE STUDY – PLANET EARTH

Planet Earth follows in the tradition of major wildlife documentaries like *Life on Earth* (BBC 1978), made by David Attenborough. Attenborough narrates but is not shown on screen; the images of landscapes and the animals that inhabit them appear without any visible human mediation. The most advanced camera technologies and particularly time-lapse techniques are used to give the viewer a sense of omniscience – we can see the inner workings of nature by controlling space and time. This way we can see deep-water fish wake from hibernation or have a panoramic view of a baby elephant lost on the plains of Africa.

Throughout, the BBC is keen to emphasise the sophistication, scale and cost of bringing the planet to the viewer. The last ten minutes of each edition is devoted to 'Planet Earth Diaries', interviewing the film crew and explaining how different shots were obtained. In TV terms this is relatively unusual – not that many programmes are reflexive and deconstruct how they were made for the viewer. However, the section is designed to do more than just satisfy an interest in the technical wizardry behind the images. It adds value, working very much like extras on a DVD for an audience which has come to expect extra-textual material. Even more than this it assures us that our licence money is being used to bring us the most advanced, most exhilarating pictures possible – whatever it takes.

One of a series of promotional films about the BBC, running on the corporation's own channels, focused on *Planet Earth*. A cameraman explains how he spent days waist-deep in bat droppings just to get a particular shot of the bats in flight. As he finishes his story the slogan 'This is what we do' appears on screen. It tells us that only the BBC is willing and able to deliver these pictures to us. It implies that commercial concerns would not care to engage in such an enterprise on the off-chance that a beautiful and awe-inspiring image may be captured at some point. We are reassured that the public service ethos is still valid, that the BBC is prepared to spend our money investing in time, talent and risk. Promotional films on *The Office* and other progammes tell a similar story, namely that the licence fee is worth it because it funds not just these programmes but an organisation that makes them happen and has the reach and power to do so. *Planet Earth* cost £11 million to produce but the first episode alone was seen by 8.7 million viewers and received ecstatic reviews, vindicating the investment (*Broadcast*, 10 March 2006).

PSB in the USA

The BBC example stands in stark contrast to the American experience of PSB. With an industry forged in commerce, the whole idea of PSB has been viewed with much suspicion in the US. Public television, as it is known, was not allowed until 1967 and since then the political pressures on the very small amount of federal government funding involved have been intense. Indeed much of the funding comes through individuals in televised pledge drives where the public TV stations try to

Planet Earth Diaries tell us how our licence fee is spent

make the most of their generally educated and wealthy viewers (Aufderheide, 2004: 1854–7).

PBS (Public Broadcasting Service) is a national programming service for public stations that now supplies a primetime schedule to most of the 350 public stations across the US, accessible to most of the American TV audience. Some programmes have entered the public consciousness, most famously *Sesame Street* (1969–) the educational show for kids featuring Jim Henson's puppets, but also Ken Burns's landmark documentaries on American history (e.g. *The Civil War* in 1990 and *Jazz* in 2001) and some of the British imported costume dramas billed under the umbrella heading of *Masterpiece Theater*. A screening on PBS affects the nature of the text: on the one hand it becomes defined by its distribution system as exhibiting some kind of cultural status, on the other can be seen as elitist or worthy.

In the new digital broadcasting environment, pressures on public broadcasting internationally will grow ever stronger and in some territories it may disappear completely. The appearance of 'choice' (whether real or not) creates an argument that all needs will be met in a free market; public service providers articulate a counter-argument that we frequently don't know what we want, or need, unless it is provided and we can find it for ourselves.

CASE STUDY – CHANNEL 4
It is useful to see how some of the issues discussed here have worked, and continue to work, in practice by looking in detail at a television institution: Channel 4. Looking at Channel 4's history, present position and future plans, will show how

structures, policy, competition, branding, ratings and the public broadcasting ethos affect the texts produced.

Channel 4 has cultivated a very specific identity within the landscape of British broadcasting, but this identity has changed in response to society and the economics of the television business. The channel has not only reflected change in society but it could be argued that it has precipitated some of that change with the programmes it has transmitted and the practices it has adopted.

The birth

We have already talked about the duopoly that dominated British television from the 1950s to the 1970s. The critics of the duopoly started a campaign for a fourth channel, arguing that it should not just be the second ITV channel but something entirely different that would break the rigidity of the industry. The differing ideas meant a long gestation period and a major report on the concept (the Annan Report, published in 1977) proved inconclusive. However, the new Conservative administration elected in 1979 championed the project, ultimately favouring the idea of an entirely new type of broadcaster and spurning the claims of the ITV companies. Channel 4 was finally launched on 2 November 1982. It was financed through payments by the ITV companies, who were compensated by being able to sell advertising for the channel in their regions, thus freeing the channel from direct commercial pressures in its early years (Bonner and Aston, 2003: 10–11).

The first Chief Executive was Jeremy Isaacs, a legendary programme-maker of flagship documentaries such as Thames TV's *The World at War* (1973–4), and it was Isaacs's vision that set the course of the channel for years to come. The channel was set up with a remit in its charter to cater for minority audiences and to 'introduce new talent, to reaffirm creative alliances, or bring together fresh ones, and to develop ideas for which the existing services have not so far found a place' (from IBA document 'The Fourth Channel: The Authority's Proposals'). Isaacs and his team certainly set out to do just that, committing to innovation but also to a connection with audiences. At a pre-launch speech Isaacs reiterated that 'Channel Four wants to entertain . . . we want in new ways, and good old ways, to entertain. We want for some of the time to reach large audiences. We want to earn our keep' (Royal Institution, January 1981).

Ratings were variable, but some programmes did well. Minorities, from black or gay audiences to special-interest groups as diverse as fans of American football and quilting, were served for the first time. Some programmes had a radical political agenda and this, together with the free use of strong language, created controversy in the newspapers – the *Daily Mail* in particular has been a consistent critic during the channel's twenty-five-year history (including dubbing the then Chief Executive Michael Grade the 'pornographer-in-chief' in the mid-1990s).

The brand

We can see that Isaacs's approach and the path laid down by the remit influenced the texts that it transmitted – often more challenging, they were different to programmes on other channels, and looked to audiences beyond mainstream mass appeal, but they were also likely to be engaging and fun. The texts were also being transmitted in the context of a clear channel identity. Despite their diversity the programmes were being broadcast by a channel marking itself out as new, vigorous and provocative and that affected the way the texts were understood – even relatively conventional sitcoms or lifestyle programmes seemed fresh when juxtaposed against an alternative comedy piece like *The Comic Strip Presents* . . . (1982–8, occasional since) or a youth programme like *The Tube* (1982–7).

Branding enhanced this identity: the multicoloured '4' ident designed by Martin Lambie-Nairn became an iconic image, and indeed throughout the channel's history the image of the '4' has retained its power. Although it has been through many incarnations (at the time of writing, a spectral moving image formed from blocks of flats or electricity pylons) it still communicates a certain cool, a feeling that we are in a place that is interesting and different.

The industry

The establishment of Channel 4 was hugely significant in the way that it transformed production in Britain, while the new modes of production influenced the nature of the texts themselves. Instead of producing its own programmes, the channel acted as a publisher-broadcaster. This meant that it would commission programmes from independent TV producers, using a staff of commissioners for specialised programme areas (Drama, Factual, Youth, etc). This provided the basis of a much more pluralistic TV system, with any number of companies pitching in ideas and competing to make programmes. Over the years this system of commissioning has become the industry norm, as the BBC and ITV have been subject to a quota of independent programming.

How does this system change texts? It allows a wider range of voices to reach the screen because it draws from a bigger pool of creative talent and employs a multiplicity of production methods. Under the duopoly, while there may be more consistency, it is also likely that a particular culture will dominate the organisation, with certain production practices always being used and a house style perpetuated across texts. It would be wrong to think that a commissioning system is not partial, however. Although it opens up the *possibility* of more diversity than if a broadcaster is transmitting programmes made by itself, the commissioner is an individual with considerable power. Programmes can be accepted or rejected because of the personal tastes of that individual – for example, if a style or subject, or indeed a producer, is not favoured. As it stands today, where there are commissioning systems operating over several different channels, this is less of an issue, but commissioners are also bound by pressures from above, and by the identity that their channel pursues. Programmes reflect where they are being shown, and in the multichannel environment distinctiveness is seen as important – both in content and style. Channel 4 can claim that it revolutionised the way television was made in Britain and that its presence has played a major part in creating a television production industry in Britain.

The audience

From its inception Channel 4's programmes reflected its iconoclastic approach and were a cheerful mix of triumph and disaster. Some of the entertainment shows created audience excitement and significant and loyal viewers (*Countdown*, Yorkshire/Channel 4 1982–, the first show to be broadcast on the channel, is still going strong). Others, although experimental, were interesting to many and pleased the minority audiences at whom they were aimed: for instance, the pioneering magazine show on black issues *The Bandung File* (1985–9), or some of the experimental work showcased in *The Eleventh Hour* (1982–8). Some of the experiments inevitably failed either to engage or attract an audience, however; equally some attempts to be popular are still notorious for their gross lapses of judgment: *Minipops* (1983), with its children posing as sexy pop stars, is perhaps the one that still elicits most shudders. In general, however, Channel 4 did offer a real alternative for British viewers, allowing them to encounter the unexpected and a range of views that did not all originate from within the establishment.

As the 1980s unfolded, Channel 4 mapped the changes in society that resulted, often, but not always, critically. After early travails the news and current affairs output offered a distinctive slant on the world, uncovering many stories ignored by mainstream bulletins. To some degree it has maintained this reputation. At the same time as receiving recognition for its serious take on world events, Channel 4 was gaining another discernible parallel identity as the home of the wild, shocking, anarchic and occasionally out of control. This developed through youth programmes like *Whatever You Want* (1982–3) and comedy shows such as *Saturday Live* (1985–7). When Isaacs was replaced by another big industry name, Michael Grade, this anarchic streak continued and does to this day. The notoriety of shows like *The Last Resort* (1987–8), *The Word* (1990–5) and *TFI Friday* (1998–2000) has became almost a badge of honour for the channel, confirming its cutting-edge status, even if some of the bad-taste antics on those shows were sometimes more puerile than radical. Such texts have made Channel 4 vulnerable to attacks from various positions but do still allow it to retain its air of anarchy twenty-five years on. The channel's success with young audiences (in 2006 26% of its audience was 16 to 34, far more than other channels; source: BARB/C4) has helped its market position as well, making it extremely attractive to advertisers.

The business

It is this commercial success that has caused some to question Channel 4's direction in recent years. Critics claim that the original remit is no longer being interpreted in a way that offers up alternative voices or produces enough programmes that are different from those on other channels. Every so often there have been threats to privatise Channel 4 – it still receives indirect forms of subsidy – and the channel has sought to deflect them by emphasising its alternative vision, its own unique brand of public service broadcasting that is very different from the paternalistic approach of the BBC. Can it still convincingly claim this?

Once Channel 4 was established, both culturally and financially, its funding position came under scrutiny. The 1990 Broadcasting Act established the channel as an independent non-profit-making trust, disentangled from the ITV companies and now responsible for selling its own advertising, with a safety net meant to ensure that its remit was not affected too much by commercial imperatives (Bonner and Aston, 2003: 289–92). This arrangement began on 1 January 1993 and the channel has proved extremely adept at selling airtime, bringing in high revenues and competing very effectively with ITV and other rivals for advertisers' money. As we have seen, advertisers demand ratings – if not always very large numbers of people then at least those with disposable incomes, who are likely to buy the products advertised. The Grade era saw a greater emphasis on quality control, as some of the least popular and more esoteric programmes were partly replaced by programmes that could compete for viewers. This paid dividends when Channel 4 began to sell advertising, although controversial and serious programmes still continued to have an impact.

Over time, though, it could be argued that texts can be compromised by success in selling advertising and maximising audience numbers. Once a degree of financial success has been attained, it has to be maintained; making a loss unacceptable and putting the organisation under intense pressures. This is compounded by the increased competition in the industry created by the rise of digital channels. As Channel 4 has continued to increase revenue and its audience share in the 21st century, a debate has developed in the television industry about its role. The arguments can be broadly summarised as follows:

Critics of Channel 4

Critics of the channel reflect a range of different positions, from radicals who feel that the freedoms and innovation it pursued as part of its remit in the 1980s have been abandoned, to those, like the *Daily Mail*, who have always thought the channel subversive and tasteless, to commercial rivals like the BBC and ITV (whose outgoing Chief Executive Charles Allan slammed Channel 4 at his lecture at the 2006 Edinburgh TV Festival) who see it as unfair competition.

One argument these critics make is that Channel 4 is protected by its public service remit but does not fulfil it. Business rivals see this as hampering their companies by taking audiences from them with populist fare, while Channel 4 accepts subsidies supposedly to make more challenging programmes. Ratings figures show that there is something in this. The gap between 'mainstream' and 'minority' terrestrial channels has closed significantly in the last few years and some Channel 4 programmes that get high ratings would not look out of place on mainstream channels: the game show *Deal or No Deal* is a recent big hit and the property programme *Location, Location, Location* (WC Media, 2000–) is hardly catering to a minority or disenfranchised market (folk that want to get very rich are well served by television).

To some critics, particularly those on the left who felt an affinity with the channel in its early years, Channel 4 has abandoned its promise to challenge, dare to be different and reach out to new audiences. It has become about money and the superficial, obsessed with makeovers, aspiration and 'celebrity'. They would argue that Channel 4 is a mainstream channel only interested in the young and affluent, selling a glossy, but ultimately deceitful view of the world. Other critics may suggest that this does not just reflect on an immoral society but helps to create it, bringing everything down to its lowest common denominator. *Big Brother* tends to be used as a totem in such arguments but other shows, from *Wife Swap* to *Hollyoaks* (Mersey/Channel 4 1995) can be used to support these points, as can event programming designed to shock and titillate, such as live autopsies (Gunther Von Hagen's TV shows) and coverage of masturbation championships (part of the channel's proposed but ultimately shelved 'wank week' in 2007). Even the original founding father of the channel, Jeremy Isaacs, expressed his doubts, saying 'today, commercial ambitions are taking Channel 4 down different paths. Is it still doing enough of what it was established to achieve?' (*Prospect*, November 2006).

Supporters

Others, notably the channel itself, but also some producers and a large number of viewers, would disagree. They would argue that Channel 4 has had to change with the times. Stagnating in an esoteric backwater was not an option as competition in broadcasting developed and Channel 4 needed to prove its worth, and its subsidy, by connecting with audiences. Anyway, they might say, it was not desirable. Some of those experiments in its early years categorically failed to engage the public and a greater professionalism produced stronger texts. To have any kind of social and cultural impact Channel 4 needs an audience – this is what makes *Shameless* or *Jamie's School Dinners* (2005) significant, while hit

> **Think about . . .**
>
> **Channel 4 and you**
>
> What do you think? You are probably in the age group targeted by much of Channel 4's output – how do you react to their programmes? What do you think of the remit and how it has operated? Does Channel 4 remain a powerful brand?

programmes like *Big Brother* and *Wife Swap* raise questions we should be asking about ourselves and the way we live.

Popular texts bring people to the channel who may then see something more challenging, and these more challenging programmes still exist in the schedule. Supporters would argue that *Channel 4 News* brings a depth of analysis and breadth of coverage unmatched in British broadcasting and would point to the tradition of cutting-edge comedy and the recent substantial investment in single drama-documentaries that try to make sense of the world today, such as *The Road to Guantanamo* (2006) and *The Hamburg Cell* (2004). It is good, they might insist, that Channel 4 caters for young people, because no one else does, at least not in a diverse way that mixes genres and speaks to them in a non-patronising mode of address. It is also good that Channel 4 sells lots of advertising, because it keeps the channel going and maintains its powerful position in a marketplace where its old practices have long ceased to be sustainable.

Scheduling

The point where the production of television and our consumption of it intersect is the schedule. The schedule – literally the order in which programmes are transmitted throughout the day – is our guide to viewing. The channel decides on a particular broadcast slot and publicises it to the audience on air, electronically or via printed listings. We decide what we want to see on the basis of the schedule – either planning our evening around a favourite show or consulting it when we return home to see what suits our mood that day. Traditionally the broadcasters control the schedule and their decisions on slots, times and frequency of transmission determine how we view.

The dominant model has been the 'mixed schedule'. The 'mixed schedule' still survives but as we have seen is being challenged, as digital channels offer 'narrowcasting' to selective audiences. What the mixed schedule endeavoured to do was to cater for all tastes, all audiences and all moods throughout the day. By putting contrasting types of programmes side-by-side, viewers could encounter new ideas and be informed, challenged and entertained by different slots. If they didn't like a particular programme, one more to their taste was likely to appear very shortly. With a mixed schedule throughout the day or evening, viewers become used to watching long sequences of different shows. The texts inform each other and become something more than the sum of their parts. This is the flow that Williams and Ellis describe. They suggest that meanings in television are not derived so much from individual texts but from the schedule and the way in which texts are seen together (Ellis, 2000: 130–8).

How we understand texts is certainly influenced by how they are presented to us. The schedule gives us certain expectations of our television viewing experiences; we become used to the juxtaposition of fact and fiction, comedy and tragedy, the familiar and the new. These expectations are quite flexible but viewers may protest if for instance, material offends them or if the schedules are too one-note, notably when there is blanket coverage of sporting events. If programmes overrun, the schedule is disrupted.

The form the schedule takes has traditionally been fairly rigid. Predictability was believed to help the viewer in finding what they wanted. Regular news bulletins at the same time each day provide structure. Some parts of the day can be less mixed (for instance, there may be a run of lifestyle programming in the daytime and then an hour or so of children's shows), before prime time offers a varied diet usually involving some drama, news and a new documentary.

Until recently programmes, with few exceptions, were broadcast weekly. Serials were transmitted at the same time each week, so building up a sense of anticipation and developing a routine around viewing. Now that is only one scheduling option. The multichannel environment, especially the 'family of channels', offers the broadcaster more flexibility in scheduling. Shows are now often repeated on other channels the week after broadcast. At the same time technology enables and encourages a culture based on instant resolutions and gratifications. A common scheduling tactic currently is 'stripping' – broadcasting a programme on consecutive nights or in more than one slot per day (particularly used for *Coronation Street*). The need to keep viewers with the channel demands inventive scheduling and schedulers have learnt different tactics to retain the audience. There is a form of control going on here: sometimes viewers' desires to find out what is happening are gratified and sometimes they have to stay with the channel and sit through the following programme to find out what happens next. In August 2006 a typical Channel 4 talking-heads factual entertainment show, *The Law of the Playground*, had its ratings significantly boosted by being scheduled between two slices of *Big Brother* on eviction night (source: BARB).

Digital channels schedule in quite a different way, and inevitably this will start to influence the mainstream terrestrial channels before too long. Typically, digital channels have less content to screen each day and so often show each programme two or three times in different slots. This still represents a form of broadcaster control but acknowledges that viewers increasingly want more opportunities to see programmes. An interesting development in scheduling is the +1 channel (E4, for instance), allowing viewers to see the same schedule one hour later.

CASE STUDY – A SNAPSHOT OF A SCHEDULE

To understand the complexity of how the schedule works and how it can affect our understanding of the meanings of texts, we need to look at it in some detail. Here are some snapshots from the schedule on one day in the autumn of 2006. Think about how the texts work with the 'flow'.

The day in question, Thursday 21 September, has been picked almost entirely at random. I did, however, avoid the weekend, when the schedule takes on rather a different shape, as broadcasters assume that viewers have access to television all day). We will look at three 'slots' in the schedule of about an hour at different times on that day, and examine the thinking behind the programmes selected for those slots and how they compete with each other.

8am–9am

TV-watching early in the morning is less established among the majority of the population than at other times of the day. This is the timeslot where radio is most competitive in the battle for audiences, and, of course coincides with large numbers of people travelling to work or school. Broadcasters have the choice here of aiming for a broad audience or targeting a specific group of viewers likely to be watching at this hour. The terrestrial line-up is as follows:

BBC1	8.00–9.00 Breakfast
BBC2	7.30–8.30 CBBC: *Roar*
	8.30–9.00 Cbeebies: *Tweenies* (8.30–8.50); *Our Planet* (8.50–9.00)
ITV	8.00–9.00 GMTV, including from 8.35 Lorraine Kelly's show *LK Today*
C4	7.55–8.25 *Everybody Loves Raymond*
	8.25–8.55 *Will and Grace*
	8.55–9.25 *Frasier*
Five	8.00–8.15 *Fifi and the Flowertots*
	8.15–8.20 *Peppa Pig*
	8.20–8.30 *Funky Valley*
	8.30–8.45 *Franny Feet*
	8.45–8.50 *Bird Bath*
	8.50–9.00 *Sandy and the Flapper*

It is clear that broadcasters are keenly aware not only of who their audience might be but also how they are watching in this slot. At this time it is quite likely that viewers can only watch for a short length of time, as they are getting ready for work or school. The BBC and ITV favour multi-item magazine shows where bitesized chunks of entertainment or information are presented to the audience, who feel they can dip in and out of the programme. The text is shaped to suit the needs of the viewer: aware that it is not practical to commit to a long, developed piece of work, the programmes offer the viewers small items that make it worth their while watching. It is interesting that as the hour progresses, possible changes in audience movement are noted. *LK Today*, a talk show featuring Lorraine Kelly, targets an audience of women whose children may now have left for school. You will note that BBC2 and Five show programmes for very young (under-five, pre-school) children. In BBC2's case they first show *Roar* simultaneously with CBBC – the corporation's channel for 5–12-year-olds – then at 8.30 when they will have gone to school it switches to Cbeebies for younger children who might be at home with a parent all day or with childminders. Five offers shows for pre-school children throughout. Frequently these are very short and allow viewers to dip in and out of the schedule. Channel 4 provides an alternative by scheduling reruns of American sitcoms. Fans will have seen them before and may feel perfectly happy to watch part of a show again.

On non-terrestrial/digital channels, this is an important slot dedicated to children's channels (as well as Cbeebies and CBBC, there are Nick Jr, the Disney Channel and others) but less so for others. Many digital channels just repeat other parts of the schedule and show reruns of US imports (*Mad about You* on Living, *Futurama* on Sky One, *Ironside* on ITV3). In many cases (for example, BBC3 and BBC4) they don't broadcast at all, only going on air in the early afternoon or evening.

5.00–6.00pm

This is an intriguing slot, situated towards the end of the working day, when children are home from school but many people are not yet back from work. Audiences are significantly higher than earlier in the afternoon and the slot has recently become competitive on the commercial channels. On 21 September it looked like this:

BBC1	5.00–5.25 *Young Dracula* (a children's comedy-drama series)
	5.25–5.35 *Newsround*
	5.35–6.00 *Neighbours*
BBC2	4.30–5.15 *Ready Steady Cook*
	5.15–6.00 *The Weakest Link*
ITV	5.00–6.00 *The Sharon Osbourne Show*
C4	4.45–5.30 *Deal or No Deal*
	5.30–6.00 *A Place in the Sun*
Five	The first half in the slot includes the end of a relatively recent American TV or straight-to-DVD film (on this day it was *Race against Time*)
	5.30–6.00 *five News*

There is competition within the slot for viewers returning from work early, or based at home. *The Sharon Osbourne Show* addresses a predominantly female audience and is designed to compete with Channel 4, which often (though not this week) screens its own talks shows hosted by Richard and Judy or Paul O'Grady at this hour. On this particular day it is screening the very successful quiz show *Deal or No Deal*, overlapping slightly with BBC2's long-established *The Weakest Link*, one of their biggest weekly audience draws. There is also lifestyle programming on BBC2 and Channel 4, long one of the primary drivers of the daytime schedule. Only BBC1 continues to screen children's programmes in this slot. ITV have been allowed to cut their statutory hours of children's programming. Five do not bother to compete with the other channels at this time with their broadcasts of littleknown American TV or straight-to-DVD movies, although at 5.30 their news bulletin is the first to go out in the early evening, possibly stealing a march on rivals. Note that on most channels the programmes in this hour are undemanding, 'light' entertainment trying to gain audiences with diverting, rather than challenging work. This may be because viewers are perceived to be busy with children or exhausted after a day's work, so just want to unwind.

Multichannels still largely concentrate on reruns and imports at this time, (*Friends* on E4, *Futurama* again on Sky One, *Charmed* on Living) and again it is an important slot for children's channels, coming to the end of their post-school schedule.

9.00–10.00pm

This is the heart of prime time – the most important hour of the schedule. Children are in bed, most people are back from work and there is a large adult audience to be fought over. Viewers expect the best programmes at this time and will make fewer allowances for product that does not engage them.

BBC1	9.00–10.00 *Ancient Rome: The Rise and Fall of an Empire* (first episode)
BBC2	9.00–9.30 *Extras*
	9.30–10.00 *That Mitchell and Webb Look*
ITV	9.00–10.00 *I Smack and I'm Proud* (a documentary examining the case for and against smacking children, with childcare experts and 'celebrity mothers')
C4	9.00–10.30 *Low Winter Sun* (second part of a thriller drama)
Five	9.00–10.00 *Ann Maurice: Interior Rivalry* (a kind of makeover game show where contestants compete to become the successor to Ann Maurice as the host of makeover shows)

Here we can see the terrestrial broadcasters lining up their big guns in competition against each other. The schedule also reveals that they are competing not just for ratings but also for prestige. These prestige productions reflect the nature of each channel. *Ancient Rome* is a very expensive drama-documentary using state-of-the-art technology and big-name actors. While accessible, it also strives to show that the licence fee is producing work that is different to commercial rivals. Similarly on BBC2, sitcom *Extras* and sketch show *That Mitchell and Webb Look* feature some of the most esteemed cutting-edge comedians of our time, proving the channel's worth as a showcase for new talent and challenging material. Channel 4's drama is another prestige work, a tough, adult genre piece that reassures viewers and opinion-formers that the channel is not all *Big Brother*. ITV and Five are reverting

Think about . . .
Would you make different interpretations of
this schedule? Look at today's schedule and
compare it to this one: are there any
significant differences? Think about how the
schedule reflects competition for viewers.

more to type in offering lifestyle shows, although *I Smack and I'm Proud* seems a strange mix of reality show (complete with its sensational title and its 'celebrity mothers') and current affairs, featuring experts and debates on social issues.

This is an equally important slot for non-terrestrial channels trying to draw in viewers who can't find anything appealing on terrestrial TV. New US drama or comedy is being offered on More4 (*Without a Trace*), E4 (*Scrubs/The War at Home*) and Living (*Janice Dickinson Modelling Agency/Out of Practice*), while lifestyle and reality shows feature on some others (*Say No to the Knife* – yet another cosmetic surgery series – is on BBC3). Documentaries are on BBC4 (*Forty Minutes On* – interestingly picking up BBC documentary stories from twenty years earlier and thus assuming an older and more teleliterate audience) and *Asbo Fever* on Sky One.

While the children's channels have closed, other niche channels are now coming into play. Movie channels (FilmFour and more than ten on Sky) are playing their biggest titles of the day at this time and sports channels are screening live coverage of events like Premier League snooker (Sky Sports 1) and boxing bouts (Eurosport).

Conclusion

We have seen how important the production process and broadcasting institutions are in the construction of texts. The television industry and the norms it creates influence the meanings that they contain and how we read them. The structures of broadcasters and channels and the economic environment they inhabit affect the programmes we watch. Competition for viewers, marketing to ensure people watch and the measurement of the audience all contribute to the way the text appears on screen. With this in mind, we now need to consider our place in the creation of meaning. How does our consumption of television affect the text and what do we bring to it, both as part of the audience and as individual viewers?

2. Audiences and Consumption

Audiences are constantly changing their relationship to television. There is a difference and sometimes a tension between 'television', as made up of companies and programmes, and how we view television as a source of entertainment and information in our home. This chapter will concentrate on considering ourselves as viewers (that is, individuals watching TV) and as an audience (a group of people engaging with the medium and its texts), and will explore the following issues:

- *The need to attain a mass audience and how this has affected texts over the years.*
- *The various ways we watch television and how that affects meaning, as we bring our own experiences, beliefs and personalities to the text.*
- *How changes in technology in the last five years and the creation of different platforms for television have already had a huge effect on our relationship with the medium.*
- *The public sphere of consumption, and the critical contexts that might influence our opinions.*

The television audience

In his book *Seeing Things*, John Ellis characterises television history and its relationship with the viewer as comprising three periods. The first phase he describes as 'scarcity' (Ellis, 2000: 39), which covers television from its inception through its development as a mass medium when TV offered a limited range of choices for the viewer, over two or three channels. Roughly this covers the period from the 1930s to the late 1980s/early 1990s. Often they would just watch what was provided, and accept it as a diversion. Occasionally they might be confronted by something unexpected that they would not normally choose to encounter.

The second period he calls 'availability' or 'managed choice' (ibid: 61). In this period (late 1980s to around the 2003 Communications Act, and for many viewers still the dominant mode of watching) we, as an audience, have a wide choice of options but we still make them from schedules and use the same hardware as in the days of scarcity. Essentially 'availability' is a natural development from 'scarcity' but our position as viewers is now a source of competition. We can now compare and seek out texts, and choose from a range of alternative texts.

The last period Ellis identifies is 'plenty', from now into the future (ibid.: 162). Much of this future is very uncertain but clearly it will involve a multitude of choices; we will control these choices ourselves to a much greater degree than previously. Texts will probably become more diverse in form and we will certainly not only be watching them on the sets in the corners of our living rooms, but interacting through a choice of hardware.

All this has changed the way we watch and the nature of texts.

Over time the relationship between viewer and programmes has subtly shifted: 'scarcity' brought mass appeal and experiences; 'availability' put the viewer in a position of control and stressed our individual requirements from TV; and 'plenty' creates new questions and possibilities that will be explored further in this chapter.

TV as a mass medium

To fully appreciate the changes in the way we watch now, we need to look back at the past and analyse how people behaved during other times of change. We also need to understand that TV has not always been about a limited diet of programmes we know we like and watching them at a time convenient for us. Until very recently our experience of TV, and as a consequence the way the medium understood itself, was very different. TV was primarily seen as a mass experience, with programmes being watched at the same time by many, many people. In the early 1960s a hit show like *Steptoe and Son* might be watched by well in excess of 20 million people – nearly half of Britain's population. In 1964 the then Prime Minister, Harold Wilson, famously tried to stop the show going out on election night because he feared that Labour supporters might stay in to view the Steptoes rather than go to the polls (Sandbrook, 2006: 15)). Popular, or cult programmes had a status as an 'appointment to view', where people wanted to see them at the same time so they could discuss their reactions with their friends. This can still happen but it is becoming the exception rather than the norm.

CASE STUDY – THE ARRIVAL OF ITV

To illustrate this further, let's look closely at a moment in viewer history. ITV opened as Britain's first commercial TV station in September 1955 after government legislation. Its creation was a response to pressure from business and in the teeth of determined opposition by many parts of the British establishment, from the Labour

Party to the Church of England (Crisell, 1997: 84–5). In contrast to the longer-running public service BBC broadcasts, which, despite favourites like *The Grove Family* (1953–7) and *The Quatermass Experiment* (1953), were seen as rather sober and worthy, ITV programmes quickly built up a reputation as populist, earthy and fun. Despite a slow rollout across the country and the complex pattern of different franchise-holders for different regions that characterised the network, audiences responded with such enthusiasm that only two years after the launch ITV had a 79% share of the British television audience. How did this remarkable achievement come about in such a short space of time? Why did large audiences overwhelmingly embrace ITV?

Inevitably there were a number of factors involved in the rise of ITV. Its launch coincided with the beginnings of an economic boom after a period of austerity. For the first time the majority of people, particularly working-class people, had money to spend on consumer goods and home entertainment (Sandbrook, 2005: 106).

Although ITV was a commercial organisation and had a close relationship with business, it also positioned itself as 'the people's channel'. The BBC's TV output still maintained the lingering legacy of Lord Reith, its stern guiding force in its first years (he was Director-General from 1927 to 1938), who stressed the need for programmes to be improving and morally uplifting. He famously believed that television should not give people what they want, but what they ought to have (Crisell, 1997). By contrast ITV stressed unadulterated fun. It promoted a line-up of top variety shows (*Sunday Night at the London Palladium*, 1955–69, perhaps being the most famous), game shows and imports from the US. This style seemed to fit an acquisitive, consumerist culture but also a more confident population who demanded some say in what they saw and considered entertainment to be as valuable as education.

ITV tapped into this irreverence, but it is a mistake to see its early output as merely vulgar populism, although many in the establishment at that time saw it as just that. The arrival of the new channel, and the viewers' response to it, led to the development of TV as a medium – that is, a system by which messages, thoughts or feelings are communicated to people. Each medium has its own unique characteristics and many ITV shows really used the potential of television to connect on an intimate basis with the viewer in their home (Crisell, 1997: 101). As well as cheeky chappies and cash prizes, there was daring quality drama in *Armchair Theatre* (ABC/Thames 1956–74) and the news division ITN made world events relevant in the nation's living rooms as well as in the corridors of power. The engagement with the mass audience that marked ITV's shows raised the game at the BBC, who had to justify their continued existence by making programmes that had more popular appeal. By the early 1960s, viewing share was roughly equal. The 1962 Pilkington Report on Broadcasting punished ITV for its 'vulgarity' and commercialism and forced the channel to take on further public service obligations, although the report was widely considered to be unfair (Crisell, 1997: 116–17). This raised questions over the possible conflict between the audience's needs and wants that are still contested today.

Certainly the coming of ITV heralded a period in which mass audiences helped to shape television. It could be argued that the new medium and the keenness with which people embraced it, buying sets and choosing TV as the primary source of entertainment (seen, for instance, in the sudden huge decline in cinema attendance), empowered the viewer. The industry needed to acknowledge and react to these patterns of consumption and was made to realise that a dialogue had to be developed with the audience about what they were watching. At the same time, as ITV found out, they had to please the government and the regulators, who were not always convinced that the desires of the audience should be gratified.

Television as a shared experience

Having a mass audience, making huge numbers of people want to turn on the set to watch the same thing at the same time as each other, gives texts a potency – the connection between viewer and programme is something to be desired, because the programme becomes something more than a product; it becomes a cultural artefact.

For its first fifty years, TV really did communicate to a mass audience. In the mid-1990s the romantic comedy *Four Weddings and a Funeral* (1994) was hailed as the most successful British film to date, estimated to have been seen by 8.8 million people. A couple of years later its first TV screening, on the 'minority' channel Channel 4, had a rating of 10.1 million (source: EDI/BFI/BARB). Sheer weight of numbers alone makes television important as a social force. For a long time TV was dismissed as essentially a throw-away medium, particularly in the early days when its artefacts could not be preserved and had little life beyond the here and now. But even then critics could not deny television's place within the rhythms and routines of everyday life. It is this position that gives television as a medium its cultural resonance and social power. Dennis Potter, often considered British TV's greatest dramatist, once said that you should 'fight and kick and bite to be on television' because of its power to impact on so many people (interview with Potter by Gordon Burn, *Radio Times*, 8 October 1970). The multifaceted nature of the medium, its potential to deliver everything from long-running fiction to live coverage of unfolding events, accentuates this.

Television's mass appeal allows us, as viewers, to share experiences. This sharing gives TV a dynamic relationship with contemporary society. TV can both influence society and reflect or embody attitudes, and changes, within it. There is a need for programme-makers to retain audiences by engaging with our perceptions of the world; if we feel that our needs are not being served, we will simply stop watching. Equally, though, our perceptions can be altered by what we see, not just individually but as a society.

Television acts as a social discourse, a way in which we communicate, make sense of our world and understand each other (Marshall McLuhan considered that it constituted 'a global village', 1964). Its shared reception can also influence what we think. This can inspire political action: for instance, *Alice* (Yorkshire TV 1974), a programme about a woman suffering a terminal illness from the effects of working with asbestos; or famously *Cathy Come Home*, whose dramatic tale of a family becoming homeless led to the setting up of the charity Shelter. It may also set in train longer-term social changes: see for example, debates about whether *Big Brother* has influenced the behaviour of young people and shattered the culture of British reserve (Biressi and Nunn, 2005; Jermyn and Holmes, 2005). Good popular TV shows can also crystallise a moment and articulate a mood or the cultural *Zeitgeist* for us. You could argue, for instance, that *The Office* captures the feeling of powerlessness at work (Walters 2005); and in the 1980s it was suggested that *Only Fools and Horses* (BBC 1982–2003) tapped into the hustling, acquisitive culture of Thatcherism.

The shared experience of watching television would seem to be in sharp decline as ratings slide and viewers are dispersed across more channels, but it can still exist and it can have remarkable consequences. For instance, characters in *Little Britain* (BBC 2003–) have become a kind of cultural shorthand (for good or bad) that we all understand. The show's character Vicki Pollard, a sulky delinquent who tries to evade responsibility at every turn with ever more elaborate excuses, is now evoked to refer to any young working-class woman. Many have argued that this stereotypes a large group of people and leads to lazy assumptions and judgments being made (Julie Burchill and Michael Collins, for example). While this is not necessarily the fault of the show's creators, it does illustrate how TV can gain a cultural currency of its own, originating from the text but generated by the interpretation of its viewers. The antics of contestants on *Big Brother* or *The X Factor* (talkbackThames/ITV 2004–) become gossip in every playground or office and fill the front pages of newspapers. At the beginning of the summer of 2006, when *Big Brother 7* started, no one in Britain had heard of Pete or Nikki – two months later they were the topic of discussions everywhere. News coverage of a disaster such as the Asian tsunami or the London bombings brings people to their televisions and creates a collective memory of its impact upon us, as did the TV footage of the moon landings and the Kennedy assassination in the 1960s.

Regulating TV

The 'threat' of TV

The power that television has as a mass medium has come at a price. More than books, cinema or theatre, television makes politicians anxious. They fear its power to communicate directly to the people and the possibility that their own message will be ignored. The instant access to millions and the presence of sets within the home (our own space where we are out of their immediate control) combine to pose a threat, both to the political order but also potentially to the moral values that authority figures feel should prevail in society. Political parties also sometimes complain about the way they are directly presented on programmes or discussed, especially through supposedly 'objective' news bulletins.

Moral panics

More commonly there is a vague criticism of the way television is apparently influencing moral values. This is usually couched in terms of the representation, or 'glorification', of sex, violence and bad language but also moves into wider debates about general antisocial behaviour. There have long been organisations, often with a religious background, that have campaigned against television on this basis.

It is worth looking at a couple of examples in detail to illustrate how this can happen. To take a notorious recent case, in a half-time performance at the American Football Super Bowl on 1 February 2004 singer Janet Jackson accidentally exposed a nipple for a split second in a dance routine while singing a duet with Justin Timberlake. Uproar ensued. Over half a million people complained and the conservative-dominated US regulator, the Federal Communications Commission, seized the moment. Notably they fined broadcaster CBS a record $550,000, but in further measures initiated a series of actions to prevent content they deemed 'immoral' from being broadcast. Punitive actions were taken against a number of different networks and their programmes. These ranged from swearing by starlets at music award shows to an episode of police-procedural show *Without a Trace* (CBS 2002–). A number of ABC affiliates decided not to show *Saving Private Ryan* (1998) for fear of reprisals by the FCC, who had refused to issue a waiver to screen the film. Most importantly the FCC and allies in Washington set their new approach in legislation, passing a bill increasing potential fines from $32,000 to $500,000 (*Guardian*, 28 November 2006).

Clearly, socially conservative forces seemed to use the Jackson incident because they feared the representation of sex (particularly female sexuality) on television. The large religious lobby in the US ensured support for a measure from those who believe that television, because it is part of the domestic environment and can be accessed by children, could be harmful to their moral welfare. They are also worried that shows will propagate ideas about morality that they do not share. The threat of massive fines to media business is not only designed to punish transgressions of the FCC's code but also appears to be intended to discourage producers and networks from

Mary Whitehouse
In Britain organised campaigns against 'the threat' of television became widespread in the 1960s with Mary Whitehouse and the Voice of the Viewer and Listener. Whitehouse launched a campaign to 'clean up TV', attacking the language in programmes like *Till Death Us Do Part* (BBC 1966–75) and sex and violence in others. She particularly clashed with the BBC's Director-General Hugh Greene, who refused to engage with her on any level. She still had some influence up to the 1990s. Following her death in 2001 John Beyer took over her organisation, now renamed Mediawatch. Christian Voice, a more explicitly religious organisation, co-ordinated a campaign against *Jerry Springer – The Opera* (BBC 2005), which they considered blasphemous.

covering contentious topics, exploring sexuality, including bad language, or questioning conservative assumptions.

Self-censorship at every level of programme-making is the likely outcome and is an interesting concept. To a degree it is inevitably present and indeed some would argue that it should be so if creative choices are being responsibly considered. However, acting according to your own moral instincts can be seen as very different from censoring your own work because you fear punishment by the authorities and the possibility of going out of business unless texts conform to a strictly defined moral standard imposed by others.

In Britain the Super Bowl case was greeted with mystification – primetime TV has featured intentional nudity for many years after the watershed and the incident was, after all, an accident on a live broadcast. British TV has had much more latitude on 'moral' content than the US networks and despite the interventions of Mary Whitehouse and complaints over *Jerry Springer – The Opera*, organised religious lobbies have much less support. In the other most complained about programme on British TV, the satirical comedy *Brass Eye*'s special on paedophilia (Talkback/C4 2001), the regulator OFCOM made some limited criticisms but no fines were levelled. However, broadcasting has still proved politically contentious in Britain and continues to been seen as a threat, again because of the medium's ability to form a direct discourse with its audience.

Political intervention

Here the controversies have been more explicitly political in nature, usually involving criticisms of government policy. Under the current Labour government the most notorious example was the radio allegations about the presence of weapons of mass destruction in Iraq that led to the Hutton Report and the resignations of the BBC's Chairman and Director-General, Greg Dyke, in 2003. However, it was television that provided political storms under the Thatcher administration in the 1980s. The BBC, as a publicly funded body 'representing' the nation, found itself in trouble over a news report by Kate Adie on the use of British bases to bomb Libya (1988), and particularly about coverage of the Northern Ireland conflict. In the 1980s a broadcasting ban was issued prohibiting the voices of those in proscribed organisations like the IRA to be heard (their words were read out by actors) and a documentary tracking the lives of Republican and Loyalist representatives, *Real Lives: The Edge of the Union* (1985), was pulled by the BBC governors following government pressure.

The most potent case in this period, however, was an ITV programme, *Death on the Rock* (Thames 1988). This documentary in the 'This Week' strand, made by Thames, examined the shootings of three IRA members in Gibraltar. It was accepted that these people (one woman and two men) were intent on planting a bomb, but the programme alleged that they had been executed by the SAS with no attempt to arrest them. It used witnesses to build its case. The government accused Thames of 'trial by television' and launched an investigation (the Windlesham Report) into the programme. When Thames lost its franchise in 1992, there was dark talk that *Death on the Rock* was to blame (although it was outbid by a competitor in the process).

Whether it concerns 'moral' content or political criticism, television is regarded as potentially dangerous. TV is often seen as part of the establishment (Hall, 1980; Bourdieu, 1998) but it occupies a much more ambiguous position than that. Certainly it can be a mouthpiece for regimes, relaying their message to the people and keeping them in their place – indeed this has been the case under some dictatorships or in the old Soviet bloc, and pressure has been exerted heavily even in some countries that are nominally democratic. It can also replicate social norms and conventional moral codes. However, it also has the power to be something else, to make us question the ruling order or its moral codes. This is because of the relationship the medium forms with the viewer, both collectively (speaking to the mass audience) and individually, approaching us in the intimacy of the home. Depending on point of view, this can make it radical or dangerous.

> Studying TV effects
> Look at *Ill Effects: The Media/Violence Debate* by Martin Barker and Julian Petley and *TV Living*, edited by David Gauntlett and Annette Hill for research, data and insights into the psychological and social effects of television on audiences.

Much research has been conducted about the effects of TV on the viewer but few conclusions have been reached.

The watershed

Traditionally TV in Britain has sought to provide some clarity to the debate and compromise between adult freedom and child protection by working to an agreed 'watershed' of 9pm. After this, moment material is allowed to be more challenging in its language, or treatment of sex and violence, and this is supported by the regulators (although oddly, 18-rated films cannot be screened before 10pm).

Needless to say the watershed affects programmes a great deal, partly through self-censorship. Normally they will be produced with a particular slot in mind, so if this is pre-watershed there will be curbs on potentially offensive content. This particularly affects genres like comedy. *Men Behaving Badly* (Hartswood BBC, 1992–8) started out on ITV as a pre-watershed comedy before moving to a post-watershed slot on the BBC, where it was able to explore its sexual themes and humour much more freely.

How we consume TV

The consumption of television is different to other media; it is more deeply entwined in our existence because of its domestic function. That does not mean that the experience is necessarily more intense than other media. Many argue that it is less so, claiming that the domestic function and the place of TV in the home makes it a diversion, a kind of white noise in the background. John Ellis states that 'Broadcast TV is extensive and ever present: it gives the impression of carrying on regardless of what anyone is doing' (Ellis, 1982: 2). Because we are at home, in our own space surrounded by all that is familiar, we do not seem to undergo the same process of submission as in the cinema – we do not forget where we are, we are not alone in the darkness transported to some other reality. We might watch on our own, or with others, which, as explored below, can result in quite different experiences. We may be doing other things at the same time, ironing for instance, or eating dinner. We may be glancing with half an eye while on the phone to a friend, or indeed keep the images on while turning the sound off, controlling the different facets of the medium to suit our requirements. We might wander out of the room for a few minutes but keep the set on, so like Ellis suggests, it carries on regardless of what we are doing.

> Think about . . .
> How did you watch TV last night? Where were you and what were you doing while you watched? Were you alone or with someone?

We need to look closer at how we watch TV. This connection with the everyday, this idea of television as something that comes to us in our own environment has obsessed scholars. It becomes a pattern of consumption that reflects and affirms our position in society. The texts we watch comment on our attitudes and our aspirations.

Viewing as a family

For a long time, watching television was an activity that involved the whole family, its presence at the heart of family life acknowledged as a fact but also, as we have seen, a threat. The idea of everyone sitting in front of the box watching the same programme may seem strange now when multiple transactions can take place between family members and different media at the same time under the same roof, but different social traditions, not to mention limited heating, conspired to force TV to deal with the whole family unit.

In pre-remote days, families were often identified as 'ITV' families or 'BBC' families, defined – this being Britain – by class. Some households were reputed to never watch the other side, and some 'BBC families', were not allowed to watch ITV out of snobbishness because ITV was seen as 'vulgar'. Television was something that seemed to confirm our identities, both what we watched and, just as important, how we watched. In the series *Blackpool* (BBC 2004) self-made man Ripley Holden (David Morrissey) declares that 'The thing I hate about becoming middle class is that we never have the telly on when we have dinner any more'.

TV can be something that binds us together as a family; it can help us create an identity as a unit. *The Royle Family*, set almost entirely in one front room while three generations watched TV every night, already felt somewhat nostalgic when it aired in the late 1990s. The show illustrated how the television is a focus for competition for space within the family. Possession of the remote control becomes important in the jostling for status and gratification. However, one episode showed how television can be a unifying force in the home, where what is shared is stronger than what divides them. This unlikely unity is caused by the *Antiques Roadshow* (BBC

1979–), a long-running Sunday fixture on BBC1. The excitement is caused by the valuations for antiques given to members of the public who have hauled their heirlooms to the local village hall. As these moments approach, the Royles feverishly lay odds on the likely price, triumphantly cheering when fixed smiles indicate that it has failed to live up to the owner's expectations.

Perhaps because of the increasing difficulty in achieving this unity today, shows that bring the family together in front of the set remain highly prized within the industry: witness some of the discourse in trade magazines around *Doctor Who* (see case study below) or *Strictly Come Dancing*. An appeal across generations is not only likely to create larger audience numbers who will probably stay loyal to the text but is gold dust to advertisers of mass-market goods.

CASE STUDY – DOCTOR WHO

Doctor Who originally ran on the BBC from 1963 to 1989. It was essentially a sci-fi drama series for children but developed a large fan base from those reared on the show. It was sophisticated enough (at least in its 1960s' and 1970s' incarnations) to have some adult appeal, and some aspects of the show, like the Doctor's spaceship (the 'Tardis') that looked like a police phonebox and the arch-villains the Daleks, entered popular culture. Although before its most recent incarnation it had been over fifteen years since the show was broadcast, a now ageing fan culture of conventions and clubs remained, as did a distant, but fond folk memory.

Plans to revive the series came in part from Russell T. Davies, one of British TV's foremost contemporary dramatists. Davies's work had included a number of children's series as well as more adult shows including some dealing with his identity as a gay man, notably *Queer as Folk*. Davies's love of *Doctor Who* was evident in the latter. Likeable central character Vince is a huge fan of the show within the fiction and this becomes a plot point: his best friend Stuart upstages Vince's boyfriend by buying Vince a model of 'K-9', a robot dog familiar to fans of the show, and Vince brings a date back home only to find him more interested in his collection of rare *Who* videos than sex.

Davies's potential involvement certainly aided plans for a revival in 2005, but it is important to remember that it was seen as a big risk prior to transmission. The last years of the original incarnation had seen ratings and kudos slump and it became a byword for bad special effects and low-budget sets. It was also unclear how much it would appeal to children growing up in a much more sophisticated technological age, where the way the media works is much less of a mystery. Perhaps they wouldn't find it in the least bit scary or exciting now they were exposed to virtual reality and videogames.

As it was, the series has proved a popular and critical triumph. This is because it constructed itself as a modern family show, uniting different audiences. It uses new technology to create convincing special effects but subordinates them to story and character. Children were able to use their imaginations and were gripped by the thrills created by Davies and the other writers. It was also pretty scary, daring to tap into childhood fears and indeed fears of children: the episode 'The Empty Child' featured zombie-like deadly children wandering around London in the Blitz calling 'Where's my mummy?'. The show also starred Billie Piper as Rose, a contemporary young London woman who offered a point of identification for the youthful audience – a kind of older-sister surrogate whose journey, and sense of wonderment, can be experienced vicariously by viewers.

The Doctor himself was played in the first series by an established star actor, Christopher Eccleston, and in the second by a rising younger star, David Tennant. The gravitas and brooding romanticism that Eccleston in particular brought to the role intrigued adult audiences, even those that had not maintained their youthful enthusiasm for the original show, or indeed ever felt such an enthusiasm before. His relationship with Rose and the implications of his own tortured past as a Time Lord, the last of his race destined to walk the universe for ever, were sophisticated enough to grip adult viewers, whether or not they were watching with their children. On paper, the move from one lead actor to another could capsize a show, but the producers were able to draw on the understanding between viewer and text and their history together.

Various actors had already played the Doctor and the change from one to another was always dramatised as a 'regeneration', where one body morphed into another. This is familiar to fans and becomes part of the logic of the series. Likewise the presence of the Tardis still seemed to work through the folk memory of the original series. Police phone boxes have long disappeared but the audience understands that the Doctor travels in one, and no more explanation is necessary. Old fans are also kept on board by intertextual references (that is references to the history and codes that have developed within the series itself) – the return of villains like the Cybermen and the Daleks or the sudden discovery in the second series of K-9 and a Doctor's assistant from the 1970s, Sarah-Jane. Younger viewers are drawn in through the reactions of Rose, who is unfamiliar with these elements, to the world of the text.

The revived *Doctor Who* succeeds because it builds up a discourse with its viewers. By applying strong scripts, convincing characters and exciting situations to a knowing humour and self-referential motifs, it links different audiences together. Its success has led to numerous spin-off programmes, from a documentary series, *Doctor Who Confidential*, to a related drama, *Torchwood* (BBC 2006–). There is frenetic web activity around the programme and a theme-park experience in Cardiff, where it was filmed. The BBC has certainly capitalised on success but that success derives from the show's ability to set up a dialogue with its viewers, using and manipulating the cultural baggage and expectations that the audience brings to the series. *Doctor Who* unites a family audience by giving different family members different reasons to enjoy the programme.

Viewing alone

Most people today probably view television alone – more people than ever before live by themselves and the majority of children have a TV in their room. Viewing alone produces a different kind of reaction to viewing as part of a group and it allows a more intense relationship to develop between the individual and the text. Without needing to consider anyone else's wishes, the lone viewer has complete control of the environment, and can exercise choice.

The remote control

A key factor in this has been the rise of the remote control. In the early years of TV, changing channels (or indeed turning your set off) involved getting up and turning a knob on the set itself. Remember that in those days a set took several minutes to 'warm up' when switched on. The remote control was developed as early as the 1950s but was not widely available until the early 1980s when video recorders in homes became widespread (Bellamy, 2004: 1918). The effect of the remote was to give power to the viewer, who could now make quick and easy judgments by switching channels when not satisfied. The remote also created commercial anxiety, as many people used ad breaks as an opportunity to sample what was showing elsewhere. The ability to have some choice over what was on screen allowed the viewer to control the viewing space (Gauntlett and Hill, 1999: 35). If they chose to keep watching a show, the act of making a conscious decision to do so meant that they invested more in the texts.

Knowing texts

Choosing to be a regular viewer of a show creates a developing relationship between you and the text. We build up knowledge of the events within it, both depicted and implied, and, of course, get to know the characters or format. This will be looked at in more detail in the second part of the book, when texts will be examined more closely, but the point to remember here is that we bring ourselves to the text – not just our own lives, identities and feelings from outside the text but also our experiences of the text. We come to know the characters, for instance, and have our expectations of the way in which they are likely to act in specific situations. We understand the internal logic of a series and producers work together with this understanding.

To take an example: in *Friends* our knowledge of the ensemble of friends over different episodes leads to certain expectations about how they will behave as a chaotic situation unfolds. Ross will respond neurotically and Chandler with a sarcastic remark, while Phoebe's mixture of insouciance and other-worldliness leaves her

> **Think about . . .**
> Watch one of your favourite shows with a friend who is not a fan – and ensure either that they have not seen it before or gave it up after an episode. How does watching with this person, who has not shared your experiences as a viewer, affect your enjoyment of the show? What does this tell you about the way in which our responses to TV programmes are constructed?

untouched by the chaos. Once we know a show, understand its internal logic and the manner in which its constituent parts work together, then the relationship between ourselves and the text becomes more dynamic as it begins to play upon that knowledge. This relationship takes time to develop (intertextual references won't work in an opening episode when we lack knowledge of character, tone and situation, for instance) and relies on an understanding that lots of people, or at least a dedicated group, are regular viewers.

This does not just apply to fiction. In a factual entertainment show like *I'm a Celebrity, Get Me out of Here* ... the format fulfils our expectations. We are aware that every day there will be a bush-tucker trial involving contestants having to undergo all manner of intimacies with spiders, snakes, rats and the like. We apply our textual understanding to build up a sense of anticipation when we see the dynamics of the group in the jungle, wondering how individuals will react when faced with the trial horrors. Knowing that we can influence this by voting for them to endure these torments heightens this anticipation.

Audience theories

Much scholarly work on television has investigated the relationship between text and audience and the degree to which it is free to decipher meanings. Scholars have also been concerned with the representation of different groups in society and the general social effects of the ideologies that TV texts seem to embody.

Structures and signs

As TV developed as a mass medium, the straightforward 'effects' model of text and audience propagated by the Frankfurt School and others seemed inadequate. The relationship was clearly a more complex one but many still argued that TV was part of a communications strategy – a way of sending messages to the masses, which they absorb and replicate in other aspects of their daily lives. The structuralist critics, such as Roland Barthes, argued that texts (whether books, films, TV programmes or photographs) were made up of deep underlying structures that worked to direct meaning (Barthes, 1972; 121–31). The structures worked with signs (a process known as semiotics) that invited the consumer to link objects, or words, with particular values. A signifier (say an image of a kindly policeman such as British TV stalwart *Dixon of Dock Green*, BBC 1955–76) creates something that is signified (an idea that the police are a benevolent force in society that keep us safe, perhaps). Together they form a sign.

Structuralist ideas were enormously influential in the 1960s and 1970s, as they seemed to be a verifiable, almost scientific, method of understanding texts by breaking them into their constituent parts while maintaining that they were ideologically controlled. However, structuralism is very deterministic. It allows little freedom for us as viewers to look at a TV text in ways that are not just defined by its structure or to bring meanings to it ourselves.

Encoding/decoding

Scholarly work has made attempts to adapt the ideological aspects of structuralism to television, while acknowledging that our responses were not just controlled by the structures of the texts. One of the most important examples of this work was Stuart Hall's essay 'Encoding/Decoding' (Hall, 1980: 121–31). Hall argued that television texts were 'encoded' with structures and codes articulating particular ideological positions. It is important to understand that this process is not necessarily a conscious one on behalf of the programme-makers; he is not suggesting that it is all a planned conspiracy to hypnotise the public into doing what those in power want. Rather it is one of the ways hegemony works, and TV producers are influenced by the urge to consent to the way society is ordered.

When we watch a TV show, we are then decoding it, 'reading' and understanding its messages. For Hall the text is powerless without this: 'if no 'meaning' is taken, there can be no 'consumption' (ibid.: 80). If the meaning is not articulated in practice, it has no effect. However, Hall stresses that no one reading can be assured, as encoding is not a foolproof process. The structures and codes will convey a meaning that most people will accept – a 'dominant' or 'preferred' reading that delivers the message supporting the status quo.

However, Hall develops Barthes's idea that some texts can be 'polysemic': that is, they may have multiple possible meanings. Some people may accept some of the dominant codes, but reject others. For example, a viewer of *24* (Fox 2001–) may object to the portrayal of Arabs but accept the general principle of Jack Bauer defending national security. This would be a 'negotiated' reading.

Other viewers might reject the text out of hand and make an 'oppositional' reading. Hall also makes the point that someone might make an 'aberrant' reading that is a personal reaction, avoiding the 'dominant' reading. For instance, while watching *Prime Suspect* (Granada/ITV 1991–2006) a viewer could be upset because a crime portrayed mirrors their own experience, or be preoccupied by Helen Mirren's appearance.

Clearly Hall's theory is true to a degree. We take on information from TV programmes and they contain explicit or implicit meanings about the world. This view of television still assumes that watching is a largely passive activity, however. The different types of reading are not equally weighted: the 'dominant' or 'preferred' reading is assumed to be by far the most likely response. Hall is a Marxist critic and so also assumes that the codes are based primarily on economic power relationships and these determine our responses.

The 'active viewer'

If we look at our own experiences of viewing, however, it does not feel that simple. This approach seems too determined, underestimating the complexity of watching TV in two key ways:

1. We are not passive in our responses to texts much of the time. For one thing, we may dislike the programme intensely and turn it off. We may like aspects of it, but not others. We might not laugh when expected to, or feel moved, or we may disagree with the points it seems to be trying to make. We may make a conscious decision to keep following a series, or to give it up. We may feel a particularly strong positive response to a scene or a character, beyond what seems to be suggested by the text. The audience is not a homogenous mass but full of individuals with very different life stories that they bring to a text.
2. The text itself may be ambiguous. It may inspire contradictory responses in one person, let alone different individuals. 'Good' TV (the definition of this will be discussed later), like any art, should be complex enough to carry more than one possible meaning or inspire more than one reaction. Barthes talked about 'open' (rich and complex) texts and 'closed' texts (limited, basic) texts. 'Open' texts are polysemic. He assumed that television texts were likely to be 'closed'. Perhaps he was wrong.

In contrast to Hall, John Fiske, in *Television Culture*, suggested that the viewer was active and that ultimately there are as many meanings to a text as there are viewers. We are all different, and bring our own experiences and personalities to everything we see thus creating our own meanings (1987: 65–72). Fiske was particularly interested in resistant readings, which have also been the focus for many feminist critics – for instance, in soap opera (Brunsdon, 2000). Here the viewer picks on something within the text that may go against its dominant message, so, for instance, while there may be an underlying idea in *Sex and the City* that settling down with a man is an aspiration worth having, the actions of Samantha in much of the series resists this ideology.

Audience studies

Some scholars have tried to put these theories to the test by working with real viewers to explore their responses and reactions to programmes in detail. Such studies have raised interesting questions about the nature of watching TV and how that might affect interpretation. They have also yielded useful data on who exactly watches what and their reasons for doing so. This has been achieved through very detailed field exercises, involving diaries, questionnaires and representative samples of viewers.

David Morley has produced a number of detailed audience studies: one, *The 'Nationwide' Audience* (1980), looked at viewers of the BBC's early evening magazine show *Nationwide* (1969–84) and examined their reactions to the programme. In his opinion, Fiske's ideas were pushing the idea of the 'active viewer' too far. Viewers exist in a society dictated by certain codes and they must be influenced by them. It is thus hard to resist entirely the meanings communicated in the structures of the texts. He argues that 'audiences do not see only what they want to see, since a message (or programme) is not simply a window on the world but a construction' (1992: 21).

Nationwide purported to present a picture of ordinary Britain to the average viewer, mixing light-hearted items with some social and political coverage. In doing so it made assumptions about how people saw society and their place within it. Morley organised different groups (all students of very different types) and gauged their reactions (Morley, 1992: 91). Although he dismissed Fiske's conception of the audience, he also found that Hall's ideas were too determined. His research showed that economic power was only one of many ways the text–viewer relationship was defined. Responses were much more complex and he concluded that the knowledge and experience of each viewer did help define their understanding of a programme's meaning (1992: 117–18). There have been many other audience studies since this work, another influential exercise being Ien Ang's work on Dutch fans of *Dallas* (1985).

> Think about . . .
>
> . . . a programme you saw this week – trace your reactions as it unfolded. What views did you form and did any of them change as you continued to watch? What kind of 'decodings' do you think you were making?

TV and identity

Audiences can respond in different ways collectively, and as individuals. As well as looking at TV viewers as a mass audience, we can also examine the behaviour of viewers as individuals or as groups within society. We bring different things as individuals to texts. This is an important point to remember, because we, and our responses to programmes, create meanings as much as the content of the texts themselves.

What we bring to texts will vary for different programmes and different viewing occasions. While some of our characteristics and tastes will stay the same, others may alter with our circumstances, or as we grow older. After all, when we see a repeat of an old programme our responses may be very different than when we viewed it for the first time. We have gained in experience and different things have happened to us in the intervening period. Perhaps some of those experiences mean that the programme will upset us now, or perhaps our critical faculties are now more sophisticated. Also society will have changed. It may seem hopelessly dated now, or even offensive, as the accepted social discourse has changed around particular issues.

We consist of a collection of different identities that we might employ at different times. Let's invent a potential viewer, Martha. Martha may watch some programmes primarily as a woman, some as a young person, some as an English person, some as a black person, some as an Arsenal fan, some as a history student, or perhaps some as a person who has experienced bereavement. Different aspects of Martha will come into play in choosing programmes and in her reactions to what she is watching. They may feel very important at certain moments and not relevant at others. What may also be vital are the tastes Martha has formulated over a lifetime of TV viewing. She may have learnt that she enjoys some types of programme – say sitcoms and history documentaries – and will seek them out. She may also have learnt that she does not care for others, maybe soap operas or makeover shows, and turns over when they come on. We can see then that Martha is bringing a great deal of meaning to texts, some of which is extremely complex, and perhaps even contradictory. Not all her tastes may conform to parts of her identity – she might be young but hate *Hollyoaks* and enjoy *Heartbeat*, for instance. As Fiske and others (e.g. Lury, 2006) suggest, the way we make our own meanings can be a dynamic process of negotiation with ourselves.

> Think about . . .
> . . . the different aspects that make up your own identity and consider how these might come into play while consuming different television texts. What do you bring to particular programmes?

Cultural identity

A particular cultural context might change how a text is viewed. At its most obvious, something that seems bland or quite tame on British TV might be subversive or shocking in another cultural setting – note, for instance, the very close control of imported programmes in regimes like China or Iran. But differences can also work on a more implicit level and this can be seen in cross-cultural exchanges between the US and the UK. While there is a shared language, a similar political process and a television history that at least overlaps, there are also fundamental differences of interpretation and response. British terrestrial TV has been notably more liberal in depicting sex and strong language than the US networks, for example, but has often felt more cautious about violence.

More than this there can be differences in identification with characters or participants on screen. In her book *Selling Television* Jeanette Steemers mentions that *The Weakest Link* failed in both the Far East and in Southern Europe because viewers found the summary dismissal of losing contestants in the quiz too humiliating and cruel (2003: 179, 202). The enjoyment for viewers in Britain of public-based shows like *Big Brother*, *The X Factor* and *Pop Idol* (talkbackThames 2001–3) is derived as much from seeing people do badly and make fools of themselves as from seeing them display their talents and reach the top against the odds. This is an intrinsic part of British culture much complained about by home-grown celebrities and often referred to as 'tall poppy syndrome' – essentially the desire to see those attempting to better themselves fail. There is also a tendency to ironically applaud either the completely self-deluded or the cheerily witless no-hoper, almost as a contrary reaction to the stated aims of the programme. Transpose the same formats, as has happened, to an aspirational culture like the US and the programmes may be different. Audiences might be willing contestants to realise their talents and become famous and not have the same perverse pleasure in failure that we enjoy so much here in Britain. This changes the meanings of the text in quite a profound way, with cultural differences reflected in the reasons why we watch.

CASE STUDY: SPECIFIC AUDIENCES – NEW TRICKS AND THE OLDER VIEWER

There are some texts that appeal to a particular demographic. They may be produced with ingredients that address that audience – for instance, characters with whom viewers can identify, who seem to be in some way like them – or employ an appropriate aesthetic, like the fast cutting common on youth shows. The targeted audience needs to respond to those ingredients, however, and make its own connections with the text. It's worth seeing how this can work. One of the big hits on BBC1 in recent years has been the detective series *New Tricks* (BBC 2003–). The show has proved to be a big ratings hit, averaging about 7 million viewers, a very impressive figure in the multichannel age. *New Tricks* defies the times and current industry thinking because it is a success made by an audience much older than the sought-after 16–34 demographic. How has this occurred and what connections is this audience making with the programme?

New Tricks is based on a cold-case squad of three retired detectives brought together to reinvestigate old crimes where new evidence has emerged. They are controlled by a forty-something female career policewoman, Sandra Pullman, who attempts to keep her charges in line, despite their contempt for modern bureaucratic policing methods. A number of unpleasant crimes are investigated and several episodes contain moving moments and some psychological realism. However, the pleasures of the series are not found in the plotlines and or in any sense of the realistic depiction of police work, unlike shows like *Prime Suspect* or the *CSI* franchise. Viewers enjoy the show largely for the dynamic between the characters. There are a couple of factors here that appeal to the older viewer.

The first is the familiar, expressed through Jack, Brian and Gerry, the three retired coppers. They are played by three popular TV actors with CVs going back over thirty years. Jack is played by James Bolam, famous as Terry in *The Likely Lads* series and for the 1970s' drama *When the Boat Comes In* (BBC 1976–81); Alun Armstrong (Brian) has been in many 'quality' dramas on British TV (*Our Friends in the North*, BBC 1996, *Goodbye Cruel World*, BBC 1992); and Dennis Waterman (Gerry) has played numerous cockney charmers over the years, notably in *The Sweeney* (Thames/ITV 1975–8) and *Minder* (Thames/ITV 1979–89). Their presence and a certain knowingness in their performances and the lines they speak make

New Tricks makes a specific appeal to an older audience

connections with previous TV texts viewers might have enjoyed and to a shared experience – of being older – common to the core audience.

Second, the mixture of incomprehension and disdain for the contemporary world expressed by the three 'old dogs' in *New Tricks* is likely to resonate and amuse the older audience. The travails of getting older and set in your ways are wryly observed. The characters express this in different ways: Gerry is an ageing lothario with a troupe of ex-wives; Jack is bereaved and talks to the grave of his dead wife; while Brian has mental illness problems and lacks social skills. Together they embody frustrations and fears about getting older.

Occasionally they face younger rivals in the police or cross swords with the bureaucratic and greasy-pole-climbing commanding officer. Sandra Pullman (played by Amanda Redman) bridges the modern world and the world of the three retired coppers. Rather than deploy a young character to create conflict with the older men, she is a middle-aged character with a rather lonely life outside work. There is a reciprocal protective element in their relationship and she takes the edge off their more politically incorrect tendencies while proving largely sympathetic to them. As a woman, she offers a different point of audience identification, especially for the older female viewer, as does Esther, Brian's bemused wife.

The success of *New Tricks* with the older audience is based on such points of identification, providing elements in the text that this older audience values. There are strong characters, witty scripts, and inter- and extra-textual references to shared histories on a number of levels – getting old, dislocation from modern life, experience of Britain in the last forty years, and, very importantly, the experience of watching TV in that time.

Fan audiences

Sometimes the connection between text and viewer can be stronger than merely making 'an appointment to view' for each transmission. Some of the audience have such a passionately positive response to a programme that they become 'fans', in the same way that other people are fans of football teams or pop groups. As well as buying DVDs and watching each episode several times, fans form their own communities that interact, both virtually, through online forums, and physically, at conventions, for example. They can form pressure groups, either to keep 'their' show going, or to comment on some new development. A remake of costume drama *Poldark* (BBC 1975–7) in 1996 was bitterly attacked by fans for not using the same lead actors.

The fan base occasionally has to be courted and won over, as we saw with *Doctor Who*. Certainly once established, it is important that a dialogue is formed between fans and programme-makers, although the relationship is not always an easy one. Fans pick up on particular things that they like about a text – setting, tone, style, individual characters or actors – and may be very loathe for anything to change. In contrast the creative talent behind a programme may want to develop and change the programme, and find themselves constrained by these expectations from their core audience.

Like lovers spurned, fans can sometimes be the most critical of audiences if they feel their programme is no longer delivering the connection that originally drew them to it. New characters can sometimes face hostile reactions if it is felt they do not measure up to their predecessors, for example.

We will look at the nature of fan cultures and their critical discourse more closely on page 84 but here we should point out how fans consume a text in a different way to the more casual viewers. The response is more intense and emotional, and instead of absorbing the text as part of 'a flow', fans are isolating a particular programme from it and understanding it in quite a different way to non-fans (Hills, 2006: 105). A fan takes the original point of connection and builds on it, actively reading the text to recreate this enjoyment so it becomes an element within the text.

Telephilia

What is the extent of our active viewership? Can we attain the same feelings of ecstasy, of resonance or of revelation as is assumed for fine art, literature or cinema? In the cinema, we have 'cinephilia' – a love of both film as a work of art and the experience of going to the cinema. Some think that television cannot inspire this kind of love. John Caughie has argued that there cannot be a 'telephilia' in the same way as there is a 'cinephilia' (2005), which he discusses through reference to his own feelings of intense delight at experiences in picture houses such as watching a Fred

Astaire dance routine. His argument seems to be connected with TV's grounding in the real world of domestic life. The medium's connection with the humdrum, with the banality of everyday existence, is thought to diminish the intensity of feeling because it cannot take us away from our lives. TV is still considered somehow 'small', its aesthetics insufficiently grand to have an emotional impact.

I beg to disagree, as others, including Karen Lury (2006), have. I would suggest that the everydayness of TV is precisely what gives it emotional power. It can convey the reality of a feeling to us in a way that cannot be disregarded or escaped easily: for instance in the news reports of harrowing war deaths or famine. TV also gains strength from its fixed place in our daily lives: it takes on the rhythms of normal, mundane existence and comments upon them.

One of my favourite shows is the 1970s' sitcom *Whatever Happened to the Likely Lads?*, which tells the story of Bob and Terry, two Tyneside men, no longer as young as they used to be, wondering what is happening to their lives. Little dramatic happens but the show's treatment of everyday life, of the compromises we make and the decisions we don't take, speak to me on a profound level – it feels liberating, it feels resonant.

What can 'telephilia' – the love of television – be then? Su Holmes and Deborah Jermyn (2006: 55) suggest that it might be the investment in 'television art' in the appreciation and collecting of shows like *The Sopranos* or *The West Wing* (NBC 1999–2006). I would suggest, like Lury, that 'telephilia' can also be an emotional response to a piece of television art that can, just like cinema and the sublime feeling we may experience watching an Astaire dance routine, be about moments as well as whole texts. A scene, or even an image, can delight, trouble or intrigue on a number of levels. At the end of *Edge of Darkness* (BBC 1985) policeman Ronnie Craven (Bob Peck) is dying from radiation sickness. As he falls, he screams the name of his daughter, killed at the start of the series. The next shot shows the place where he fell, now full of strange black flowers. This closing image raises as many questions as it answers, leaving us to consider its strangeness and emotional impact on us as viewers.

We can often feel haunted by things we have seen on television years earlier. In many years of dealing with enquiries from the public about television, I have often been contacted by people trying to identify something that stirs in the corner of the memory – a storyline, a scene, a piece of dialogue, sometimes just an image. This may be, like *Edge of Darkness*, a piece of work seen as 'quality television' and admired by many, or it may be something more obscure – a one-off single play, or an episode of a cult children's drama perhaps. It may be a moment in something otherwise totally unmemorable, even not very good, that made a connection with us.

Here again the domestic context is all-important. Our response is tied in with how we watched the text, what was going on that day maybe, what stage we had reached in our lives, perhaps the juxtaposition with what we had just watched

Craven's dying cry of love. Strange black flowers grow at the spot where he died. Meanings are left open.

Think about . . .

. . . your own TV memories. List three 'moments' and think about why they made such an impact on you.

previously. The intimacy of television, its entrance into our everyday life, is a factor in making these moments impact on our memory. Far from 'telephilia' being an impossibility, I would suggest that it can be very intense, but that it differs from 'cinephilia' – in part because of the influence of the context around the text. Look at the nostalgia market for some old children's TV programmes, for instance. The continuation of *Bagpuss* in British culture over thirty years on is not so much the text itself, charming though it is, but the context that surrounds it – a kind of folk memory of growing up in the 1970s that is being passed on to new generations.

Evaluating TV

Of course, just having a response to something doesn't make it good. It is time to enter one of the thorniest debates in studying television: What is 'good' TV? How do we recognise it?

There have been two rather contradictory modes of thinking about evaluating television within television studies. Much academic work on television, until relatively recently, has been primarily concerned with the social effects and mechanisms of the medium. Value judgments are sometimes considered to be suspect because they are inevitably subjective – that is, seen as just personal opinions. On the other hand there have been debates well beyond the academy about the idea of 'quality television', a phrase that has been applied to various types of programme at different periods of television history. The term has been applied to investigative documentaries, costume adaptations, single plays or serials by particular TV dramatists on social issues, and to some long-form US dramas.

Studying TV Evaluation
Read Sarah Cardwell's essay 'Television Aesthetics' and Robin Nelson's contribution 'Quality Television' in *Critical Studies in Television* vol. 1 no. 1 (2006), which looks at the critical arguments around evaluation <www.criticalstudiesintelevision.com >.

More recently academics have been re-examining the role of evaluation in studying TV. These have stressed the importance of making evaluations based on close readings and interpretations of the text (as, to nail my colours to a mast, I hope this book does too). Evaluation is, of course, subjective, but it can also be informed and perceptive. It isn't just about what we like.

With other art forms, there is much less wariness in making judgments about texts. People are quite happy to go to major art galleries, because they understand that the paintings are in some way 'great'; or they appreciate that Shakespeare's plays are superior examples of dramatic art. Film is a heavily evaluated medium with a valued canon of titles made by auteurs. Art-house films are marketed on the basis that they are somehow 'better' – more profound, more crafted – than most multiplex product.

Why then is there such reticence to evaluate television positively? Partly, I would suggest, this is tied in with a self-image problem that has beset the medium since its birth. Because TV is seen as 'everyday' and 'domestic', and a 'diversion', there has been a tendency to dismiss all its output as undifferentiated rubbish – a view still occasionally heard by those rather smug folk who proudly boast that they do not own a television set and are much the better for it (actually they are missing out, as we know).

However, clearly some television texts *are* better than others. This is not to say that these 'quality' texts are somehow not connected with the rest of television production and consumption. They were not beamed down fully formed as works of art from some other dimension, but came from the same processes as everything else we see.

So what, then, might make them better than others? Consider something that you felt was a good work of art and examine what you think made it so. Originality could be a factor: it may experiment with the form, raise new questions or have a particular aesthetic quality that hasn't been seen before. However, of course, not everything original works well, and indeed some work that is not original can still be good, even great. It could be something that works well within its particular remit: that, when compared to similar programmes, fulfils our expectations better. A thriller could be very thrilling, a comedy very funny, or a documentary very interesting.

Most of all it could be something that Jason Jacobs describes as having 'strong engagement, intense viewer proximity and concentrated attention' (2001: 431). If this resonance applies to a large section of the audience, it may be a pointer to a work's inherent qualities. What, of course, does not equate with quality is popularity itself; a programme may be very popular but not very 'good'. It may be watched purely because it gives some kind of instant gratification without having much impact on its audience. However, that doesn't mean that the popular can't be good, far from it. *Coronation Street* has been the top-rated programme in Britain for years, and while it certainly is not always good, there are frequently good things in it such as witty lines of dialogue, well-performed scenes, emotionally realistic situations and so on.

Many shows that most would agree are 'quality' have had degrees of popularity (*The Singing Detective*, BBC 1986, *Cracker*, *The Office* and *The Sopranos*). Others have not, however – some series are cancelled because of poor ratings but the series or two that was broadcast still lingers in the minds of those who watched it.

To take one instance, *Buried* (World Productions/C4 2003) was a complex series set in a British male prison. It wove together a number of storylines, featured some immensely powerful performances (such as Lenny James as its protagonist, Lee) and raised difficult emotional and moral questions. However, perhaps inevitably, it was very dark. While those who kept viewing found it a rich and rewarding experience, many were put off by the prospect of watching prison brutality. Ratings were thus low and despite critical acclaim it was not recommissioned by Channel 4 (many would argue it should have been and that its low figures did not mean that the series was not of the highest quality). Complexity can also be a factor in defining a TV text as 'good' or better than others. *Buried*, for instance, refused the route of easy answers to the dilemmas that it put forward. A complex text can mean a richer text (although it has to be well crafted and structured or it can just become impenetrable). It allows more ambiguities and is more open to interpretation.

Evaluating a programme can (and should) be a challenging business. We have to consider what we bring to a text – our background, prejudices, tastes, history and social context – and think about how that might affect our judgment (Nelson, 2006: 61). Clearly no evaluations are entirely objective, divorced from our own contexts, but that does not mean that all such evaluations have the same weight. An informed evaluation (interpreting the text and rooted in the experience of it), mindful of one's own position, does have more weight than an uninformed opinion based on a very superficial reading. Not all opinions are equally valid in such circumstances: the opinions may be interesting as part of a body of criticism, the people themselves may be equally valid as commentators, but the responses need to be thought

> **Think about . . .**
> Read TV criticism from a number of different publications – broadsheet paper, tabloid, online blogs and academic texts – what kind of assumptions does each make about 'quality'?

through and interrogated to achieve validity. Fiske's analysis was problematic because it did not take this into account sufficiently.

Making meanings

Equally this applies when texts are read for meanings. David Bordwell and Kristin Thompson, in their classic film textbook *Film Art*, suggest four levels of meaning 1979: 49–52). This model can be applied perfectly well to television programmes and I shall do so using *Buffy the Vampire Slayer* as an example. The four levels are:

1. Explicit – meanings that are clearly discussed within the text. For example, in *Buffy the Vampire Slayer* the notion of adolescence, of becoming an adult, is referenced by the characters in the dialogue and, given the high-school setting, is fairly undeniable.
2. Implicit – meanings that are implied within the text. In *Buffy*, it could be argued that the series implies that the dark side, represented by the various vampires and demons, is something within us all, or within our society, that we have to confront.
3. Referential – meanings within the text that refer to events or knowledge outside of it. *Buffy* refers to aspects of the lives of contemporary young women, to the public education system in the US and to the ancient lore of vampires and the occult.
4. Symptomatic – meanings, whether intended by the programme-makers or not, that reflect society or replicate particular ideologies. Thus a 'rich text' like *Buffy* could be said to critique conservative cultures in the US of the late 1990s, or indeed to unwittingly endorse some of the ideological values of that time and place.

As these examples show, meanings can be contested, particularly the implicit and symptomatic levels, where it may be perfectly possible to have two completely contradictory views that are both justified from readings of the text. It could be argued that *Buffy* is a feminist text or one that reinforces female stereotypes, for instance, with textual references to both.

However, while particular programmes can elicit a number of valid interpretations, not every meaning can be accepted. Every meaning has to withstand some kind of scrutiny in relation to the text. For instance, if someone suggested that *Buffy* was actually an allegory about the war in Iraq, it would be hard to support (not least because it predates most of the events). Equally an attempt to paint *Buffy* as a piece of pro-neo conservative propaganda would probably falter on the show's positive gay characters and distrust of organised religion.

Stuart Hall's idea of the 'preferred reading' – an interpretation of meaning from texts that does not preclude other, or even contradictory, readings, but describes an understanding that most people would derive from seeing a programme – can be very useful, albeit developed from its rather rigid original conception (Hall, 1980: 134). This is something to bear in mind when attempting to evaluate programmes.

Changing consumption

So far I have mainly discussed well-established ways of consuming television – an individual or group at home watching programmes, chosen from a schedule, on a television set. While this remains the most common way of watching TV, times are changing very fast.

In the last five years there has been a gradual shift in viewing habits that seems to be accelerating, with new developments on the horizon or about to move into mass usage. Our adoption of new technology and the options that it brings can radically change our relationship with texts. Media is all around us and we are building up our own media profiles, selecting texts from various sources that we feel complement each other – a process Abercrombie and Longhurst call 'mapping a mediascape' (1998: 170). TV is having to adjust from being the dominant mode to competing in this 'mediascape'.

In this section I will examine these new developments and how they might already affect our understanding of programmes. First, though, it is useful to look back at TV history and note that this process has always gone on and that some of the viewing patterns common these days were once radical and far-reaching developments.

How the VCR changed TV

We have already seen how the remote control allowed viewers more freedom to create their own environment – changing the channel or turning off the sound – and represented an incremental shift in the power relations between producer and consumer. The advent of the video recorder (VCR) was another extremely important development that affected viewing habits. When most households started to acquire VCRs in the early 1980s, it revolutionised how we understood texts. In Britain, although apparently much less so in the US, VCRs were primarily used for timeshifting – that is, recording TV programmes and playing them back at a more convenient time. Necessarily this diluted the mass experience of everyone watching the same programme at the same time (although people would often catch up relatively soon afterwards).

More importantly the mechanics of the recorder allowed us to see programmes in a different way. Previously a show would only be seen once, with perhaps the possibility of a repeat a year or so later. We might miss some of the complexities of the text, and the lack of availability made it hard to study programmes. However, if we recorded a show, we could rewind, freeze-frame or fast-forward. Think about what this meant for viewers. You could go back over a scene if you hadn't quite grasped what was going on, zip through parts you thought were a bit boring, and, crucially, skip the adverts. You could freeze the frame to appreciate the image or gain more information, or, of course, stop the transmission whenever you wanted to go to the loo or go out and see it in different sections than those prescribed by the broadcaster.

In addition, instead of just recording programmes you would have otherwise missed over each other *ad infinitum*, you could keep programmes and build up libraries of particular titles. 'Owning' a text in this way marks it out from the 'flow' of broadcasting and precipitates a new kind of relationship – it might become something treasured, a cultural artefact. Although viewers were still bound by the schedule and what is broadcast, television texts are no longer things that happen beyond our control. Instead of being thrown once into the world and then existing only in a vault or in the recesses of our memory, they can be captured, returned to and retained.

Let's now look at some newer developments and how they might be complicating our understanding of programmes, as well as changing our viewing habits.

Digital multichannel

'Digital', or 'multichannel', is now the broadcasting environment in which texts are negotiated. The two terms are often used as a compound word, but they are two different innovations that have happened to coincide and combine at the same time. Digital refers to the transmission technology, the ability to use computerised technology to send pictures to screens digitally rather than lines of data through analogue transmitters. Multichannel is the industrial organisation of the TV industry into an unlimited number of channels and broadcasters, a process enabled by digital technology, which does not have the limited spectrum of terrestrial analogue, where technical constraints mean that only a limited number of services are possible.

The technological advances in delivery and choice represented by digital/multichannel have become established very quickly over the last few years, to the point where over 75% of UK households now have access to digital TV in some form (either Sky, Freeview or cable; *Broadcast*). Choices, in terms of channels, have of course grown with this advance. As a consequence, it also threatens some of the available familiar viewing modes, although it could be argued that these consequences are linked to its innovations, rather than an inherent part of the technology. For instance, there is nothing technically to stop the ever-spiralling number of channels being modelled on BBC1 or ITV1 (mixed schedules appealing to a broad audience) but that is not by and large what has occurred. Instead channels have aimed either to present one particular type of programming (UKTV History, Sci-Fi Channel, Five Life) or appeal to a clearly defined demographic (E4, BBC3, ITV3).

The amount of TV watched has not increased with this profusion of viewing choice – average daily viewing remains just under four hours. Interest is simply dispersed over a wider area than previously, hence the ratings fall of established terrestrial favourites as some viewers presumably decide to cease their relationship with them, or possibly view them in some other form.

Interestingly *Broadcast* has reported that ratings for individual programmes on new digital channels remain low and do not seem to be rising, implying that viewers are spreading their attentions quite thinly (source: *Broadcast*, 14 October 2005). This makes the case for a licence fee, for instance, more difficult. Lower audiences seem to show that there is less social benefit from public service television because fewer people are experiencing it. The BBC has tried to counteract this by allocating resources for the launch and maintenance of digital channels with a public service role, which either develop cutting-edge new talent (BBC3) or take a serious and discursive view of world affairs and high culture (BBC4).

What are the consequences of this new type of viewing? Within the industry these are already being felt. Smaller audiences mean smaller budgets for a start. As well as affecting the look and ambitions of the text itself, these smaller budgets impact on the capacity of production companies to continue in business, at least on an independent basis. On the other hand it does mean that there are more options for placing your programmes, and in some circumstances it could be argued that ratings pressure will drop when the industry gets used to more diffuse audiences. This might allow more experimentation.

The rise of digital also affects our relationship with the medium. The shared experience of television will certainly lessen and some argue (mistakenly I think) that it will disappear altogether. With a larger schedule, and a culture that has less rather than more free time as work continues to dominate most people's lives, we will have to work harder to form relationships with texts. Veteran producer Tony Garnett, while welcoming the new television world, considered that marketing work – making its existence known – was the foremost challenge (Garnett speaking at the TV/Fiction Exchange Conference, Crewe, September 2006). We may be aided in this, but probably through different delivery systems from the traditional TV set.

Think about . . .
What do you think the future might hold for television in terms of what we choose to watch? What impact will this make on the medium – will TV still offer any kind of shared experience?

The tendency may be to stick with the familiar: to watch only the genres we know we like or stay within our own demographic group. The diversity of what we consume could narrow, and as a consequence our view of the world become more limited. Or, of course, it may develop in a different direction that we cannot as yet foresee – perhaps TV will still be as important in our own lives and society.

Whatever happens, digital and multichannel TV has been established as a road map for the future. The analogue signal will be switched off over a period of four years, concluding as early as 2012 in the UK and 2009 in the US. The government and broadcasters have expended energy and resources in convincing the nation of the benefits of digital and have largely succeeded, partly through the success of

Freeview, which had the advantage of one purchase and no contract commitments, unlike Sky or cable where you buy the service, not the hardware. It will be interesting to compare what happens in Britain to the experience in the US, where, through cable, viewers have long had multiple choices. It is interesting to note that although there are frequent complaints that, as Bruce Springsteen sang, there are '57 channels and nothing on', network TV does survive and, as discussed, channels like HBO do show challenging material.

PVR

PVR (personal video recorder) technology has been available for a few years but is only now starting to become a mass consumer item in the UK (it is more established in the US). PVR brands like TiVo or Sky+ are becoming an accepted part of viewing and the way this technology is used can significantly alter the understanding of texts. PVRs contain a hard disk onto which programmes can be recorded and either viewed directly from the disk or copied to blank DVDs. You can preset specific material you want to watch but you can also programme the device to record a range of programmes of particular genres, or it can do so itself based on previous preferences. Instead of hunting through the schedule for shows we might want to see, it does this job for us, in effect creating our own channel just showing the programmes we like.

Some of the functions are, of course, similar to recording on video, which most people have been doing for the past twenty-five years. However, as well as doing away with the impracticality of hoarding vast numbers of tapes with no idea of what they contain, it does promote a different kind of consumption. The ease by which material can be stored means that some viewers will watch almost everything at a different time to its original broadcast, again weakening the power of the schedule. When watching programmes, a facility allows you to stop the live broadcast to visit the toilet, pop to the shops or complete other mundane tasks. This dramatically changes our power relationship with the text: instead of being part of the broadcasting 'flow', something that happens regardless of what we do, it now becomes a tool under our control.

The television experience is now something we can tailor to suit ourselves. PVR is creating a certain amount of trepidation in the broadcasting industry because of this. The control over the nature of the broadcast – stopping it, fast-forwarding over the dull bits to watch just the key climactic moments – changes the nature of the text as it was made and intended to be consumed. It is the video experience on a much larger scale, replacing the schedule rather than being an alternative to seeing a programme when it is being transmitted. As shown in Chapter 1, there is particular disquiet in the advertising industry, and therefore among the commercial broadcasters who rely on this revenue.

DVD

The rise of DVD (Digital Versatile Disc) as a new format for video, replacing VHS tapes, has also revolutionised TV consumption. Here the emphasis is specifically on our understanding and appreciation of the texts themselves.

You could, of course, buy TV series on video but the tapes were bulky and, with usually only about three episodes on each one, trying to build up a series could necessitate moving house. The DVD disc format, with a far higher storage capacity through digital compression and its slim-line packaging, is much more sympathetic to TV material and purchases have risen greatly as a result. Production costs are also lower, making a wider range of material obtainable.

DVD gives TV texts a new life. Experiencing texts away from the 'flow' changes our understanding of them.

In these circumstances the major point of contact between the viewer and shows with a considerable cult or critical reputation, such as *Deadwood*, is through DVD. It may be no coincidence that these shows are so critically esteemed. This mode of consumption removes them from the stigma of broadcast TV and allows them to be seen almost as *objets d'art*, something you own and which reflect your taste, rather than just something you view at the same time as everyone else.

This notion of ownership seems important: to own something is to make it special, and gives you something to aspire to. Adverts for DVDs often emphasise 'yours to own', promoting the value of controlling your personal access to the product. One very happy result of the DVD revolution for many of us is that the high sales and low production costs have encouraged broadcasters and rights holders to open their archives and make a lot of old television material available again. The explosion in availability in the last couple of years in the UK has been remarkable, going well beyond commercial successes or recent titles to take in the obscure, the challenging and the quirky, right back in some cases to shows from the 1950s.

Archive TV

This is great news, as many exciting and unique pieces of TV had not been released before. One of the reasons that television has always been something of a poor relation in the arts is that work seemed to have such a short life in the public domain. Alan Bennett, author of some of the greatest works, complained in the 1980s that 'a BBC Television film has no history. It is an incident, with luck and occasion, the bait for the writer a nationwide audience and his work a topic of general discussion that day' (*Sight and Sound*, 1982: 121). Thereafter, however, it becomes just a memory, a text that is not quite tangible and we are left searching for evidence. In the absence of the text, it was difficult to evaluate or study it, and so interesting work was neglected and the story of the form overlooked.

Now older television can be reappraised to see whether it still holds up as a text. We can evaluate its emotional impact, assess its ideas, appreciate its writing and performances and use it in the classroom in the same way as we do old films. The inclusion of extras like interviews with participants or related shorter material can also be illuminating. This way the text lives again, but it is important to remember that it is living in a new form. The experience of watching, say, an old Dennis Potter play on a DVD is very different from catching it by chance on a wet Tuesday night after the news and before a late-night variety show. Similarly the meanings we make from the text may be different from those made by the original audience.

Only a small amount of material has this new life — almost entirely drama and comedy. Other TV texts were designed for the moment and hold little ongoing relevance.

Internet

Perhaps the biggest technological change in our understanding of what television means is the Internet. The ubiquity of the Internet is having a profound effect on television, being seen variously as a commercial threat, an alternative delivery system, a branding opportunity or indeed a force that removes the point of TV as we know it.

Certainly the idea of the Internet as a threat has some validity. The media is all around us like never before and the Internet is the fastest medium, constantly changing content to deliver new information all the time. While it does not reach some sections of society (notably the poor and some of the elderly), to others, particularly the young, it is becoming the dominant medium in their lives, available through a number of systems and a work tool as well as a form of entertainment. In these circumstances the Internet can take over television's established role as the information provider and what might be called 'delivering the moment'. If the web is quicker and as reliable in giving us details of news events, sports results, immediate images, gossip or music, then those functions become less important and less impressive on television. One of TV's most important facets, its 'liveness', the sense of being party to a moment in time and connected to events watched with millions of others, is diminished (there is a discussion on 'liveness' in TV in Lury, 2005: 99).

The buzzword at industry events these days is 'content'. 'Content' essentially includes the TV texts discussed in this book – programmes, commercials, trailers –

but makes them non-medium specific. Increasingly such content, although created for television, can be accessed away from the TV set. IPTV (Internet Protocol Television) can enable TV texts to be seen on home computers or via Internet connections to TV sets, to create something like a video-on-demand service.

Now that more and more people have powerful broadband connections, computers are emerging as an alternative way to experience television viewing. Broadcasters are determined not to be left behind on this one. Channel 4 is now streaming all its output through its website as it is transmitted. The BBC is streaming particular shows that it hopes to promote and offering preview clips. In 2007 it will launch the BBC iplayer, a catch-up service for all programmes broadcast the previous week, and has long-term plans to make its archives available digitally. This presumably will work in a similar way to PVRs but encourages a brand loyalty to the corporation.

All these innovations have largely been based on streaming, allowing viewing access only to material in circumstances controlled by the broadcaster, rather than downloading, where the material is copied and kept. As with the music and film industries before them, broadcasters are afraid of downloading and the threat of copyright theft, worried that it might take revenue away from rights holders like themselves and ultimately from the individual creative talents involved in production. However, downloading as a legitimate method of consumption is now under way: in the US ABC and NBC are already selling programmes, while in the UK Channel 4 is now planning to put the bulk of its archive up for download sale and Five is offering *CSI* episodes to buy electronically. ITV is adopting a different model, putting programmes up free but carrying adverts.

The creative archive
The BBC and Channel 4 have been involved in the creative archive scheme, where a small amount of non-rights sensitive material, typically old news reports and wildlife footage, is made available for download and can be used in student projects, art works and so forth.

If you want to look at streamed extracts of classic British TV programmes, the BFI's Screenonline website makes them available, and offers interpretative text. They can be accessed throughout most schools and universities in the UK.

Companies have had to get involved in providing downloads because it was happening unlawfully anyway. Many TV programmes were being downloaded prior to the UK transmission, especially hit US shows like *Lost* or *Desperate Housewives* or texts with a fervent cult following. This is done illegally, often from pirated copies uploaded onto the web, and broadcasters will increasingly co-operate with anti-piracy bodies to curb this trade. At the same time they have to embrace this new revenue model, as the music industry ultimately did after battling with sites like Napster, and as the Hollywood studios are currently exploring. Also broadcasters with a public service remit are coming under increasing pressure to digitise older material and make it available to all, but the issue of rights is still a hurdle that needs to be overcome.

The Internet and 'clip culture'

As well as being a new way to deliver content, the Internet could change the way we understand texts. For one thing it encourages a kind of 'clip culture', an environment where viewers expect to engage with short pieces of content for instant gratification. For an audience that becomes used to accessing YouTube regularly, or perhaps a *Little Britain* sketch or premiership goals on your mobile, this could become the norm. In a society where we are overloaded with media, information and sensory possibilities, it is easy to see how we could just come to accept a sort of television greatest hits. This is a trend that broadcast TV has also encouraged in the last few years, with the 'best ever' clip shows frequently a marathon fixture on Sunday nights.

Enjoyable though these shows are, and as convenient as the consumption of clips rather than full programmes is, ripping a scene from its context changes the nature of the text and diminishes its pleasures. When PCs and mobiles across Britain played the minute or so footage of David Brent's ridiculous dance from the second series of *The Office* in 2002, it offered a moment's giggle. When seen in the context of the entire episode, it becomes something much more. It becomes quite a profound statement about loneliness and self-delusion, advertising Brent's inability to judge a situation or his own limitations. Watching him dance after his loathed boss's sleek efforts and feeling the stunned silence of his colleagues and the half-hearted applause makes it funnier, as does the accumulated knowledge of Brent throughout the series, and his immediate predicament in the episode.

The extent of the Internet's impact on the business of television and the way we watch it remains to be seen, but clearly it exists. In some cases, notably shows like *Big Brother*, the Internet is an integral part of the broadcasting experience. We are able to access events in the house at any time through streamed footage, are able to share opinions and revisit our favourite clips. What remains to be seen is whether broadcasters can make money directly from it or just hope that it makes people aware of what else they can offer. The problem is that the Internet has developed around free content and people expect this to continue. At this stage it does not look as if web use is going to be another way of funding programmes, for example.

Mobile TV
The screening of TV material through mobile phones, sometimes with original work in mini-episodes that can be accessed as 'mobisodes' is an interesting phenomenon. 'Mobisodes' almost parody the experience of TV and the anticipation of waiting for the next episode, but they are inevitably limited by the aesthetic restrictions of a tiny screen. Similarly it is not at all clear that TV, whichever way we choose to receive it, is suited to viewing on the move. Unlike music or radio it does not translate easily from our domestic environment and sustained mobile consumption beyond the two–five-minute clip is still untested. For all the focus in advertising for phones on their audiovisual content, it is still in terms of goals, gags or 'moments' (Nicholas, 2006: 158)

Interactivity

An important factor in the changing consumption of television is the rise of interactivity. We have talked about the 'active viewer' of television, who constantly evaluates what they watch. Another, very visible, sign of this in

A famous scene from *The Office*. The whole, however, has a greater meaning than the moment

recent years has been the participation of viewers in texts, an explicit on-screen intervention between the programme and its audience.

It is easy to forget that this is a recent innovation. For television's first forty years the demarcation between appearing on TV and watching it was pretty rigid. As a member of the public you were only going to be on screen if you were the contestant in, say, a game show, where you would have written in and been graciously invited to appear by a producer, that is unless you were part of a social problem, in which case you might encounter a documentary crew. Your only other chance was if you had a particularly irritating laugh and could end up in the studio audience of a sitcom. Texts were created entirely by 'professionals' and you had no influence as a viewer on how they were constructed or on their content.

All this has changed. The popularity of makeover shows where film crews invaded the homes and gardens of their viewers, and docusoaps, which followed people in their everyday lives, were an important part of the change in the mid-1990s. This developed further when reality TV shows began to dominate the schedules following the success of the first *Big Brother* in 2000. Members of the public could either be contestants in these real-life game shows or, in programmes like *Wife Swap*, they could be the centre of a programme, creating their own dramas (see Chapter 4). The mystique of being on television has now gone. You no longer need to sing, act, have any discernible talent or occupy a position of power to be on TV. Everyone knows that everyone can do it – it is becoming considered almost an inalienable right to appear on the box.

It is not just our physical appearance on television that forms an intervention by the audience. Technological changes have given us the opportunity to intercede in programmes and change the nature of texts (Jermyn and Holmes, 2006: 50–1) . This can happen in a couple of different ways:

- Voting – many programmes now allow us to decide the outcomes of what we watch by voting, whether by phone or increasingly via the Internet. By doing this we are creating or altering the text ourselves, choosing from a variety of options devised by the producers. The range of programmes this can be applied to is now very wide. We may think initially of casting out a disliked contestant in *Big Brother* but it can also include everything from choosing the goal of the month, to selecting the top films of all time, to electing which crumbling building to save, or not, in *Restoration* (BBC, 2003–5). We are given the power of controlling what will happen. It is often noted that more people vote in *Big Brother* than in general elections, but we should think about the limitations of this power. When we say that our vote does not matter in an election and complain about being the pawn of forces we cannot control, is this also the case in our new role as text creators on television? Is the 'democracy' that voting on TV seems to represent really a sham and are we being manipulated to produce the 'right' (i.e. most profitable) result?

    There are other ways we can insert ourselves into texts apart from voting on the outcome. Text messages from the public are now a common sight on screen, particularly during moments like the live feed on reality shows. While most of these are statements like 'I think Pete is Gr8 – Natasha', they illustrate the expectation of interaction. The public now assume that they will be involved in many programmes and this is deferred to by producers, desperate to retain viewers. The intervention of public opinion, long established on talk radio, is now very much part of our understanding of certain TV texts. This will be discussed more fully in Chapter 4 which considers news and factual TV, but it has now also become a feature of genres like sport and light entertainment.

- The red button – a physical manifestation of the interactive age is 'the red button'. This is a literal description of the button on remote-control devices for digital television that provides an alternative version of the text on offer. We have the choice to find out more information about the image on display (say, some text about the habits of an animal on a wildlife documentary) or a related but different text altogether – an alternative football match, for example (Lury, 2005: 165). The rise of the red button has not been altogether straightforward – Channel 4 abandoned their service recently, while the BBC push theirs relentlessly – but it says something interesting about our quest for more content as viewers: rather like the purchase of DVDs with interminable extras we know we will never watch, it makes us feel as if we are getting value for money.

Interactivity is now a given as part of the viewing experience. Some consider that the battle for control will be won by the viewer – a key concept now is user-generated content, material made by viewers and shared among them, bypassing the 'industry' altogether. Some feel that this is the future and that sites like YouTube are a more inherently democratic way to create texts. News broadcasts are actively working with so-called 'citizen journalists' – members of the public who are filming material, usually on mobile phones. Certainly technology is making all this possible. An article on the Media Guardian site by Jeff Jarvis (2 October 2006) positively promoted this as the way forward. He claims that 'all the old definitions of TV are a shambles . . . the limits of television – of distribution, of tools, of economics, of scarcity – are gone. So now at last, we can ask not what TV is but what it can be.' He ends with a call to arms: 'Television has already exploded. So now let's build the new TV.'

> Think about . . .
> What do you think of Jarvis's remarks? Is TV as we know it a thing of the past? Will it be something that everyone can have a part in creating?

CASE STUDY: THE DECLINE AND FALL OF TOP OF THE POPS

An interesting illustration of the effects of the changing nature of consumption, both within TV and beyond, can be seen in the sad end to one of British TV's great institutions, *Top of the Pops* (BBC 1964–2006). First broadcast on 1 January 1964, the show became a part of the national culture; it was an essential part of growing up, must-watch viewing for younger teens who spurned it in public as they got older but were still excited when their favourite bands appeared among the rest of a line-up they dismissed as rubbish. Its format, based around the published weekly singles charts, seemed to be its strength, ensuring a diversity of talent and a reflection of the times. It featured some seminal cultural moments – David Bowie performing 'Starman', the Sex Pistols, the Smiths – that inspired people to take a new direction in their lives and others to make music. It took its strength from the television medium. You could hear the records on the radio but you didn't know what the band looked like until you saw them on *Top of the Pops*.

As times changed, it was still something everyone understood, but the public stopped watching it. Many of the technological changes we have discussed played a part in its decline. The Internet frequently meant that people could hear and download songs, and indeed videos of promo films or live performances, long before their official release. In such an environment the idea of the chart began to lose its potency and the format of the show became a hindrance rather than a help. The rise of multichannel saw a proliferation of dedicated music channels, usually offering a more rigidly defined style of music so that viewers were likely to get more of what they knew they liked. This is exemplified by MTV, long established on cable and satellite, which seemed a slicker and hipper home for music-loving teens. The interactivity of sites like YouTube and MySpace and the sharing of music material created communities that did not need a weekly show to tell them what was out there.

The programme's ratings declined steeply, leading to a move from BBC1 to BBC2 and an unwise attempt to combine latest teen sounds with archive clips for older viewers. As ratings fell to just 1 million, the show was summarily axed in the summer of 2006. Although it was felt to be a natural end, there was something sad about its demise. It was a symbol of what old-style mixed-schedule TV at its most powerful could do – suddenly stun an audience with something unexpected. Unlike dedicated stations pumping out promos, it took its power from its position in the middle of prime time, somewhere between the news and a sitcom, and its ability to insert the uncomfortable into the cosy. It remains to be seen how the new TV environment shaped by our changing patterns of consumption will do that.

Critical contexts

We do not just evaluate texts in a vacuum, where we make judgments purely on the basis of our own opinions. We are surrounded by other people's opinions that may challenge or endorse our own feelings about a programme, or indeed about television as a medium itself. This discourse around texts is conducted in different ways that might affect us: criticism of programmes by professional opinion-formers in newspapers or on TV itself; peer opinion from those we know or from other members of the public through the media, especially online; and from the general critical received opinion that builds up both from the top-down and the bottom-up.

Professional TV critics

Newspapers have long had TV reviewers. There is usually a daily column (or weekly for Sunday papers) commenting on the previous night's viewing in just a few hundred words. Some of these reviewers hold positions for a long period of time and become acknowledged experts on the medium, while being accessible to the more casual viewer. Many of these (Nancy Banks-Smith in *The Sun* and later the *Guardian* is an example) are astute commentators who build up a body of admirers who want to read their copy no matter what the subject. In more recent years there has been a trend to hire reviewers who are either jobbing journalists who take the job as a rung on a career ladder and position themselves as 'the man or woman on the street', approaching the texts like any other viewer; or already established personalities, either writers, cultural commentators or those working in television – examples in the UK include Will Self (the *Observer*, then *The Independent on Sunday*), Victor Lewis-Smith (the *Evening Standard*) and A. A Gill (*The Sunday Times*).

The continuing existence of the daily review is really something of a bizarre anachronism. It developed for purely practical reasons: many programmes went out live and there were few advance tapes available, so the journalist had to watch it at the same time as everyone else. Now these technical obstacles are overcome it still continues, although it becomes something of a pointless exercise. After all, the audience has often either already seen the programme or is likely to have missed it (Lawson, 2006).

Increasingly over the last few years there has been a rise in previews of programmes. Sometimes these are short items summarising press releases but often they are more analytical pieces making a case about a text – usually in magazines like *Time Out* or in the Saturday editions of the papers. The general critical snobbery about TV in relation to the other arts has often meant fewer long-form pieces on TV programmes than about film or theatre but this is slowly being rectified, with work by Mark Lawson in the UK and David Bianculli in the US. Lawson is also a regular TV face but there are currently few opportunities for TV pundits to investigate TV as a medium.

It is interesting to look at some particular critics and to interrogate the angle they take on TV and their influence. Programme-makers will claim that critics have no effect, and this may be true in terms of popular programmes and their ratings. They can, however, influence the general critical climate, and in the case of say, a prestige production, they can cause problems if they decide that it has failed to match its aspirations. Similarly championing a series can bring it some kind of recognition.

Three interesting current British examples are Garry Bushell, Victor Lewis-Smith and Charlie Brooker. Bushell, now with the *Sunday People* but most famously with *The Sun*, is a polemicist who uses television as a subject to expound his political views (essentially right-wing populism). Although he is very knowledgeable about the medium, he positions himself in the role of a kind of archetypal tabloid reader: a discontented, English white working-class man who sees much television as elitism and champions traditional popular entertainment. Some of his arguments about the contempt of the TV industry for ordinary people may well be valid but there is also a feeling that many of them arise primarily from his political position rather than any considered judgment of the text.

Bushell began in the music press but Victor Lewis-Smith was already a relatively successful TV and radio satirist before he started reviewing. Again he is very knowledgeable about television but also adopts a persona based around biting derision, his pieces being part critique of the programme and part comic routine. He will frequently choose obviously 'bad' TV to comment on, such as shopping or quiz channels, but also will often adopt contrary positions to the general critical mood – he attacked *The Office*, for example.

Charlie Brooker, by far the youngest of the trio, sometimes takes a similar line in his preview column in the *Guardian*'s supplement 'The Guide' and his BBC4 show *Charlie Brooker's Screen Wipe*, attacking the iniquities of bad TV in colourful and lurid prose. To my mind (and you should read their reviews and make your mind up) Brooker is the more engaging – his anger at dumb TV is palpable but so is his enthusiasm when he finds something he thinks is good.

It is important to bear in mind the context of such reviews. Bushell's work is geared to the readers of the popular tabloids for whom he writes, Lewis-Smith's column is for a London evening paper rather than a national title, and Brooker's column in 'The Guide' is part of a publication aimed squarely at metropolitan, liberal 18–34-year-olds. Readers have a relationship with their paper in the same way as they do with TV programmes, and reviewers can sometimes perform for them. Audiences get used to a certain style and range of views and so a particular persona is expected (this is known as 'performative' behaviour, of which more in Chapter 3). There is also a business rivalry and historic tension between TV and newspapers and this can sometimes be reflected in their coverage of television – it is sometimes in the interest of news barons to paint TV as stupid or vulgar or subversive.

Online fan communities

Increasingly peer opinion is becoming as influential as professional critics. There always was an element of this, of course: you may have pretended to like, or even watch, a show when you were at school purely because everyone else said they were doing so. Particular series built up committed fan followings, who organised clubs and conventions, but recently this kind of exchange of opinion and enthusiasm has found its natural medium on the Internet. Now fans, or even critics, of a show can communicate and debate from all around the world at the same time on fan sites. In many cases there are forum boards where conversations about shows take place, and indeed some develop this much further: for instance, in the writing of fan fiction (or 'fanfic'), where characters from the show are imagined in new episodes written by aficionados.

The scale of this can be enormous. If you put 'Buffy the Vampire Slayer' + 'Fan forum' into Google, for example, it comes up with 24,100 hits. Huge varieties of subject exist within such forums, with extensive conversations under each, spiralling evermore into new conversations. Some may be simple information requests ('Is Buffy still on where you live?'), some are paeans of praise to favourite characters ('Spike is really sexy, that's all there is to say!'), others debate what are the best and

Think about . . .
Is there a particular reviewer whose opinions
you seek out? If so, why? Do you take part in
online fan forums? What do you get from
participating in a fan community?

worst things about a show, while yet others pick at problems in the plot or subtext ('Why didn't Angel tell Buffy?') (all examples from <www.fanforum.com>or <www.buffyworld.com>).

These textual communities are a fascinating phenomenon and the shared enthusiasm stops it from degenerating into abuse, which is the plague of other kinds of web message boards. Clearly they add something to the text, making it greater than merely what is on screen, because the interaction between the text and the viewer is so powerful and resonant for much of the audience (Hills, 2006: 106). We have already seen how influential fans can be on their particular texts but they are also important beyond that in reinforcing television's status as a medium.

Critical fashions

We can also be influenced by a pervading critical climate. This can apply to whether the consensus is that a particular show is good or bad, or whether it is past its best. Variances may exist here between particular social groups – for instance, *Big Brother* is no longer as fashionable as it was in some circles but is far more popular. It can also apply to general ideas about television, where some opinions can be repeated as accepted wisdom. One good example is the relative merits of British and American TV. In the 1970s and 1980s it was commonplace to declare (in the UK) that American TV was all rubbish and that British TV was the best in the world. A Conservative politician, David Mellor, warned that the new TV age might result in 'wall to wall *Dallas* and *Dynasty*'. By the early 2000s the critical consensus had turned around completely. Now, mainly through the influence of HBO series like *The Sopranos* and *Sex and the City*, American TV is hailed as streets ahead and British drama and comedy, routinely damned in comparison.

Needless to say the truth probably lay somewhere in between, but it can be hard to argue against these internalised 'truths'. This is where criticism (whether professional or peer) is at its most powerful, building up a body of opinion defining the medium.

Conclusion

Television is the first truly democratic culture – the first culture available to everybody and entirely governed by what the people want. The most terrifying thing is what the people do want. (Clive Barnes, New York Times, 1969)

Think about . . .
Consider the implications of this quote and
apply it to the modern television landscape.

We, as viewers, are vital agents in conveying meaning to TV texts, bringing our own interpretations and understanding to them. This can transform the experience of the text from individual to individual. As a collective audience, we define the texts in part by how we consume them, and this process, once gradually evolving, is now one of rapid, even frenetic change.

If we are motors of this change – if it is changing to match our desires – then we have the capacity to demand the most fulfilling and challenging texts. Conversely we have to take our share of the blame if it turns out that our desires are just for the easy, the obvious and the superficial.

II Texts

What's fiction and what's fact?

In this, the second part of the book, I want to move away from talking about the contexts in which we understand television texts – what we bring to the texts as viewers and the framework in which they are produced. Instead I intend to look closely at the texts themselves and the meanings that might be drawn from them. This will involve some close analysis of particular TV shows, selected inevitably in part because they are familiar to me, but also because they are 'rich texts', open to interrogation and interpretation. The types of analysis employed here can, of course, be applied to other texts too, and you should try and do so as you encounter them.

I have divided this section into two: 'TV Fiction' and 'TV Fact'. This seems to me to be a logical organisation of material, because these are the terms by which we approach texts when we sit down to view. If we understand a programme to be fiction, then we will look for some kind of narrative engagement and anticipate having an emotional response, whether that be laughter, being moved or upset, gripped or terrified, or feeling some sort of empathy with the characters. If we understand that a text is factual, we may also experience some of the above but we will also expect to be informed about something, to be more distanced from the material so that we can make judgments about its truth and understand what it is trying to say (Nelson, 2006: 74–5). Fiction and fact are also a method of organisation within the industry, so demarcated as different from the start of the production process.

Needless to say life is not always this clear-cut. There are points where the separation of fact from fiction becomes blurred and problematic, and this tendency has increased in recent years as the traditional TV genres become less defined in the digital age. There are – and have been since Peter Watkins's *Culloden* (BBC 1964) and *The War Game* (BBC 1966 but not shown) – drama-documentaries that have

Drama-documentary

Drama-documentary is a controversial form, which is often criticised for its uneasy line between fact and fiction, particularly if it involves recent events or people who are still living. Mark Lawson explores some of these issues in a piece on *The Government Inspector* (Mentorn/C4 2005), a drama-documentary on the alleged suicide of weapons inspector David Kelly after revelations that he was a source of newspaper stories – particularly the inclusion of a scene in which Tony Blair plays guitar down the phone to adviser Alistair Campbell (*Guardian*, 14 March, 2005). Have you seen any drama-documentaries where you felt either the drama or the documentary were compromised?

used dramatic forms to present depictions of real events. In the UK particularly this has been a rich form, producing *causes célèbres* like Jimmy McGovern's *Hillsborough* (Granada/ITV 1996), which challenged audiences to look again at accepted versions of recent history, often with the aim of rectifying injustices.

It could be argued that drama-documentary of this type was, despite its practical aims and righteous fury, primarily about the drama. It used real people and events to present compelling stories and resonant themes that work in the same way as purely invented fictions. Increasingly, though, the traffic between fiction and fact is two-way. Documentaries use reconstructions as a matter of course to illuminate information and present it in a clearer way, and there has been a rise in using dramatic effects and fictional scenarios to explore factual theses about the world we live in – the *If . . .* series (BBC 2004–5), for example. Also we can (and I will) argue that much factual entertainment on contemporary TV is creating a fiction rather than reporting facts. We will consider all these ambiguities but in spite of them fiction and fact are still recognisably different to us most of the time.

3. TV Fiction

So first of all let's take a look at what makes up TV fiction, how we respond to it and what guides those responses in the texts. This chapter considers three main areas:

- *Performance and character: characters are our way into the world of the text (this world is known as the diegesis in critical writing) and actors' performances make those characters, and thus the text, credible for us as viewers. We need to look at this process through detailed analysis of performances in texts – how actors illuminate the characters they represent and allow us to create meaning.*
- *Narrative structures: we will look at a range of different structures in TV fiction and the effect narrative structure has on our position as a viewer.*
- *It is often assumed that meanings in texts are created by an author. I will look at the complexity of authorship in television fiction and consider some of the debates on ascribing ownership to authors, particularly writers.*

I will also consider the future of television fiction in the light of some of the changes we talked about in Part I. Will TV fiction retain its place in our affections in years to come?

Traditionally fiction has been the most popular form on television – soap operas, crime dramas and sitcoms most frequently top the ratings. As viewers, we understand that different forms and structures deliver those fictions to us in distinctive ways that affect our responses to the text. We will examine how they work and what we draw from them later in this chapter.

First, though, how do we understand fiction on television differently to other media? After all, theatre and film are almost entirely fictional modes of art and entertainment. What can television, full as it is of other types of communication, like news, reality shows and sport, give us that these forms cannot, other than easy access? The answers are complex but the medium of television offers us its own routes into fiction, and gives us experiences from fictional worlds that film or plays cannot.

Theoretical considerations

Interpellation

Interpellation is a term originally coined by French thinker Louis Althusser and developed by Roland Barthes, and is much used in film studies. It is the French word for 'hailing', as in 'hailing a cab' or shouting a name in a crowded street. What Althusser means is that we are 'hailed' by the text to take an interest in it (2001: 86). He saw it as an ideological process but it can be used more generally to describe how we become involved in the text, caring what happens next or about the emotions of the characters we meet.

Interpellation happens in all fictional forms, including literature, but the manner in which it can develop in television is helped by a couple of unique factors, which rely on the particularities of the medium.

The first of these is space. As discussed extensively in the previous chapter, television derives much of its power from its domestic environment. Instead of going out to find it, television comes to us. As television fictions arrive in our living rooms in the context of our ordinary daily lives, they may lose the spectacle and awe that could result from seeing pictures of light on a giant screen while we remain hidden in darkness. The fictions may also lack the immediacy and vivacity of seeing real people perform live in a theatre. What they gain, however, is a further level of intimacy from being part of our space. By being played out within our space, the stories can feel like part of our own lives, and we might feel that extra surge of empathy when we see someone suffering, the scale helping us to suspend our disbelief.

The second element making TV fiction special is time. Time is crucial to understanding television's distinctiveness in fiction. Films and plays are bound by clear limitations when it comes to time, usually two hours or so. Deviation from these norms is very unusual and this dictates narrative form and consequently our expectations. Essentially they use a three-act structure of establishment, defining action and resolution in telling the story – we come to expect a strong narrative line and closure, where all the different strands of the tale come to a satisfactory conclusion.

TV does use this model sometimes, notably in the single drama, but other forms at its disposal create a quite different set of expectations. Remember that audience expectations and texts feed off each other – we react to what we understand may happen and texts build up a dialogue of anticipation, fulfilment or surprise with us as we watch. The dominant TV fiction forms are longer, offering us plenty of time in which to understand the fictional worlds presented. These forms will be discussed in more detail later but at this juncture the key points to consider are that they offer:

- More time. Instead of being confined to two hours, there may be six (as is often the case with serials), or thirty (if a series runs to three or four seasons) or indeed almost unlimited time (as with soaps and 'continuing dramas').
- More flexible resolutions. In some of these forms there does not actually have to be an end at all. In others it can be more diffuse: instead of everything coming to a neat full stop, there is a sense that, while some matters have been resolved, this may be a gradual process with a lot of loose ends. There is a feeling that these lives that we have been involved with for a time will carry on unfolding, even though we are no longer privy to them.

What effects does this have on us as viewers? Well, it allows us to build a much closer relationship with the fictional world. Karen Lury says that 'the perception of time by the audience is understood as experience' (005: 71). Thus in fiction, time gives us more knowledge and information and the possibility of developing many different perspectives. We know much more about the people and the places from a series than we possibly could if they were featured in a two-hour film. Film narratives realise their time limitations and make sure that everything we see is pertinent to the plot. There is simply no time to show anything not directly relevant to the story. TV fiction is not bound in this way: storylines can be introduced that have little to do with the central narrative arc; there can be a much larger cast of characters, some of whom do not have direct narrative functions, and we can see depictions of the everyday. This mirrors our own life experiences, which, by and large, do not have a straightforward narrative arc – creating something that at best can be both engaging and profound.

Characters and performance

Characters

Characters are one of the principal ways by which we engage and respond to texts, and of course, performance is the mode by which we understand them. Actors take on the task of these fictional people created by the writers and turning these constructs into real, living beings for the time we are watching them on TV at least.

The point of connection between ourselves and the text is, after all, primarily about the people we see on screen. We want to be like them, or we desire them or are amused or frightened by them: it is frequently character that dictates the drama, that makes things happen, things we are interested in precisely because we know and have gradually aligned ourselves with their character. The history of television fiction resonates with audiences because great characters made it so: Basil Fawlty, old man Steptoe, Columbo, Buffy, Frank Gallagher in *Shameless*, Samantha in *Sex and the City*, Bree in *Desperate Housewives* (Cherry Prods/Touchstone TV/Channel 4 2005–), Yosser Hughes in *The Boys from the Blackstuff* (BBC 1982), Dot Cotton and George Costanza from *Seinfeld*, to name but a few, speak to us about our own selves, who we are, what we could be or who we know.

Performance

All these characters made an impression on viewers not just because of how they were written but also because of the way they were performed. Actors need to make characters credible for the audience, even if, looking at the list of characters above, they may be playing people who initially seem extreme or ridiculous. Acting is a craft just like being a camera operator or a sound recordist, and it works with those other skills to contribute to the text. Performances need to complement the composition of the frame, or the music, or the quality of the image – they are an integral part of screen language and cannot be divorced from it. It is the combination of these elements that allows us to make meanings and derive an emotional response when we are watching TV fiction.

Like any craft, acting can be applied in different ways to different forms. Theatre acting requires an engagement with a live audience, so relies on clarity of voice and expansive gestures. Film acting works around the different demands of cinema – being projected onto a huge screen allows a more subtle and naturalistic type of communication of character. Television acting is different again. The screen is smaller but the actor has more time with the audience to establish and develop performances.

TV technology has played a part here. In its early years, as discussed in Chapter 1, production was to a large extent bound to the studio. As Jason Jacobs discusses in his book on early TV drama, *The Intimate Screen*, this meant that the range of views we enjoy as a cinema audience are restricted in TV – the long shot, in particular, is not normally possible in the studio (2000: 117–18). TV drama then concentrated on the medium shot (usually focused on the head and shoulders of one or more figures) and especially the close-up (a roughly life-size shot of the human face). Even after the advent of lightweight cameras and location shooting, this still remains a defining style in TV fiction.

As a result, importance is placed on expressive acting, emphasising subtle movements of the facial features. This gives performances an intimacy, which actors can use to draw the audience into an intense relationship with their characters. Equally, as commentators such as Lury (2005: 78–9) and others have suggested, the way we consume TV domestically leads to a greater emphasis on sound as a means to draw attention back to the screen. Thus voice, tone and delivery can be extremely powerful.

Strangely little has been written or studied about TV characters or acting on TV up to now. This is, I believe, an important area to consider, because it guides and defines our responses to the texts we consume, and this critical neglect should be rectified – hopefully we can start to consider it here. There are a number of different types of performance on television, closely bound to the fictional forms in which the characters appear. We will look at examples of these in some detail, referring to the context of the character within the text and the performance style adopted by the actor representing that character, examining closely those moments in which they appear and communicate with us. Again it is important to stress how time affects our responses. We spend a great deal of time with many of these characters to the extent that we know more about their lives than those of many people we know. This intimacy allows the character to display all their ambiguities and contradictions.

Good television performances need therefore to be very subtle, enabling us to grasp every nuance as the characters' lives are presented to us. This creates an ambiguity in our response as we watch: we assume an almost omniscient position where we can take an overview of their predicament and foibles, a view that might be beyond the person themselves. We may also know information that they are not yet party to that will affect them deeply, creating a tension as we see them blithely unaware of what is to come. In such circumstances the relation between the viewer and the character can become very close, even intense.

CASE STUDY: THE SOPRANOS

A good example of this is James Gandolfini's performance as Tony Soprano in HBO's much-acclaimed series *The Sopranos*. The show tells the story of the Soprano family, a New Jersey mafia gang, headed by Tony and the story of Tony's actual family: his wife Carmela and his teenage children Meadow and AJ. Tony is our link, as viewers, to the world of organised crime and the domestic environment. The series has had six seasons, usually of thirteen episodes, each lasting an hour. This is a lot of time to spend with a character, and Tony is at the very heart of the drama, appearing in the majority of scenes.

The Sopranos is a very rich text, attested to by the large amount of critical attention it has received (e.g. Lavery, 2006). It has multilayered narratives, strong explicit and implicit themes, and raises many difficult questions about both contemporary society and individual morality. Moments of reflection and links between Tony's two worlds are conveyed by the conceit of his sessions with analyst Dr Jennifer Melfi. This opens up a third sphere of action for Tony, one unconnected through plot with the other two, where Tony can consider his actions.

The Sopranos has a large cast of characters – Tony's gang, other mafia families, Carmela and the other wives, the children and their circle, FBI agents and others. The centre of our experience as viewers, however, is Tony; while the other characters and their contexts are all interesting, the focus is on their relationship to Tony and how their actions might impact on him. This is a very heavy weight for one character, and one actor, to bear and for our interest to be maintained they have to be complex, ambivalent and surprising. Fortunately the character of Tony as written, and as performed by Gandolfini, is exactly that.

The focus on Tony means that when we watch we are aligned with him, we see things at least in part from his point of view. This is problematic, because Tony is a gangster. In the course of the series he has personally killed people and ordered the deaths of many more, has a brutally violent temper, runs protection rackets, bullies his minions and has contempt for the law. Why then should we care what happens to him? We feel aligned to Tony in part because of how we are positioned by the text, in a number of ways:

- Narrative – much of what we see is related, directly or indirectly, to Tony, either his family or his position as head of the criminal 'family'.
- Aesthetics – the camera moves to follow him, often placing him in the middle of the frame. Tony is on screen most of the time, frequently in medium shot or close-up.
- The sessions with Dr Melfi – these scenes privilege Tony's view on events and his emotional problems. They set the stories into a reflexive context where we are encouraged to understand Tony's point of view.

Thus we are sometimes made to feel like we have an allegiance with Tony. Our positioning by the text shines some chinks of light in the darkness of Tony's world; his intelligence, occasional kindness and humour make things morally uneasy for us. At times we might feel we like Tony, as reasons to understand him are presented to us. However at other points in the text, such as when he orders punishment killings, undertakes petty acts of revenge, makes some bigoted comment, or lashes out physically himself, we might feel he is monstrous.

These complexities are in the scripts, in the direction, and in the concepts and structures laid down by series creator David Chase, but we need something more palpable to become so engrossed in Tony's character. Ultimately it is James Gandolfini's embodiment of Tony that makes his ambiguities convincing and unpredictable for the audience. He is eminently believable as a man torn asunder in a multitude of ways. On the one hand, Gandolfini's large, bulky frame makes him a very credible thug – we know that he is capable of inflicting violence and that he can be intimidating and threatening. However, on the other hand, he has a lightness of touch, a sensitivity, that makes us understand how the panic attacks and depression that lead him to Dr Melfi arise from deep internal conflicts. This life was chosen for him, after all (his father was a mafia man), and his murderous mother has not helped his moral sense.

There is a lot of emphasis on Gandolfini's face, as well as his imposing physique. The nature of the character offers a number of challenges to the actor in conveying emotion. Tony frequently has to say things he does not mean to protect his interests or to maintain the kind of macho, in-control, front necessary for a criminal boss. Equally facial gestures often have to be very subtle – they express feelings that cannot be shared.

Let's look at how performance and character work within the text by examining three scenes in detail. They come from the last two episodes of the fifth series, 'Long Term Parking' and 'All Due Respect', as a number of storylines begin to converge on Tony. His cousin, Tony Blundetta, has killed the brother of a capo in one of the New

York families, previously allied to Tony's mob. The rules of the mafia mean that Tony must allow his cousin to be killed in revenge for this breach of the natural order. Meanwhile his nephew Chris's girlfriend, Adriana, reveals to him that she is an FBI informant. On the home front Tony is reconciling with Carmela after a period of separation.

Scene 1

This is a very short scene at the end of the penultimate episode, 'Long Term Parking'. Tony has arranged the killing of Adriana, a woman who he liked and, although he never acted upon it, found attractive. He also knows that the laws of the mob mean that his cousin Tony must die.

The scene begins with a panning shot over apparently deserted woodland – very similar to the place where we saw Adriana killed by Tony's deputy Silvio minutes earlier. The camera pans downwards to a close-up of the woodland floor (just like the spot where Adriana has been buried). Into this scene walk Tony and Carmela, and it becomes clear that this is a piece of land Tony has bought for his wife to develop as part of their terms of reconciliation. We first see Tony's legs followed by a shot of his back, as he walks in a slow, burdened manner. Then the camera changes direction capturing Tony and Carmela in long shot, but with Tony facing away from his wife and towards the camera. The camera moves into a medium shot but with Tony in the foreground, his back still to Carmela.

Look at the composition of these frames. Carmela is talking but Tony is at the front of the frame in medium close-up. Our attention is on his face, which seems shocked and desperate. His eyes and mouth are downcast and Gandolfini makes himself suddenly seem older and almost broken by emotional pain. He appears to be on the verge of tears.

When Carmela asks him if he is alright, he says 'Me? Yes! absolutely' and smiles at her in a reassuring way as if nothing is wrong.

but when he looks back, his face once again displays its previous anxious expression.

A song ('Wrapped in My Memory' by Shawn Smith) starts up on the soundtrack. This is a melancholy tune whose lyrics include the line 'I could have been a better man'. The camera pans up from Tony's tormented face into the treetops.

Gandolfini's face expresses Tony's inner turmoil and makes us imagine what he might be feeling. Is he guilty about Adriana's death? Are the woods reminding him of the place where he knows she died? This guilt is not something he could express verbally: his crew now regard her as a traitor who deserved her demise; he needs to protect Carmela from the news; and he can't discuss it with Dr Melfi, as she would be compromised and could tell the police. Tony's expression and silence may communicate these repressed emotions to us. His torment at the inevitability of his cousin's death adds to the character's isolation and despair. Gandolfini gives us something profound to think about as viewers of this scene, working with imagery, camera movement and sound to create a response. We should hate Tony for organising Adriana's death but, although we don't forget it, his performance here implies that he recognises the enormity of what he has done and we feel a small spark of sympathy for his predicament.

Scene 2

The second scene is in the final episode of the season, 'All Due Respect'. Tony visits his crew at a formal birthday party for one of their number (who we know is an FBI informer). He takes the opportunity to address them as their leader about the situation with the New York mob and his cousin. The crew are sceptical about his handling of the problem and are frightened of retaliation. Tony tries to be statesmanlike here. He adopts a body language and tone of address that mark him out as their leader. He slaps a lot of backs, and gives the birthday boy a bottle of his own family wine, in a show of paternalistic bonhomie.

He is calm, assured and dressed immaculately. He tells his men that he is merely protecting his cousin as he would anyone of them and pronounces that 'we are a family and even in this fucked-up day and age, that means something'. Gandolfini is showing us here the mob boss side of Tony; he is performing as Tony the performer – the front he puts on to control his men and direct his business. He conducts the scene in an exaggeratedly formal way, addressing them as 'gentlemen', and using words like 'irregardless'. Tony's act is meant to reassure and defuse the

internal criticism of his actions. Gandolfini's bearing, delivery and composed facial gestures recreate this show of paternalistic distance between him as leader and them as followers, emphasised by leaving straight after his address. Although he claims to have a meeting, he returns home – the immaculate outfit was part of the show.

Scene 3

The final scene takes place in the same episode and includes a consultation between Tony and Dr Melfi. These scenes stand alone in *The Sopranos*, offering a place for reflection and analysis, both for Tony and us as viewers. He is able to unburden himself of some problems, particularly his domestic ones, but not others, because they involve details of crime. We are fascinated by these intermissions partly because we are interested to find out when Tony will tell the truth and when he will lie, and how Gandolfini will express the unguarded Tony. To start with here, Tony is nonchalant, feeding Melfi a lie about his son working hard at school. However, she delves further and uncovers his anxiety about his cousin, and accuses him of falling back into sentimentality. Here Gandolfini's face initially expresses rage before dropping into an almost childlike despair, the camera closing in on him as he tells her 'I am very confused' and then 'it's my mess, all my decisions were wrong'. Suddenly his couldn't-care-less attitude and the sanctimonious rage seem very far away. His voice drops and his eyes fix on the floor, as he seems to sink in on himself. His performance in this scene reveals both his vulnerability and his limitations.

TV and film performance
It is interesting to compare Gandolfini's performance as Tony with Al Pacino's portrayal of Michael Corleone in *The Godfather* films. Because of the necessities of the form, even though the films form a trilogy and have a long running time, Pacino's justly famous performance seems to me to be a sketch to Gandolfini's oil painting. The confines of time mean that we only get impressions of Corleone's contradictions and dilemmas as they are pertinent to the narrative. In contrast we know everything about Tony, every detail about his life.

Gandolfini's performance as Tony creates emotional responses beyond the script. The complexities of his character, both as written and performed, engage on all sorts of levels, making us interrogate our own moral positions.

CASE STUDY: INSPECTOR MORSE

The character of Tony is central to the text of *The Sopranos*, but it also leads us into other stories and other lives. There is a different kind of dramatic portrayal where the performance dominates every aspect of the text. One such is John Thaw's performance in the title role of *Inspector Morse* (Zenith/Central/ITV 1987–2000). Morse is a policeman in Oxford and the show revolves around his investigation of various murder cases. To this extent we move into other lives, if only for the course

John Thaw conveyed Morse's despair partly through facial expression and this was emphasised by frequent close-ups

of an episode, but other than the solution of a puzzle these are rarely that engaging. As a police procedural *Morse* is unrealistic, often engaged in a sort of murder-mystery English neverland that sells well abroad. However, for many (it was a huge hit) it was compelling viewing and I would suggest that again this was due to the power of performance.

Thaw invests Morse with tragic depths. Behind his supposedly quicksilver mind (in fact in many cases he gets it wrong and has to be bailed out by his deputy, Lewis) it is made clear to us as viewers through Thaw's performance that Morse is a deeply lonely, unhappy, almost tragic figure.

The mystery narratives and the show's aesthetic, with its leisurely pace and opulent settings, play a part in portraying the complexities of Morse's failure. He is positioned by them as a man who loves women but can never commit or be loved; a man with a brilliant mind unable to adapt to changing times; and a man who loves the finer things in life (vintage cars, classical music, real ales) but seems unable to derive happiness from them. Most of all this is conveyed to us in Thaw's performance and the device of frequent close-ups of his face. Frequently a full-screen close-up is used to underline his pain. The concentration on his rugged face and hooded eyes, often for several seconds, coupled with the use of moments of silence present Morse as ruined and desperate, unable to discard his self-loathing. It is the power of this performance that resonates rather than the storylines or events portrayed.

CASE STUDY: DEIRDRE BARLOW – CORONATION STREET

A very different kind of performance again is present in continuing dramas, such as soap operas. Here the emphasis is not on one central character but on an ensemble of performances. The dynamic within the text revolves around the interdependence of the characters with others in the group, as the focus of such shows is largely on a community. Because there is no resolution to continuous dramas, character is not bound up in the demands of narrative to a great extent. There are arrivals and departures, sometimes as a consequence of plotlines, but these are often created to fit the requirements of the production, or the wishes of an actor, rather than the natural development of the drama. Characters can be in the programme for decades, creating a very different relationship between character, text, performance and viewer.

Anne Kirkbride has spent her entire screen career in the part of Deirdre Barlow in Coronation Street, which she has played since 1973. She remains a key member of the *Street*'s cast, having embodied a fictional woman from teenager to mid-fifties. In that time she has had three husbands (one of them twice and one of them murdered), countless affairs, been unjustly sent to prison, and spawned a deeply unpleasant daughter, Tracey. Appearing two to four times a week over this period, she has been a regular part of viewers' lives for as long as they can remember. In such circumstances the detail of the interaction between character and viewer is extraordinarily intense. We know absolutely everything about Deirdre – her hopes, fears, disappointments, even her daily routines. The popular success of the show means that she is instantly understood as a feature of the cultural landscape. One reference to her trademark large glasses will identify her even to non-fans and a shorthand develops around her in relation to the show: we know that Deirdre is essentially nice but naive and unlucky.

The performances in soaps reflect the demands of the form. Sometimes Deirdre will be the main focus of a long-running storyline or an episode, or sometimes she will merely appear in the background, functioning maybe to say a line or two that will move someone else's story on. The performance style needs to complement the ensemble and fit in with the fiction. Within a large cast there may also be a tendency for particular performances to be rooted in particular emotions. In Deirdre's case this is often anxiety, so Anne Kirkbride spends a lot of time looking worriedly off-camera as the latest crisis affects her clan.

Anne Kirkbride's thirty-plus years in the role makes her almost a national neighbour – there are many stories of viewers who simply forget that Deirdre, or other regular characters, is a fictional construct and not a real person. This is hardly surprising: in some ways soap characters exist in lives parallel to our own. If you were a teenager in the early 1970s, Deirdre would have been there as one too, now you are a wife, mother and grandmother in your fifties, there she still is, having been part of your life for the whole intervening period. This kind of performance is almost internalised by the audience; it is a constant in their lives that becomes part of our understanding of the world in which we live. Such is the power and intimacy of television.

CASE STUDY: COMIC PERFORMANCES – EXTRAS

Comic performances are different again. Comedy as a form of entertainment relies on a tension between the realistic and the extraordinary, and performances and characters need to express both these functions. They must be realistic enough to be credible and have some kind of resonance with the audience, but they also need to be extraordinary enough to be funny. Steve Neale and Frank Krutnik talk about 'comic verisimilitude' and 'comic transgression' – that is, comedy as representing something of real experience and comedy as something that works against expectations of acceptable behaviour within our experience (1990: 83–8). I want to look closely at Ashley Jensen's performance as Maggie Jacobs in *Extras* to illustrate how this might work.

Extras is Ricky Gervais and Stephen Merchant's follow-up to the worldwide success of *The Office*, and so came out with a great deal of pressure attached to it. Fortunately it was also a success with critics and audiences and much of this was attributed to the performance of Jensen, a relative unknown. The first series is set in show business among the struggling ranks of extras or supporting artistes who work alongside stars but can only dream of their fame or lifestyle. Gervais's character Andy Millman is a former bank manager in his forties who yearns to get a line in a production. His best friend is Maggie, another extra, Scottish and in her thirties, who is less starstruck than Andy but who harbours her own fantasies of meeting a suitable man.

Within the sitcom format, even a very sophisticated one like *Extras*, performances have to function in particular ways (Mills, 2005). Jensen as Maggie fulfils a number of roles:

- She is a foil for Andy, pointing up his failings and mistakes, but also laughing at his jokes, as although we may read him as deluded, we are also encouraged to see him as witty.
- She is the source of much of the comedy, being somewhat slow on the uptake and lacking any discernible tact.
- Her actions are sometimes a motor for the plot: for instance, in series 2 episode 4 her unfortunate revelation about why Andy dumped her to his ex-girlfriend at the BAFTA awards leads to this woman denouncing him in her acceptance speech.
- Most importantly her comic failings enable the writers to explore particular comic themes, notably embarrassment and social unease.

For her to be able to make us laugh, we have to understand and identify with the character. Sitcoms (and some sketch shows) rely on recognition to be funny –

recognition of what a character we have come to know is likely to do in a given situation and recognition of the human truths their behaviour represents. Jensen achieves this through her performance. First, she gives Maggie a kooky but likeable demeanour, aided by her unkempt curly hair and taste for bohemian berets and scarves. She plays her as individual and quirky, without being at all pretentious, with an easy manner and ready smile. This gains our sympathies, as does Maggie's position in the text as a perpetual loser, often a feature of comic performances in Britain.

I'd like to look at a couple of scenes in detail now to illustrate the way character and performance can work together in TV comedy.

The first scene is from the second episode of the first series and presents Maggie as rather slow, albeit conscious of her intellectual shortcomings. It illustrates 'comic verisimilitude' in Jensen's performance, as nothing happens here that is not realistic; instead it is a comic spin on everyday miscommunication.

The episode features former *EastEnders* star Ross Kemp, playing Lord Nelson in a costume drama in which Andy and Maggie are extras. Maggie confuses Ross Kemp with Martin Kemp, another former *EastEnders* actor who used to be a pop star. Andy tries to explain that while they are not related, Ross is, however, famous in the soap as one of a pair of siblings, the Mitchell brothers. Maggie is utterly stumped by the revelation that the Mitchells are not really brothers in real life. As she desperately tries to untangle fact from fiction, we see a close-up of Jensen's face – her stare blank and her lips faintly moving in puzzlement. It is a display of comic reaction acting, for Andy has most of the dialogue. Our attention is on Jensen, however, as the comic impetus comes from her pained look to Andy, imploring some explanation from him, and the way her voice raises in pitch to implore 'Yes they are brothers – the Mitchell brothers'.

When she realises her mistake, she and Andy josh each other and she reveals her insecurities about her intelligence, worrying that it will put off the man she desires in the cast and telling Andy that in a pub quiz she once said that Columbo discovered America. The beginning of the next scene sees her trying to impress her would-be beau by ostentatiously reading the *Financial Times* in front of him. When he quizzes her on the markets, she tries to bluff, her face set in an anxious picture of concentration as she advises 'buy low – and sell low'.

The scene reveals one of the principal sources of Maggie's comic function – her occasional dimness – but we see her as more than the butt of the joke partly through the empathy that Jensen engenders in her performance. Her glazed look, as she loses the thread, makes us feel that she is more unworldly than dense, and her knowledge of her own foibles endears her to us. Naturally the fact that it happens in Regency costume makes it all the funnier, adding an element of absurdity that conversely draws attention to the realism of the exchanges, which are rooted in present-day ordinary life.

The second scene is from the fifth episode of that first series and is a *tour de force* of comic embarrassment, marking out Jensen's performance as 'transgressive'. Maggie goes on a date with a handsome young black man, which goes very well, and she takes him home. As they are about to kiss, she notices with horror her childhood golliwog doll on a shelf of toys (the toys seem credible with our knowledge of her slightly childish quirkiness). She is caught attempting to remove the golliwog, emitting an audible gasp of pain before fixing her face in an attempt to hide her panic.

She makes the situation worse by over compensating, stressing her anti-racism and attempting to 'mate' the golliwog with a white Barbie figure in rather an alarming fashion. While doing so she makes strange sexual moaning sounds, mortification digging her yet deeper into trouble.

Her suitor wisely decides to leave, very reasonably pointing out that 'the black thing seems to be getting in the way' tonight and maybe they should meet later in the week. Maggie compounds her errors first by saying that she 'hardly notices' he is black and then suggesting going dancing and asking if he is a good dancer, before painfully qualifying this with 'not that there is any reason you should be'.

The scene illustrates Maggie's lack of tact and comic inability to say the right thing in any situation. It also works as a good example of Gervais and Merchant's comedy, which often uses subjects of social unease, like race or sexual orientation, to explore the humour in our failure to react with confidence and understanding in unfamiliar social situations. Failure is always a good subject for comedy and Gervais and Merchant mine the gap between what we mean to say and what we actually come out with to maximum effect. Comedy is transgressive in this regard, for as Gerald Mast suggests, it 'expose(s) human folly and present(s) no cure, for folly is an incurable human disease for which there is no cure' (1973: 338). Indeed we can go further: Howard Jacobson argues that 'we gain ascendancy over what is vile in us by relishing it with coarse laughter' (1997: 38).

Maggie is certainly not a racist but she is paralysed by the fear that she might be thought one – in her desire to avoid offence she ends up giving it. Rather than being relaxed around her potential lover and engaging with him as an individual, she can only see his race as a difficulty to be surmounted. This could, of course, just as easily be a serious situation; Jensen's performance helps to make it comic, to make us 'relish it with coarse laughter' by recognising her all-too-human failings. Her face expresses her agony as she is caught spiralling out of verbal control, unable to stop the wrong thing coming out of her mouth and snatching defeat from the jaws of victory. In the last frame her realisation of how she has spectacularly blown her big romantic chance is palpable as she closes her eyes, her mouth slightly agape, wishing the last five minutes away.

Her performance retains our sympathies and puts us into her position, feeling her pain while laughing at her awkwardness. Most importantly at all times she makes Maggie credible, and it is that credibility that makes us find her funny.

When we know particular performances well, both in drama and comedy, they take on degrees of performativity. This means that the nature of the performance forms a dialogue with the viewer. We come to expect specific things within it (such as Maggie's tactlessness or Tony's violence) and the actor works with those expectations, sometimes delivering them and sometimes surprising us by working against them, building up the performance into a complex text in itself. John Caughie (2000) noted that unlike film, television subordinates time and space to character, not narrative. Character is the motor driving television fiction and creating a discourse between the text and the viewer.

Narrative structures

Television, like other media, is made up of different forms and different genres.

A wide range of different forms are used to convey television's narrative fictions. As discussed, time and space are available to construct a more diffuse and complex narrative than is possible in the dictates of a two-hour feature film or a stage play. For one thing theatre and cinema are media forms designed to be experienced in one sitting in real time. Television is not subject to these limitations – we can see it in the manner that best suits the needs of the text, whether that be one slot, over two nights, one hour every six weeks, in several parts over seasons spanning a few years, or indefinitely.

TV fiction forms all create very distinctive relationships with the audience and offer different possibilities in telling stories. It is important to understand these forms, how they work, the distinctions between them, and what they do, so I will examine each one, using appropriate examples.

Single dramas

Single dramas, or single plays as they used to be called, are the TV fiction form least specific to the medium. Over one self-contained transmission we are introduced to a set of characters and circumstances. A narrative line appears, develops and is concluded within a single broadcast. This is, of course, pretty much the model for a film or a theatre play.

The single play was a key form in the development of television, establishing that TV could produce and deliver serious fiction that could illuminate the human condition and raise complex ideas. This was the case both in the US and the UK. In 1950s' America plays by Budd Schulberg, Paddy Chayefsky and Rod Serling made a national impact and established TV as a creative hub. In Britain *Armchair Theatre*

Genre theory

'Genres' are types of text that can be linked together in certain ways, either by the way they are constructed or by their theme and content. Theories about genre emerged in film studies in the 1970s as a way of explaining how films worked upon their audiences. Audiences come to recognise patterns in narratives – in Westerns or horror films, for example – and, if they enjoy them, try to seek out more of the same. Media industries acknowledge this market by making more of these types of films to satisfy this desire. The texts themselves work on the audience's experience of the genre by incorporating certain codes and conventions (the shoot-out in the saloon in Westerns or the teenage camping trip in horror, for instance). Audiences use these codes to create meaning. This triangular relationship between text, industry and audience has been explored by Turner (1988/2006: 124). Genre has been of particular interest to structuralists as there is a need to identify these underlying codes within the text.

Much of this is also applicable to television, as long as the different modes of consumption are taken into account. TV has definable genres too, such as crime series, sitcoms and so on. However, unlike film, TV has a myriad of different forms, and form and genre are much harder to untangle. Steve Neale argues that TV genre theory needs to class the different forms in TV as genres in themselves (2001: 3).

on ITV on a Sunday night brought challenging work to a mass audience, and this was underlined through the next couple of decades, particularly by the BBC strands *The Wednesday Play* (1964–70) and *Play for Today* (1970–84). Throughout this period the single television drama, whether shot on tape or film, gave the medium prestige, as it included examples of agreed excellence that broadcasters could point to when they were accused of pandering to populism. Some of those working in the form, the above-named American writers, British dramatists such as Dennis Potter, Trevor Griffiths, Mike Leigh and David Mercer, became acknowledged as artists equal to anyone working in film or theatre. The form gave opportunities for talent to develop through its sheer scale: in the early 1970s there were over a hundred single plays a year on the BBC alone (Cooke, 2003: 91). While there are similarities to the film or the play, there are also important differences that come from television's intimacy as a medium.

However, as scarcity moved to availability in TV it became harder to make single drama work commercially and by the 1990s the idea of a regular slot each week to showcase single dramas was fading in Britain. There are still occasional single dramas on British TV, but they appear fitfully and are more limited in their scope. The BBC recently ran a small number of self-contained dramas on Friday nights but these tended to be mainstream, undemanding comedy-dramas (*Aftersun*, *Angel Cakes*, both 2006). Conversely Channel 4 has invested recently in single drama but these are predominately drama-documentaries such as *The Road to Guantanamo* and *The Queen's Sister* (2005). ITV1 still screens some 'single' works, notably psychological thrillers, but presents them differently by splitting them in two and showing the two parts on consecutive nights.

Given the form's glorious past this decline is sad, but unsurprising given the economics of the television industry. TV drama is expensive, and becoming relatively more so compared to reality programming. Single dramas by their nature have no potential to build an audience – they exist for one moment with perhaps a DVD sale to follow for those who enjoyed it. Their brief life on screen makes them difficult and costly to promote in an increasingly marketing-led world. Unlike longer forms like the series, they cannot continue to bring revenue in to offset the costs of production and the more inherently televisual forms of the series and serial allowed more time and space to develop a fictional world.

Series

The series is perhaps the most purely televisual of all the forms, and traditionally one of the most successful in television history. In its purest terms a series is a fiction that offers recurring characters and an established situation, but in which each episode has a self-contained storyline. Viewers, once they are familiar with the former, can dip into and understand the latter element at any time. A series is intended to run for a number of seasons and if successful – and we have discussed the pressures of ratings, especially in the US, that determine this –

develops a loyal audience base which returns to the series year after year. Over this time incremental changes may be introduced, such as a supporting character leaving, or a new one arriving, but the essentials of the show remain.

As we saw when discussing fans, the producer and the consumer build up a discourse on what makes the text work. This discourse may accept some changes as long as the tone or the dynamic of the programme stays the same. *Moonlighting* (ABC 1985–9), the series that launched Bruce Willis on an unsuspecting world, was based on the comic romantic tension between leads Willis and Cybill Shepherd. Famously when the characters finally got together, the pleasures of the show were lost and it could not carry on much longer. Each hit series has this 'DNA', a unique set of characteristics – exciting set-ups, wry, laconic scripts, engaging characters, emotional address – that appeals to a section of the audience.

CASE STUDY: THE ROCKFORD FILES

Let's take an example that shows the purer narrative forms of the series and analyse its 'DNA'. *The Rockford Files* was a popular American series that ran for a number of years in the late 1970s. It was a hit in Britain and other territories too, and is still being rerun on British TV (both terrestrial and digital channels). The series features James Garner as Jim Rockford, an LA private detective who lives near his father, 'Rocky', in a trailer on the coast and takes cases that often do not improve his tense relationship with the police department.

Each episode begins with a pre-credit sequence that unusually presents a kind of trailer for what is to come highlighting some key events and acting as a thumbnail for that week's plot. The credit sequence opens with a close-up of Rockford's desk. We hear his answerphone message, followed each time by a different message from a prospective client. Interestingly these are usually comic and not pertinent to the episode. Then the uptempo catchy theme tune begins, accompanied by a montage of stills of Rockford in various situations and poses. The series is essentially circular in structure – at the end of each episode we return to the status quo.

The Rockford Files does not therefore have much, if any, plot or character development over its run. There are a lot of action sequences, particularly car chases, but little real violence and, it is a given that Jim will emerge safe and sound from any peril. What then is the series appeal if it does not depend on plot, spectacle or suspense? The answer is tone. Viewers might watch the show for its charm, wit and, in many senses, its subtleties. The series is dominated by its central character

> James Garner
> James Garner (1928–) is one of the first and most enduring stars made by TV. Although he had a lot of success in films, he made his name in television and his intimate style was very well suited to the medium, finding hits first with *Maverick* (ABC 1957–60) then *Rockford*. In *The Encyclopedia of Television* Mark Alvey says Garner 'has been called the United States' finest television actor; he has been compared more than once to Cary Grant' (Newcomb, 2004). Other big stars who made their name through TV series include Clint Eastwood (*Rawhide*, CBC 1959–66), Johnny Depp (*21 Jump Street* Fox, 1987–91) and George Clooney (*ER*, NBC 1994–9)

and the performance of James Garner; as we saw earlier, performance can drive a text.

Jim Rockford is easy-going, witty, handsome and charming. He is also endearingly something of a loser, very much at the low end of the Los Angeles private-eye spectrum. While fundamentally decent, even a bit of a soft touch, he sails close to the wind as far as the law is concerned, creating a sense of ambiguity. The scripts rely on witty repartee between Jim and his friends and his ripostes to foes or the police, especially his long-standing contact Lt Becker. The audience comes to the series to experience the atmosphere and tone the writing and the acting create. We become comfortable with this situation and these people and it is this that makes the series popular – the actual storyline of each episode is very much secondary.

Some series have less rigid formal structures and feature a different balance of self-contained incident and developing actions across episodes. This seems to be increasingly so as formal boundaries become blurred in the new television landscape. An example is the BBC's hit series *Life on Mars* (Kudos/BBC 2006–7). There is an established situation here: modern Manchester policeman Sam Tyler is hit by a car and is mysteriously transported back to the same place in a different time – 1973. The appeal of the series is partly through this culture clash between the Britain of today and the nation's values over thirty years ago, but there is also some development. Each episode features a self-contained element – an investigation of a crime in 1973 that Sam and his nemesis, Detective Inspector Gene Hunt, solve. Additionally across each show is the running storyline about Sam's attempts to return back to his own time and also to investigate why he has been transported back to the 1970s. Different narrative devices mark this out for the viewer – when Sam watches TV in his bedsit the little girl on the test card seems to speak to him and at various points he hears voices from 2006 talking to him while he is in a coma in a hospital bed. Also interwoven in the plot are his attempts to connect with his own family in the 1970s to find answers about his predicament. This culminates, in the final episode of the first series, in a showdown with his father, who is revealed to be a ruthless criminal. When watching *Life on Mars*, part of our engagement derives from the suspense of this developing plot – a mode of viewing we associate more often with the serial form.

Serials

The idea of the serial – an unfolding story appearing in parts where we have to wait for the next one – of course predates television. There have been examples of the serial in cinema, but it is understood as originally a literary form. The great Victorian novelists like Dickens and the Brontës published their novels in serialised forms in magazines before they appeared as books, creating a sense of anticipation in their readership. From their beginnings as a mass medium, serials became a feature of the television schedules, whether adaptations of classic or popular novels, or original works. Over the years serials have remained an important part of TV fiction. The form includes literary adaptations of the classics that reinterpret great literature for new generations, often emphasising slight nuances of tone or narrative. The 'classic serial' is an important subgenre of British TV, and one that exports well to different territories, becoming a key constituent in the image of British television abroad. Some classics are dramatised frequently (*Jane Eyre*, for example), others are unearthed after decades of neglect by television (*He Knew He Was Right* by Anthony Trollope, BBC 2004, or *Twenty Thousand Streets under the Sky* by Patrick Hamilton, BBC 2005). One television writer, Andrew Davies, has built a reputation mainly from his adaptations of novels, putting a modern slant on period drama to make it vital for modern audiences by stressing the undercurrents of sex and power.

Serials have also been important for genre work in television, especially thrillers, where a sense of anticipation can be built up by the tension of waiting for the next episode (*Five Days*, BBC 2007, for example). In addition serials have enjoyed a significant role as a prestige form in television. This is particularly the case from the 1970s, when TV writers like Dennis Potter, Troy Kennedy Martin and Jim Allen felt constrained by the limitations of the single play and wanted to explore ideas that required more time and space. The result was work like *Pennies from Heaven* (BBC 1978) and *The Singing Detective, Edge of Darkness* and *Days of Hope* (BBC 1975) – all now established in the 'canon' of great TV drama. The serial form allows such writers to develop a complex web of narrative lines feeding a central problem or thesis.

CASE STUDY: BLACKPOOL

A six-part serial allows a gradual build-up of tension and the chance to immerse the audience in a world populated by sometimes ambiguous characters and events. A recent example is Peter Bowker's *Blackpool*. In the first episode Bowker's script establishes:

- A situation – the place: Blackpool, a large, rough-and-ready, hedonistic seaside resort that has an iconic place in British popular culture; the time: the present, as that popular culture is in a state of flux;
- A key event that kicks off the narrative and acts as a causal agent – the dead body of a petty criminal is discovered in entrepreneur Ripley Holden's amusement arcade. This necessitates the arrival of out-of-town detective Peter Carlisle to investigate the crime;
- The characters – we meet Holden, his wife Natalie and his teenage children. We also see Carlisle enter their lives. In addition minor characters are introduced who will illuminate the motives and problems of the main trio of players (Holden, Carlisle and Natalie). These include Holden's daughter's boyfriend Steve and the ageing preacher who protests outside Holden's gambling establishments.

Over the next six episodes this establishing situation is developed into several different narrative strands that gradually converge. The central love triangle between Holden, Natalie and Carlisle frequently ebbs and flows before Natalie and Carlisle eventually come together. On the way secrets are revealed, often acting as cliffhangers to keep us guessing through weekly episodes. The serial form allows the relationship between text and viewer to be dynamic and shift with events. As we watch, our alignment shifts gradually from Carlisle to Holden, and we end up surprising ourselves with our empathy for a man we had probably considered the villain of the piece at the beginning.

Serials, then, offer audiences the pleasures of complexity and of suspense. Although the television industry likes them for the prestige they bring, they also present challenges. By their nature, serials limit their audience – unlike a series it is difficult to dip in and out and if we miss the first episode we are unlikely to bother to catch up.

A recent development that has invigorated the serial, at least commercially, is the event serial. Texts like *24* and *Lost* make a virtue of being must-see-can't-miss programmes and high production values, labyrinthine plots and the endless deferred gratification of closure through the use of extreme cliffhangers create a powerful buzz among the audience, especially with the Internet community that has developed around TV shows. These texts, along with the long-form serials made by HBO like *The Sopranos, Six Feet Under* and *Big Love*, show the power serials can have with audiences. The HBO shows concentrate more on character than the plot-led *24* or *Lost*, but still build up a complex set of narratives across their run. Often this can be in the most subtle and patient of ways: in series 5 of *The Sopranos* there was an unresolved subplot about the homosexuality of one of Tony's captains, Vito. Over a year later, in series 6, this story was revisited, this time with devastating repercussions. This mix of series (self-contained) and serial (continuing) elements has become an increasingly common template in TV drama.

It is interesting that this revival of the serial has occurred when we are moving away from the idea of TV as a shared mass experience. The growing opportunities to view programmes – online, DVD, PVR – make the fear of being unable to catch up less of a problem, although the sheer time investment involved in following these shows still means there are limitations, as long working days mean viewers cannot follow too many serials at one time.

Soaps

At the opposite end of the spectrum to the serial, with its cohesive narrative and sense of closure, is the soap opera or continuing series. This has no end in sight – it can (and sometimes does) go on for ever without reaching a resolution. The 'soap opera', so-dubbed because of early sponsorship by soap companies in the US, has proved a defining genre for TV as a medium.

'Continuing series' is a relatively new industry coinage encompassing soap operas but also including some other texts we might not think of as soaps. *The Bill*, for example, is shown all the time, and *Casualty* and *Heartbeat* fill the schedules for large chunks of the year. The continuing series is defined by its longevity and its place as a constant in its audience's lives. Think how long the examples of the form on British TV have been running: in 2006 *Coronation Street* will have been on our screens for forty-six years; *Emmerdale* (admittedly in a very different incarnation) for thirty-three years; *EastEnders* for twenty-one; *Casualty* for twenty; *The Bill* for twenty-three; *Heartbeat* for fourteen; and *Neighbours* (Grundy TV/Channel 10) for twenty years. That is a long time to be part of something and the communities that are the currency of the continuing series may well be more vivid to viewers than the one in which we live.

Naturally over this time there are changes – characters come and go and their circumstances evolve significantly, as we discussed when we looked at Anne Kirkbride's performance in *Coronation Street*. There is a mix of finite resolved storylines that converge at some points and spawn new plots at others. Each storyline works in tandem with others to create the text; some may be particularly gripping and generate excitement beyond the hardcore audience, but typically the development will be interspersed with other plot strands. These will often be very different in tone, so *Coronation Street* will weave a big slow-burning ratings-grabber, such as Richard Hillman's murderous campaign in 2003, together with some youthful romance and witty banter among the street's old folk.

Yet despite the numerous resolutions that occur in a continuing series, there is no central resolution. This is because it is a permanent space that is the focus of the form: the street, the square, the village. That is why the lead role of the village policeman in *Heartbeat* has changed three or four times with little noticeable effect. It simply does not really matter what character fills that function, it is the show's defined time and place that matters – the Yorkshire Dales in the 1960s (a 1960s that has gone on far longer than the real 1960s did). The viewer looks to be immersed in a beautiful place and a time gone by, a time seen very much through the prism of contemporary life but on which they can project their own memories or desires. Even when there is an attempt at a year zero, such as the *Emmerdale* plane crash that killed most of the long-serving characters, resolution merely creates new unresolved scenarios. Only when the commission is removed, as with *Brookside* or *Family Affairs* is there really any sense of closure for the viewer.

In Britain continuing series remain the most popular fictions. Viewers like their permanence and the ability to inhabit lives rather like their own. Much has been made of the British audience's preference for the gritty, grimy and humdrum over the glamorous and exotic. American soaps have tended to depict the lives of the ultra-rich and chic (*Dallas*, CBS 1978–91, *Dynasty*, ABC 1981–9, and *The Bold and the Beautiful*, Bell-Phillips 1987–). *Footballers' Wives* (Shed/ITV 2002–6), a home-grown attempt to bring their particular over-the-top plots and conspicuous consumption to British screens, was eventually cancelled due to low ratings, with a suspicion that those who did watch were metropolitan sophisticates hunting kitsch rather than a mass audience. In the US, soaps are now largely a daytime phenomenon, but primetime hit texts like *Desperate Housewives* and *Sex and the City* use some of their defining features to create a similar relationship with their viewers, although their aesthetics and thematic complexity are very different.

Comedy forms

Comic fictions have their own forms, derived from those above but driven by the demands for a very particular audience response – laughter. Characters, stories and formal features like running time are defined by this very basic requirement in the relationship between text and viewer.

Sitcoms

Sitcom has traditionally been the dominant comedy form on television. Sitcom is a contraction of 'situation comedy', where the comedy flows from a particular established situation. Rather like the continuing series, sitcom works best by building up a long-term relationship with viewers. The lines become funnier when we get to know the people saying them and understand the position they are in. Some classic sitcoms, such as *Only Fools and Horses, The Office* and *One Foot in the Grave* (BBC 1990–2000), took a series or two to become really popular but then became an intrinsic part of the culture. Now when people refer to 'Del Boy' or 'David Brent' or 'Victor Meldrew', we know exactly whom they are referring to and the implications of the reference. Del Boy Trotter from *Only Fools and Horses* has become emblematic of the amiable but untrustworthy hustler; 'David Brent' is used as shorthand for bad bosses but also for crass, unaware behaviour; while Victor from *One Foot in the Grave* represents our frustrations at the iniquities of everyday life.

Sitcom is a form that has produced some of television's most memorable work, because its concern and connections to the audience resonate with viewers. Good sitcoms can stand up to the ravages of time and innumerable repeat viewings because their characters and situations say something to us about our lives. Take two classic examples: *Steptoe and Son* and *Dad's Army* (BBC 1968–78). In *Steptoe* a father and son, Albert and Harold Steptoe, run a rag-and-bone yard in west London. Now rag-and-bone men (horse-riding junk collectors) had virtually died out by the time the series ended in the early 1970s and are now an almost forgotten folk memory, but this does not matter. The situation we are involved is Harold's torment at the ties that bind him to his manipulative old Dad, and this is something we can relate to our own lives and those of people we know. Enjoyment comes from the interplay between the duo (there are no other major characters) and the cutting black humour of Galton and Simpson's scripts. *Dad's Army* is even more popular today, and is still a regular repeat fixture in the schedules, despite being about a World War II Home Guard platoon full of old men. Again this does not matter, because all ages can relate to the squabbling for the crumbs of status, the deluded ambitions of the commanding officer, Captain Mainwaring, and the perilous scrapes the ensemble cast get into.

Sitcom is also interesting because, at least in the UK, its form has been substantially reinvented. Previously sitcom had a fairly rigid structure, the loosening of which has been in response to a changing audience that was adopting a different mode of viewing. The sitcom is a form particular to broadcasting, born on the radio and raised on TV. Only an intimate medium with lots of time can produce something like a sitcom, with its slow insinuation into the lives and expectations of consumers. The conventional model was that each week the established situation would be revisited, a threat to that situation would arise, usually of a comic nature, then be overcome and the status quo reinstated. Importantly no one learned from the experience and no one escaped – we are in a prison of our own making endlessly replaying our failure (literally a prison, of course, in the case of *Porridge*, BBC 1973–7). Sitcom's strength in part comes from the truth of this scenario; viewers could relate to the never-changing environment. It was never quite as rigid as is popularly believed, however, – two great sitcoms from the 1970s, *Whatever Happened to the Likely Lads?* and *The Fall and Rise of Reginald Perrin* (BBC 1976–9), were narrative in form with events unfolding week by week.

Certain stylistic traits went with the dominant cyclical structure. The shows were very much part of the studio system in television, designed to produce large amounts of material quickly within a defined space. Aesthetically this meant full lighting, shooting on video with three cameras, heightened performance styles and a stage like a three-wall studio set with a studio audience forming the fourth wall, their laughter audible on the soundtrack.

As the 1990s progressed and technology developed, this rigidity of form, and especially the style in which sitcom was made, began to look anachronistic. Audiences were now used to dramas with more location shooting, more mobile camera styles and less theatrical performances. They were also used to docusoaps and other documentary forms that provided a route inside people's everyday lives too. Forty years after most households had acquired a television set, viewers were much more familiar with the nature of the medium. Where TV used to possess a certain mystery, now we all knew (or at least thought we knew) how the industry operated, were used to seeing ordinary people on screen and maybe even possessed the technology to make a programme of our own.

While traditional sitcoms still exist (and sometimes still do well – witness *My Family* (DLT/BBC 2000–) and *The Vicar of Dibley* (Tiger Aspect/BBC 1994–2004), new versions of the form have taken over as the norm. Stylistically the key text that prompted this was *The Royle Family*, which eschewed the studio audience, and lighting and camera styles, although it very much kept the studio set – most of the programme took place in the sitting room around the Royle's own TV. Instead of performing to the audience through the proxy of real-life people watching the studio performance, the acting style remained low-key, communicating to the viewer through repetitions and the tiniest gestures to get laughs. The camera moved around the living room and over the faces of the characters and the image had a grainy, filmic look far removed from the harsh lighting and static camera positions of earlier sitcoms.

This new style chimed with the expectations of audiences and served the humour of the show well. Famously an unscreened pilot shot in the old way did not work at all – the audience laughter broke the complicity we are encouraged to feel watching the family interact. Similarly Gervais and Merchant's *The Office* developed the sitcom further as a form. The show was made to look like a docusoap, although (at least for the first two series) the crew were not seen or heard. The device allowed the characters to address the camera and talk about their feelings in a way that would otherwise seem unnatural, and it was shot in the fluid, fly-on-the-wall style recognisable to viewers. The use of moments of silence, where we see long shots of the office at work with just the whirr of the photocopier, establishes a new sense of pacing. The most significant point again was the absence of a studio audience and their laughter: the comedy of *The Office* is based on our immersion in the world of the staff and frequently relies on the inappropriate response or the embarrassing pause; howls of laughter from without would ruin that tension between text and viewer as we hold our head in mortification over David Brent's latest gaffe. In the US, however, the traditional model still reigns supreme on the networks and the American version of the show retains some of these elements, including the laughter, altering the viewers' perspective.

The studio audience is now deeply unfashionable but I would argue that it might still have a place in our responses to texts. While it would be wrong for *The Royle Family* or *The Office*, it still works for some shows – after all, the great sitcoms of the past used it successfully. Something like Victoria Wood's *dinnerladies* (Pozzitive TV/BBC 1998–2000), set among the workers in a northern factory canteen, thrived on the connection between the performers, the solitary canteen set and the audience in the studio. It relied on Wood's distinctive humour, based around an absurd view on the everyday and the banal and a shared sense of the ridiculous. Its appeal was in being inclusive, rather than distancing, making us feel part of something. It had a very specific pace that worked like a call and response with the jokes and resultant laughter. Elements of farce were used in the way the performers moved on the single canteen set, with much being made of comic entries and exits. Taking away the audience would make it a very different programme and work against this atmosphere of warmth and inclusion.

The cyclical structure has also been a casualty of these changes in the sitcom. There is now often some kind of narrative development across episodes: Denise has a baby; Brent gets fired; Tim and Dawn get together; even in *dinnerladies'* second series Bren and Tony's romance dictates events. Sitcom is now a much more fluid form and, despite reports of its demise, it can still reach audiences and has the power of resonance. It now frequently tries to communicate in a different way, no longer trying to capture a mass audience but seeking a select but devoted band of followers. As a result sitcoms have proved to be one of the most successful television forms in addressing the concerns of contemporary society, anticipating and reacting to the changes in the way TV is watched.

Sketch shows

This comic revolution has also been aided by sketch shows, which have risen to new heights of popularity in the last decade. Sketches can either be self-contained (many of those in *The Two Ronnies*, BBC 1971–87), riffs on a theme (best seen in Dave Allen's visual gags about the priesthood in the 1970s) or be based around recurring characters and situations. It was this latter variant that has proved dominant in recent years. *Harry Enfield and Chums* (Tiger Aspect/BBC 1994–8), *The Fast Show* (BBC 1994–2000), *Little Britain* and *Catherine Tate Show* (Tiger Aspect/BBC 2004–) have introduced characters that have struck a chord with the *Zeitgeist* and caused a million playgrounds and offices to echo with the sound of 'It's so unfair', 'I was terribly drunk' 'Scorchio!' 'Yeah but no but yeah' and 'Am I bovvered?'. The convergence of character and a situation that we know will always end in the release of a learnt catchphrase is a powerful example of the dynamic between text and viewer.

A popular example of the recurring sketch as text is *Little Britain*'s Lou and Andy. Despite its moments of extreme bad taste and vast quantities of ribald innuendo, the series has been phenomenally successful in the UK. Lou and Andy are particularly popular, with one of their sketches being voted the best ever in a recent Channel 4 show (*50 Greatest Comedy Sketches*, North One/C4 2005). The set-up of the sketch never varies. Lou is a carer, looking after wheelchair-bound Andy, a sulky Scouser who makes constant demands on his friend, pointing at objects and insisting 'Want that one', then saying 'Don't like it' when at great trouble or expense it is provided for him. The joke is always the same – Andy is not really disabled but merely idle. When Lou's back is turned, he gets out of the chair to dive into a swimming pool, beat up a passer-by or appear on a TV quiz show. We always know what the joke will be but our response to the text is anticipation at the way this resolution will be presented to us, and gratification when our expectations are met. The humour of the sketch works precisely through understanding that that is what our response will be, playing variations on the theme and delaying our gratification until we finally see Andy rise up and walk. While there is a resolution in this, there can be no resolution in the situation – Lou must always be unaware that Andy is shamming or the joke is over.

Some recurrent sketches develop into mini-sitcoms, where, despite the short time, we are building up a relationship with characters and getting to know them more. *The Fast Show*'s sketches featuring Ralph, the closeted squire, and his monosyllabic Irish handyman, Ted, are perhaps the most sophisticated examples, becoming a hilarious and poignant series of fleeting moments depicting a love that dare speak only of the drainage in the lower field.

The League of Gentlemen (BBC 1999–2001) took this further. Originating in a stage and radio show based on recurrent character sketches, the TV version fused sketch and sitcom together by placing the character routines in one place – the fictional small northern town of Royston Vasey. This alters our understanding of the sketch format, as the sketch is no longer a single entity, but interacts with other stories.

New narratives

Changes in the industry, as discussed in Part I, are making TV narrative forms less defined and encouraging influences on each other. Robin Nelson argues that across all TV fictions there is instead something he calls 'flexi-narrative', describing this as 'the fast-cut, segmented, multi-narrative structure which yields the 90-second sound-and-vision byte form currently typical of popular TV drama' (Nelson, 1997: 24–5). This new aesthetic is transforming narrative through faster editing and greater numbers of scenes. This faster-paced fiction (developed in the 1990s by *ER*, among others) is now the norm and changes our expectations of texts as viewers – suddenly the older conventions of longer, dialogue-heavy scenes seem anachronistic. Television is finding new ways to tell stories.

Authorship

So who is creating television fiction? You may be familiar with the various debates around film authorship, which emphasises the director as the principal creative force.

Critics have discussed authorship in television very differently. In television fiction the writer has traditionally been considered the most important figure. There are a number of reasons for this, one of which is that historically the more limited visual canvas of the small screen and the more prescribed nature of the studio has made the director a less powerful figure. The director is also frequently a hired hand who comes on board quite late in the production process. The key creative partnership is often between the writer and the producer. This could be because a work of television fiction originates from the commissioning of a script, and because the process of rewrites familiar in the film industry is less common in TV (at least in Britain). The kudos that came from the single plays in television's earlier years derived from the writing, giving some

---

Auteur theory

Young French critics in the 1950s (including many, such as Jean-Luc Godard and François Truffaut, who would become leading film-makers) identified certain directors as 'authors' of their films. The director was seen to be the most significant role as s/he co-ordinated script, camera and performances to produce a unified text. Their ideas were developed further by American critic Andrew Sarris in the late 1960s. Sarris designed a strict hierarchy, designating some directors 'auteurs' (such as Alfred Hitchcock, John Ford and Howard Hawks) but suggesting that others were merely '*metteurs en scène*' (essentially hired journeymen). This view of authorship is problematic because

- it ignores the parts played by other roles/people in the construction of a text;
- by identifying authorship in recurrent thematic concerns and links between texts, it discriminates against film-makers who make films across genres and who may explore a range of different ideas.

television dramatists a certain amount of power in ensuring their vision reached the screen.

In Britain this view of the writer as author was particularly established through the work of Dennis Potter, usually considered the greatest dramatist in UK TV history. Potter made his reputation with single plays for the BBC in the 1960s and 1970s – *Stand up Nigel Barton* (1965), *Son of Man* (1969), *Blue Remembered Hills* (1979) and the notorious (and banned) *Brimstone and Treacle* (1976), for example – then two serials, *Pennies from Heaven* and *The Singing Detective* (described as 'Television's *Citizen Kane*' by Glen Creeber, 2007). Potter's work was both popular and controversial and he demanded, and frequently got, a high degree of creative control: indeed in his later years he directed some of his own pieces like *Blackeyes* (BBC 1989), although this was generally held to be the result of too much control and received far less critical acclaim.

Potter's status as an author was partly due to his critical reputation, his creative involvement and his public profile, but it was also due to the nature of the texts he produced. They are full of recurrent themes – the loss of childhood innocence; sexual desire; the fear of death and disease – and devices that are employed time and time again, such as the use of popular song. Many of these traits are very specific to Potter himself – his Forest of Dean childhood and the fact that he suffered from the skin disease psorias for example – encouraging us as viewers to see an authorial voice. When a new piece was aired, it would be considered in relation to his previous work and viewers would expect to encounter these recurrent Potter obsessions.

Most of the prominent television fiction writers have been read in the same way – we look in the texts for evidence of their authorship. To take some examples: Jack Rosenthal material was usually funny and often influenced by his Jewish identity; Jimmy McGovern has a reputation for fierce left-wing polemic and his work is informed by his Liverpudlian Catholic background and his past gambling addiction; Alan Bleasdale and Paul Abbott are both interested in northern working-class life and how politics can corrupt the individual.

Much of the early writing on TV drama took the writer as author as the basis of study, notably George Brandt's *British Television Drama* (1981). Cultural studies and structuralist approaches disputed this idea of authorship, arguing that meaning was something that came largely through textual and social structures, or through the viewers themselves. The work of John Tulloch (1990) has argued for a middle ground, accepting that the writer has an important role, but insisting that this is limited by the contexts of production and consumption. The writer is but one agent, one author of the text.

> **TV writers**
> Some examples of work by these TV authors:
> Jack Rosenthal – *Bar Mitzvah Boy* (BBC 1976), *The Knowledge* (LWT/ITV 1979)
> Jimmy McGovern – *Cracker, Hillsborough, Dockers* (Parallax Pictures/C4 1999)
> Alan Bleasdale – *Boys from the Black Stuff, The Monocled Mutineer* (BBC 1986), *GBH* (GBH Films/C4 1991)
> Paul Abbott – *Clocking Off* (BBC 2000–3), *State of Play* (Ensor/BBC 2003), *Shameless*

CASE STUDY: RUSSELL T. DAVIES

I would like to look in more detail at how the processes of authorship operate and the influence this has on texts through the example of another important contemporary television writer, Russell T. Davies. His work has already been considered with reference to *Doctor Who* and its audience in Chapter 2, but this success was built not just on the importance and resonance of that show's history and brand, but also on Davies's vision as an author and his critical reputation.

Russell T. Davies's career has been built on some intriguing contradictions. Much of his work has been very popular, and on mainstream channels, but he is acknowledged as a writer of depth and a daring stylist. He developed as a writer by working on children's drama and still, through *Doctor Who*, maintains an interest in children as viewers, yet some of his work has been controversial due to its explicit sexual content and challenges to bigotry and conventional thinking. Davies's writing has always explored his identity as a gay man and became infamous with *Queer as Folk*, which followed the stories of some gay men (including a teenager) exploring their desires on the Manchester scene. A later series, *Bob and Rose* (Red Productions/ITV 2001), considered sexual orientation in a different way through the tale of Bob, a gay man, who is confused to find that he is falling in love with a woman. This fluid sexual identity has become a trope of Davies's writing and is something we have come to expect as viewers of his work. Even *Doctor Who* has inferences to this, and in the spin-off series for older viewers, *Torchwood*, this becomes much more explicit, with hero Captain Jack's brazen bisexuality to the fore.

When Davies tackled another piece with its own history and associations, *Casanova* (Red Productions/BBC 2005), his gayness is employed effectively to make us think about the text. This is a historic piece about a famous womaniser but his script produces something that comments on our own time, in both its self-conscious, post-modern form and its approach to sex. Instead of being a cold-hearted masculine seducer, Davies's Casanova (played by David Tennant, later to be his Doctor Who) has a much more polymorphous sexuality and a more sensitive nature, motivated more by a desire to follow his heart and subvert authority than collect notches on his bedpost. Dennis Potter also wrote an adaptation of the Casanova story that was very different (BBC 1971), and in which he also brought himself as an author to the text and made it his own.

There is much more to Davies as an author than his sexual identity, important though that is. He also wrestles with child–parent relations, the supernatural and questions of morality. His serial *The Second Coming* (Red Productions/ITV 2003), for example, imagined the son of God (played by Christopher Eccleston) as a bloke called Steve working in a video shop in Manchester who performs miracles at a football ground. This also illustrates his fearlessness at flouting convention and taking risks, which seems to cohabit very happily in his work with his popular and vibrant approach to material and his willingness to engage a mass family audience as well as gain critical prestige.

Davies is a television author, then. He brings a particular approach and a distinctive voice to the text and in turn, his involvement influences our response. In a recent documentary about him he revealed that: 'The hardest thing in TV is to get the vision right, the tone of it, the temperature' (source: *Time Shift – Russell T. Davies: Unscripted*, BBC 2005).

His desire to do just that, even if it is not always successful, makes its mark on the text. Like Potter his contribution is not limited to the page; he becomes involved in the whole production, taking an executive producer role on many of his shows and engaging with the media business. Even before the success of the revived *Doctor Who* he had the power to get his scripts made, because broadcasters could expect quality, critical interest, innovation but also resonance for the viewer, and, often, good ratings too.

Alternative authors

Clearly, though, the assignation of Davies, or Potter, or any other writer as the author of a television fiction is problematic, just as the primacy of the director as the creator of a film has its problems too. Television (like film) is a collaborative medium. A lot of people are involved in its making and they must have some influence on the outcome of a text too. Davies may be the person who 'sets the vision' but he is assisted by others, both technical and creative personnel, in realising it on screen (Prys, 2006: 20–5).

An important role in TV fiction is that of the producer, who makes the production happen financially and organisationally, and is frequently the link to the broadcasters, ensuring that the original vision is not compromised. Davies's work has frequently been produced by Nicola Shindler and her production company Red, and her role in establishing the texts is very significant. Actors Christopher Eccleston and David Tennant have appeared in different shows Davies has written and also bring something to the text – and the text influences subsequent readings of them as performers.

> **Think about . . .**
> Who else involved in producing a programme could have authorship of a text? Consider other creative personnel (actors, composers, directors of photography, for example) and the organisations that may claim part 'authorship' – production companies, channels and so on.

The broadcasters themselves can be an important creative force, dictating aspects of the text and, of course, commissioning it in the first place. As discussed in Chapter 1 with reference to HBO and Channel 4, a culture can develop to empower creative personnel and make sure that original work reaches the screen; equally they can favour particular kinds of fiction or seek to serve a particular demographic. This will influence the kinds of fictions that are produced.

TV directors: the case of Alan Clarke
As we have discussed, the writer is given primacy in TV fiction and the role of the director is often underplayed. The one real exception to this norm in the UK is Alan Clarke (Ken Loach and Mike Leigh have also had an impact but this derives mainly from their feature film work, and Leigh also writes, or 'devises', his material). Ironically Clarke's reputation has grown enormously since his early death in 1990, with younger film-makers like Harmony Khorine citing him as an influence and a number of studies published (Kelly, 1998; Rolinson, 2005). While he worked with a variety of writers on some very different projects, there is a unifying vision to Clarke's work seen in its energy (often violent). He pushes at the form's boundaries to create a new television aesthetic with his mobile camerawork (he was a pioneer of Steadicam, where the camera follows characters around) and use of imagery to convey meaning. You should try to see at least *Penda's Fen, Made in Britain* (Central/ITV 1983) and *Christine* (BBC 1987).

Authorship in American TV

In America the focus has been much less on the individual author. For a sitcom, for instance, still largely produced in the UK by one or two people, there is traditionally a whole team of writers to hone the script. In drama, too, there may be different writers across episodes, although they will try and maintain a consistent tone. This tone may be established by one writer, or a producer (frequently both) who has devised the programme and sets its course. Joss Wheedon with *Buffy*, David Chase with *The Sopranos* and Alan Ball with *Six Feet Under* are obvious examples. Frequently these 'series creators' are ascribed as authors. Again many other people are involved in creating the text but there is an overall authorial voice.

In a medium where texts are born from a commissioning process, produced for large commercial concerns, and distributed through a schedule controlled by the broadcasters, authorship is always going to be a contested subject. The primacy of the writer in TV has perhaps unfairly diminished other creative roles, and the contributions made by the producer and indeed, in some cases, the director and others need to be taken into account. However, the importance given to writers has meant that they have been ceded some creative power on occasion – giving them the status of authors has led to a greater degree of authorship.

Conclusion

Television fiction uses the medium's strengths to produce complex and rich texts. Time, space and flexibility of form can be employed to create a dynamic relationship between the viewer and the story, and an intensity in creating characters that develop with us and resonate. TV allows a wide range of narratives that take advantage of the way we watch and the intimacy of the viewing environment. We can be transfixed for a couple of hours but we can also be gripped over six weeks or grow up with people and a place in a kind of parallel universe for the length of our lives. No other form can offer that kind of variety and sophistication, and traditionally fiction has been the main point of engagement for viewers, delivering the highest ratings and the most prestigious shows.

However, there are signs that this may be changing as the modes of consumption detailed in Chapter 2 unfold. Audience numbers for TV fiction, despite the excitement over a *Doctor Who*, a *Shameless* or a *Desperate Housewives*, are dwindling. New shows have a harder time attracting an audience and despite the expense involved in making them, broadcasters are increasingly cutting their losses, axing shows or moving them into 'dead' slots. Inevitably this will mean that fewer are made, because fiction is very expensive, requiring script and development time, large casts of well-paid actors, big crews, and costly sets and locations.

In Autumn 2006 US network NBC announced a drastic cut in scripted shows, no longer screening them in the first hour of prime time and in the process laying off 700 staff and cutting its budget by $750 million. It has decided it can reach more audiences with much cheaper unscripted programming like reality and game shows (source: Latimes.com). In some ways this has already happened in the UK, although fiction still brings awards, prestige and public service brownie points for broadcasters. Sometimes it can still come good, but shows like *Doctor Who* and the revivals of *Cracker* and *Prime Suspect* that pulled in good audiences in 2006 were able to work on high recognition factors from older successes. For new material it is much harder to build audiences who get to know characters like the Doctor, Fitz or Jane Tennison and want to find out what happens to them.

Why is this? There are now such demands on the audience's ever-decreasing leisure time and so many more potential sites of content that perhaps we are unable to give as much to texts. Fiction requires effort. We need to invest a lot of time in watching, getting to know the characters, the situation and anticipating the actions that could take place. We need to care about it but the resources for caring may be diminishing. At the start of a new series or serial we have to decide very quickly whether we want to invest any further and give up more of our valuable time. This demand alters the nature of the text and is inclined to make it more simplistic so that it grabs us early on and maintains our interest. Some of the best TV dramas (*The Singing Detective* for one) deliberately work as a slow burn, so that later revelations are all the more powerful and the impact more resonant.

> Think about . . .
> How much fiction do you watch? Is it less than you used to? Why do you think audiences for TV fiction are declining?

Television drama has delivered extraordinarily powerful and profound experiences and continues to do so, so it would be sad if it lost its audience, thereby losing its power and its likely future. Perhaps new technologies will find new forms and new ways to re-engage that audience before it realises what it has lost.

4. TV Fact

This chapter will unpick the modes of factual address in the following ways:

- *By looking at the idea of 'reality' in reality television.*
- *By considering authored fact, a form of TV where an individual, often positioned as an 'expert', relates their version of the truth.*
- *By examining forms that purport to report something close to objective truth like news and current affairs.*
- *By acknowledging, as with fiction, the importance of performance and looking at this in the factual context by considering the role of the television personality.*

While television fiction is relatively easy to define, what constitutes factual TV is surprisingly ambiguous. What do we mean when we say a programme is 'factual'? We might think of news bulletins or documentaries but plenty of other types of text are strictly speaking factual as well. Game shows are 'fact', in that they are really happening (if perhaps not quite in the form we are experiencing). Chris Tarrant really does ask questions on *Who Wants to Be a Millionaire?* to someone who really is a surveyor from Milton Keynes. Light entertainment shows are records of real events: if Ant and Dec are appearing as themselves, they are a fact, a reality; likewise a contestant's toe-curlingly bad audition on *The X Factor* also really happened. These texts are not television fiction as we understand it – they are not acted or written in that way – so they appear as some form of factual TV. As we will see, this idea of 'fact', of what is true, can become opaque and problematic, and it can be argued that this is increasingly the case.

There is, then, a wide range of what constitutes fact on TV. It covers a variety of genres, many kinds of narrative structures and different types of engagement between the viewer and the text. Fact on TV offers endless possibilities – think about the following actual or potential examples from contemporary British TV:

- Footage of nesting seagulls on *Springwatch* (BBC 2005–)
- A nurse from Warrington 'being' Beyonce on *Stars in Their Eyes* (Granada/ITV 1990–)
- Jeremy Paxman interviewing the Home Secretary on *Newsnight* (BBC 1980–)
- David Tennant exploring his family tree on *Who Do You Think You Are?* (Wall to Wall/BBC 2004–)
- Chelsea v. Barcelona on Sky Sports 2
- Matthew Wright discussing the stories in this morning's papers with Lowri Turner on *The Wright Stuff* (Princess Productions/Five 2000–);
- Jeremy Clarkson test-driving a new Mazda on *Top Gear* (BBC 1978–)
- A round-up of headlines on *Five News*
- Monty Don planting a shrub on *Gardener's World* (BBC 1968–)
- Manchester University beating Newcastle University on *University Challenge* (Granada/BBC 1994–)
- The final of *Strictly Come Dancing*
- *Cosmetic Surgery* (2004–5) on Five
- Simon Schama considering the background to Caravaggio's work in *The Power of Art* (BBC 2006)
- An investigation into children's vaccination programmes on *The Real Story with Fiona Bruce* (BBC 2003–6)
- Gillian McKeith shouting at a fat person on *You Are What You Eat* (Celador/C4 2004–)
- Jamie Oliver cooking a pasta dish for schoolchildren in *Jamie's School Dinners*;
- Alan Sugar firing a hapless would-be executive on *The Apprentice* (talkbackThames/BBC 2005–)
- Said hapless would-be executive being interviewed by Adrian Chiles after they have been fired
- Twelve strangers meeting for the first time inside the *Big Brother* house.

Over the course of this chapter we will interrogate some of these factual texts, or ones like them. How are they constructed? What are we looking for when we watch them? Do we want to be entertained, or do we want to be informed about something we did not know previously? Probably both. I would suggest that we want to encounter some element of truth. 'Truth' is, of course, a complex concept, open to many interpretations. Certainly not everything in these programmes is 'true' in the sense of being absolute and verifiable and, as will be shown later, we constantly need to interrogate the nature of the truth presented to us. However, I think we could say that we expect a measure of truth within factual TV. We would be shocked if we found out that on *University Challenge* the Manchester University team had been shown their questions in advance and were not really students; if 'Gillian McKeith' was a part played by an actress; if it was not really David Tennant's family tree being investigated; if a plane crash reported on the news had not really occurred; or for that matter if Alan Sugar actually intended to hire all the apprentices and went out drinking with them. At different times, in different kinds of factual programmes, we search for different kinds of truth and our understanding of that truth is flexible. We expect more from the news than from *Big Brother* perhaps, but the rows that develop in the press and among viewers when there are suspicions that a contestant is not what they seem indicate that we still imagine the latter to be substantially true.

Factual entertainment

The most commented-on phenomenon in television in the last decade, at least in the content rather than the delivery of programmes, has been 'reality television'. Within the industry this kind of programming is also known as 'factual entertainment', although this category may include other forms beyond what viewers would recognise as reality texts.

> Objective and subjective
> Think about the terms 'objective' and 'subjective' and consider their implications. In the *Oxford Popular Dictionary*, objective is defined as 'not influenced by personal feelings or opinions' and subjective as 'dependent on personal taste and opinions'. Many would suggest that to be truly objective is not possible – we cannot divorce our emotions, background and social context. However, it could be designated as a desirable aim, even if it is not attainable. We are used to many factual programmes at least attempting to be objective, and it would be a surprise to us if, for example, the anchor of a news bulletin suddenly expressed their personal views on the Prime Minister. There is also a place for a subjective interpretation of events, but we expect the difference between the objective and subjective approach to be marked out by different formal constructions for reasons of clarity.

Docusoaps

In the mid- to late 1990s there was a vogue for 'docusoaps' – series that followed people in particular places or doing particular jobs. *Airline* (LWT/ITV 1998–), *Hotel* (Lion TV/BBC 1997–8), *Driving School* (BBC 1997), *Life of Grime* (BBC 1998–) and *The Clampers* (BBC 1998) were successful examples: texts that took a more populist spin on the traditions of 'fly-on-the-wall' documentary long established in British television (Kilborn, 2000: 111–19). They did this by building up particular stories for their entertainment rather than informational value, and inserting influences from other forms to engage viewers. For instance, Maureen's bad driving in *Driving School* was emphasised for comic effect, while in *The Clampers* the team were filmed after issuing tickets singing along to the Queen song 'Another One Bites the Dust'.

The shows purported to offer a window for the viewer onto specific real worlds but also strived to be entertaining. Their structures focused on 'characters' they found in their environments like Jeremy Spake, an air steward on *Airline*, or Maureen in *Driving School*. Viewers connected with these people and they (briefly) became household names. The texts inevitably began to reflect that connection, concentrating on narrative lines or personalities they knew to be popular. The relationship between text and viewer still hinged, however, on the idea that we were being offered at least a version of the truth, in part because viewers were responding to seeing ordinary people on TV for once, and not, as Brian Winston pointed out, as 'social victims or problems' (2000: 55).

We may be vaguely aware that editing is weighting the world that we were seeing in a particular direction, but we accept this because we understand that this is done to entertain. However, there are lines that viewers assume will not be crossed when we are encountering what purports to be the truth. There was an outcry when it was revealed that Ray, the larger-than-life leader of the clamping team in *The Clampers*, actually worked at a desk when the cameras were not rolling and did not spend his time on the streets removing vehicles. Viewers felt cheated and there has been tension throughout the development of reality TV about the balance between actuality and constructed reality in TV fact. As Su Holmes and Deborah Jermyn argue, 'this debate . . . has very much foregrounded an awareness of the format's manipulation of the real' (2005: 26–7).

The 'docusoap' format mutated over time into other textual styles presenting 'reality' as entertainment. A significant strand that has come to dominate the genre moves away from simply representing a situation that exists outside television in an entertaining way to creating a 'reality'. These shows put real people in a situation constructed specifically for the programme or embark them on a course of action they would not normally anticipate. An example would be a programme like *The 1900 House* (Wall to Wall/C4 1999), where a contemporary British family has to live as if it was 1900 and endure the same privations a family would at that time (except, of course, for the presence of a film crew). This is a situation that would be most unlikely to happen without the production of a TV show called *The 1900 House*. Slightly different are shows like *Castaway 2000* (Lion TV/BBC 2000) or *Beyond Boundaries* (Diverse/BBC 2005–). While it would be possible for a group of people to live on a Scottish island for the year or for a group of people with disabilities to trek across Africa, the events are facilitated by television and scenarios are created by selecting that particular group and filming what happens. Such programmes rely on being able to build a narrative that engages the viewer. Typically this involves conflict, whether between individuals in the group, or from setting challenges that involve hardship and crisis.

It is often claimed by both critics and participants that television sets up this conflict to ensure the success of the programme. Sometimes texts reflect a tension between producers and participants on this basis. *Castaway 2000* saw struggles between one contestant, Ron, and the others that he blames on the production (and he successfully claimed that they had misrepresented him – he threw a chair at a wall and on TV this was construed as throwing it at a person). The television text and the real events that are happening exist in a dynamic relationship where those involved are aware at particular times of the artificial elements in the whole enterprise. At times they rail against this situation, at others they seek to take advantage of it. Indeed the winner of *Castaway 2000*, Ben Fogle, has built a successful career as a TV presenter since the series.

Reality TV

The tensions are inherent in the form. In a very early example of 'reality' television, long before it became an established part of our TV landscape, a group of families were thrown together to live as if they were in the Iron Age, in a show called *Living in the Past* (BBC 1978). One of the families was vegetarian and this led to tension and arguments because they refused to hunt and prepare meat, which seemed to the others a necessity for survival in this environment. Perhaps producers might have selected the family precisely to create such situations. While most viewers are aware of the constructed nature of these real-life situations, there is a level of understanding that the setting up of conflicts is what makes them entertaining, and occasionally illuminating, texts.

Programmes like *Big Brother* develop these ideas yet further. We completely understand that the situation is on the one hand real, because there is a set of disparate individuals who have never met previously in the *Big Brother* house at the time we are watching. On the other hand we are clear that it is unreal: we know that it is entirely set up for the cameras and would not happen otherwise, and we understand perfectly well that the housemates have been selected to provide conflict and crisis (Biressi and Nunn, 2005: 91). There are many reality shows following different formats based around experience, or competition. *Big Brother*, which has completed its eighth UK series and spawned a host of international versions from the original Dutch format created by Endemol (and unwittingly George Orwell, who first coined the phrase 'Big Brother' to describe the oppressive regime in his novel *1984*), has transformed the way we understand reality on television.

The public on reality TV

This may particularly be the case in our approach to the people we see on screen. The housemates (in the non-celebrity version of the show) are almost all unknown before they appear on screen in the house, yet immediately stories about their lives appear in the press. We are invited as part of the programme's format to pass judgment on them by voting on whether they should be evicted from the house. The televised evictions feature crowds of viewers who react at the appearance of the housemate by cheering or booing and hurling abuse (occasionally this must have been frightening and threatening for the competitors). How much are we seeing them as 'real people'? Plainly we would not like this to happen to us but it is seen by many as part of the deal – housemates take a gamble by agreeing to participate in the show and fame is exchanged for privacy. As part of that process the participants forfeit any right to sympathy.

This seems rather harsh but comes from the way we understand the participants through the text. Su Holmes says that 'it is certainly important for the programme to claim that at some point we will witness the display of real selves in the house' (Jermyn and Holmes, 2005: 124). But do we ever really see that? Even in shows like *Big Brother*, where there is live feed of events as they unfold, we are still receiving a version of that person seen in the context of that text. A housemate is positioned in a particular role in the house, through camera close-ups, editing and the juxtaposition of images, and by repeating certain scenes in different contexts. The house, is remember, a completely unnatural environment – when in normal life would you be prevented from leaving your house for two months, or from having any time alone? As viewers we forget this and understand a person purely because they act in a certain way under these circumstances.

In the first series in 2000 it was understood that it was an artificial situation in a more fundamental way – partly social experiment and partly a competition to see who would win with the public. At various times in the house the contestants sang a made-up ditty called 'It's only a game show'. At the same time one of the contestants, dubbed 'Nasty Nick', was disgraced for acting as if it was a game show and trying to ensure that he won by building up information on nominations. This opened up a paradox in the possibilities of reading the text – we know that it is a contest but we do not wish the contestants to acknowledge that it is. In subsequent series this desire has increased, so although it is essentially a game show we like to think of the programme as being something else, positioned somewhere between reality and light entertainment.

Participants now have a much more obviously performative role, existing in the text in terms of the expectations of the viewers. Viewers are encouraged to assign roles – camp gay man, predatory older woman, wild 'ladette' – and respond to them in this context, often as they 'perform' this role and are judged on the basis of it. There is a grey area in separating the real world from the television world and sometimes we cannot be sure whether we are seeing something that has actually happened or a very partial version of that event constructed by television. Participants often complain that they have been demonised through editing, and there are points where this can seem acute, such as the montage of their 'best' house moments they have to sit through with presenter Davina McCall after eviction.

Viewers see ordinary people on television through the text and remain oblivious to their existence away from it. Why do they volunteer to be on television? Do they think TV might sort out their problems? It would be interesting while watching programmes like *Wife Swap* to know this, to understand the process whereby they decided to volunteer and why the producers saw them as good subjects. There can be a misunderstanding of the benefits of TV – many viewers mistakenly think that members of the public are paid large amounts to appear, which is rarely the case. Certainly there are discussions to be had about whether the public are being exploited on television. Are people being led into situations that they cannot control?

In particular there are questions about representation. In some cases this might be the absence of particular groups of people from such programmes; in others it may be the way that the text chooses to present participants. You could make a case (and some have, for instance Palmer, 2005) that reality TV creates a spectacle around class, exaggerating and ridiculing some traits for the amusement of affluent viewers. As discussed in Chapter 1, sometimes the motives and positioning of the programme-makers can be questioned, as well as those who appear. We also should consider our own role in this – are we wallowing in other people's misfortunes and trying to set ourselves apart from them through TV? We need to unpick our own responses and question how we are being made to feel.

The rise of reality TV has been a subject of great interest to academics and social commentators alike. The discourse surrounding *Big Brother* and other reality shows like *Wife Swap* sees them as representative of society, both in the tensions depicted in the text and in our understanding of the media. When situations are created and members of the public inserted into them, are we actually seeing a fictionalisation of fact? John Corner has argued that this is an example of 'post-documentary', where documentary ideas and styles have dispersed across all types of programming (2002: 153). Equally are the things that we have traditionally enjoyed in fiction – character, plot, closure, conflict – being transposed to factual programming as reality becomes a form of entertainment? Holmes and Jermyn

> Think about . . .
> Does TV exploit people? Is the way reality shows are constructed fundamentally unfair to participants?

see this as 'a very self-reflexive and self-conscious interplay between different programme forms' (2005: 6). No doubt there has always been a measure of this but reality TV appears to have accelerated this process and asks questions about what becomes 'true' or 'not true'.

CASE STUDY: THE APPRENTICE

It is worth looking in some detail at how a reality show works and how we understand it when we are watching. The text I want to explore here is *The Apprentice*. The series is based on an American series of the same title (Mark Burnett Productions/NBC 2004–) featuring entrepreneur Donald Trump. Twelve contestants (six men and six women) compete to get a job working for Trump at a high salary. To get the position they form teams and are assigned particular business-related tasks. The losing team is summoned to Trump's boardroom and one of its members is summarily fired. The last four contestants compete individually against each other in tasks and extended interviews and one is hired to work for Trump.

The programme format was sold to talkbackThames, who were commissioned to make a UK version for the BBC. Two series have been broadcast in the UK on BBC2 and have proved to be ratings successes for the channel – so much so that the following series moved to BBC1 (a common practice with popular programmes).

The British version of *The Apprentice* is intriguingly positioned as both a business series and as a factual entertainment programme with a game-show element. Another business-based series, *Dragon's Den* (BBC 2005–), occupies similar territory, also allowing the space for the viewer to engage with a competition and, it must be said, to take a detached position laughing at the ineptitude of some of the contestants – a kind of *X Factor* with spreadsheets. There are elements of this in the British *Apprentice*, which slavishly follows the American format but uses well-known British businessman Sir Alan Sugar instead of Trump.

Sugar's persona as a gruff, straight-talking Jewish Londoner and self-made man is important to the experience of the series. His boardroom demeanour is tough and brittle and creates fear in those who enter. Each episode centres on the task, following the two teams, organised by a designated team leader, as they try to complete it successfully. This is usually broadly business-related but also visually interesting and something conceptually easy for viewers not involved in business to understand, so running a market stall rather than selling shares via the Internet, for example. The winning team is quite simply the one that makes the most money. The losing team leader nominates two other members of the team to accompany him/her to the boardroom, where one will be fired.

In the penultimate episode of the second series (tx 3 May 2006) the format changes. The four remaining candidates undergo extensive interviews with some of Sugar's associates and two of them are then eliminated from the competition in the boardroom. In the final episode the final two candidates go head to head in a task and one is then chosen by Sugar as his assistant with the words 'You're hired', an inversion of the 'You're fired' we have heard throughout the series.

I want to look at this penultimate episode in some detail, isolating key moments and examining how our responses may be being guided. The episode, like all the others, was followed by a spin-off programme on BBC3 (and sometimes also shown on BBC2), called *The Apprentice: You're Fired*, a studio-based show hosted by Adrian Chiles, where the fired candidate has their say and various business experts weigh in with their opinions, as does the studio audience, which votes on whether Sugar's decision was right.

The title sequence contains some interesting paradoxes, mixing establishing aerial shots of Canary Wharf and the City of London with images of the apprentices and sound bites from Sugar. This is odd, because the headquarters of his company is actually in suburban Essex, and not the financial centres of London, but their image of high-profile deal-making presumably fits the mood the producers are trying to create.

The sound clips in this sequence feature Sir Alan telling the twelve apprentices on their first day that 'This is not a game . . . this is a twelve-week job interview. There is no phone-in, no texting, no panel of judges – it's me who decides who gets hired.' Straight away, then, the programme marks itself out as distinct from other types of factual entertainment that do employ these methods of selection. Sugar asserts his control over the result and over the purposes of the show, as far as he is concerned.

Clearly, however, our experiences of the text are quite different. We do not have a stake in whether the winner will be a good employee for Amstrad and improve their profit margins. Frankly we don't care, although we accept that Sir Alan does and we are interested in his reactions to the candidates. While some may be fascinated by the presentation of business and the excitement of seeing whether the task is successfully completed, what many viewers want to see are actually the same things that attract viewers of other reality shows: conflict, tension and the chance to see some deluded egos get their comeuppance or to root for someone we find sympathetic.

However, we also appreciate the slightly different position we hold in *The Apprentice* in comparison to reality rivals such as *Big Brother* – we cannot directly influence the result and the aesthetic of the show reflects this distance. It is shot in cool, stark blue tones with the use of a number of strongly composed static images. Take the point when the final four candidates enter the boardroom.

Alan Sugar's associate Claude criticises Michelle's reliance on 'gut feelings'

The scene is formal and austere, with the emphasis on the vast expanse of table between the candidates and Sugar and his associates, as he explains the rules of the episode. Three associates will interview the four candidates: two women, Michelle and Ruth, and two men Paul and Ansell.

During the interview sections the camera cross-cuts between the candidates and the three interviewers, sometimes juxtaposing their responses to the same questions. For the viewer the process is fascinating as we have so far only seen the apprentices in the context of a team and this gives an opportunity for us, just as much as for Sugar, (who receives only a verbal report of the proceedings), to judge them as individuals. Enjoyably for us, this can be a painful process.

The consultants report back to Sugar. They are unanimous in dismissing Paul, whose attempts at bravado backfired spectacularly. They all agree Ansell is an extremely nice person and, despite reservations about their veracity, rate Michelle and Ruth. The exercise proves very satisfying for viewers reinforcing opinions likely to have been formed across the run. Paul has consistently been on the winning team but for many would have seemed largely charmless and chauvinistic on screen.

The press and reality TV
In the final programme Michelle was announced as the winner, gaining a job with Sugar's company. At this point tabloids started to print stories on her troubled past, and coverage continued when she had a relationship with one of the other contestants, Syed. In the autumn it was announced that she would not continue working for Sugar.

Paul says to the interviewer 'I think I'm brilliant

Ruth admits that people resigned when she became a manager

Sugar asks Michelle, 'Are your family proud of you?'

Ansell had been likeable throughout, while opinions are likely to be varied on the two women. Back in the boardroom, Sugar quickly fires Paul and then, after struggling with the decision, chooses Ruth over Ansell. He has already selected Michelle, making references to her tragic family background in a rather coded way (we did not know her story until after the programme had aired).

The Apprentice offers us the pleasures of reality television while posing as something else. It allows us to feel that we are engaged in something real, rather than contrived, as there is a job at the end of it, yet clearly Sugar would not normally go through such an exercise to recruit staff. The series is essentially a form of game show but its setting in a business environment, and the fact that the contestants are claiming some appropriate experience instead of being plucked off the street, make us feel differently about it. This is also reinforced by its cool, detached aesthetic, its place on BBC2 and the relatively low-key commentary. However the tabloid storm around Michelle indicates its similarities with other reality programmes, and its success as gripping popular entertainment that resonates with its audience. You're Fired is a spin-off programme very much like Big Brother's Little Brother (Endemol/C4 2002–), and seeks to involve the audience with the contestants and sate their desire to have some kind of say on events. The Apprentice is 'good television' – we want to watch what happens – but is it 'real' or 'true'?

Authored fact

When we look for 'truth' in factual television, it can be presented to us either objectively or subjectively. The subjective mode has an interesting, and long, history in TV, setting out a thesis or a particular view on events. It does not pretend to be the only possible interpretation of a story but tries to convince us that it is the best one, the one that gets beneath the surface and feels most 'true'. Subjective factual television, or as I call it here 'authored' fact, communicates a point of view on what we see on screen to a greater or lesser extent. The 'author' operates in a fashion not dissimilar from the authors discussed in Chapter 3: he/she can be a film-maker, or on-screen presenter, or both, but they build up their case to the viewer about what they are seeing. There are three different types I want to explore here:

- Authored documentary
- Author as participant
- 'Expert' – author as interpreter

Authored documentary

There is a long tradition of authored documentaries, texts where the film-maker tries to communicate their artistic vision by creating a sense of how they perceive life as it really is. Cinema documentaries by film-makers like Robert Flaherty, John Grierson, Humphrey Jennings and Frederick Wiseman have done this for decades, taking us inside a world to gain a better understanding of it. Sometimes this would be about people (Flaherty's film about the Inuit, *Nanook of the North*, 1922), sometimes about places (Wiseman's film about a mental hospital, *Titicut Follies*, 1967) or activities (Grierson's 1929 film *Drifters* about trawler fishing). They do this not by a simple explication of the facts but by making an artistic statement through images and editing. Grierson thought that its purpose was to 'pass from . . . descriptions of natural material, to arrangements, rearrangements and creative shapings of it' (1979: 36).

This form is ideally suited to television and has been used extensively. The time and space that TV has in its armoury allow film-makers to present very detailed portraits over a series, or impact on viewers through the intimacy of the home. Film-makers like Denis Mitchell produced poetic documentary work, such as *Wedding on Saturday* (Granada 1964), in which a wedding between a young couple in a Yorkshire pit village is portrayed in a way that sheds light on the life of a community.

In the 1960s and 1970s, 'fly-on-the wall' techniques (inspired partly by Wiseman's work) became an important form of expression.

Paul Watson's *The Family* (BBC 1974), allowing us access to the minutiae of life in the Wilkins's household in Reading, is a key text here, as is Michael Apted's *Seven Up* (Granada 1964–). *Seven-Up* has followed the lives of some children who were

Documentary ethics

Sometimes the tensions between the creative and actuality elements of documentary result in controversy. Brian Winston points out that 'documentary is not fiction, but neither is it journalism exactly' and goes on to say that its creative elements 'permit a measure of artistic "amorality" ' (2000: 132). Inevitably time frames can be simplified, stories of different individuals can be conflated, and some detail can be omitted; however, there are limits. Winston's book *Lies, Damn Lies and Documentaries* (2000) details the case of *The Connection*, an ITV documentary purporting to be a true story of the international movement of cocaine, that turned out to be largely constructed.

There have also been controversies about how the participants in documentaries were treated. A Channel 4 documentary *Against Nature* (RDF/C4) about environmentalists got into trouble because some of the people interviewed felt they had been misled about its aims – their contributions were used against the ideas they were expressing and they were filmed in a way they felt undermined them.

seven years old in 1964 by making films tracking their progress every seven years. The model has been used in several other countries since.

'Fly-on-the-wall' programmes situate us in the middle of the action, as if we were there. They imply the absence of a camera, convincing us that we are experiencing unmediated reality. There is lot of time in which to get to know the subjects and pictures are presented without much, if any, commentary. Of course, however, the cameras *are* there and we are being shown an edited version of what happened. Towards the late 1980s some film-makers started to change the mode of address of the 'fly-on-the-wall'. While positioning us in the middle of the action, they also inserted themselves, owning up to their presence and then becoming acknowledged by the subjects. Nick Broomfield, a much-hailed documentarist, began to appear in his own films. Sometimes he acted as a catalyst to instigate events, deliberately annoying or challenging his subjects. In *Tracking Down Maggie* (Lafayette Films/C4 1994) the subject of the film becomes his inability to make a documentary about Margaret Thatcher. Another example is Molly Dineen who does not appear in her films but her voice is heard and people address her – not the 'camera' as an abstract entity but her, 'Molly', specifically. You may be familiar with some recent exponents of this kind of authored fact such as Jon Ronson, Michael Moore or Louis Theroux. They often set themselves up as provocateurs, promoting a polemical case by making themselves a causal agent or site of action in their programmes. In Theroux's shows he spends time living with particular subjects (often fading celebrities) to see what effect his presence has on them.

A very different example of modern authored documentaries is the work of Adam Curtis. Curtis does not appear on the screen but tries to put a very subjective argument, nevertheless. He takes a thesis, tells a story to support it and invites the viewer to think about its implications. He does this through a barrage of images, usually stock footage or pieces of popular entertainment that underpin his commentary, never hiding the fact that he is not attempting an objective approach. Curtis argues that 'TV is not inherently biased against ideas' and that 'people love the idea that they are being pulled back to make sense of their feelings' (Edinburgh Festival speech, 2005). His most influential work, *The Power of Nightmares* (BBC 2004), used his trademark techniques to argue that the terrorist threat was overstated by plotting a parallel course between the rise of Islamism in the Muslim world and the rise of neo-conservatism in the United States.

Author as participant

In many factual programmes we are experiencing people, places or events through a presenter. In some cases the focus of the text is the participation of the presenter – their journey (either literal or metaphorical) is the reality we are experiencing. How are we positioned in these programmes and how do we negotiate the truth in them?

CASE STUDY: TRIBE

Michael Palin's travel series and celebrity family history show *Who Do You Think You Are?* are both examples of this kind of text, but this case study focuses on *Tribe* (BBC 2005–7), a series presented by and featuring Bruce Parry, a forty-ish British explorer and ex-army officer. In the first series he journeyed to a number of remote communities around the world, usually indigenous peoples, to understand and take part in their customs. In the second three-part series he travels through Southern Ethiopia's Omo Valley, living with different tribes in each programme. In the last of these, which I want to consider in detail, he stays with the Dasenach people, who live in the arid delta of Lake Turkana.

Bruce meets Abenach

Bruce speaks to camera in the tent, saying 'The girls are definitely in control here

The programme starts in the same way as the rest of the series: in a voiceover Bruce Parry describes how he wants to find out about how other cultures work 'and I believe the best way to do this is to live with the people I meet on my journey, to experience their culture first-hand, to become for a short while one of the tribe'.

After some context about the area and Bruce's journey (including graphics of a map), he is shown entering a Dasenach settlement. The chief is away and the matriarch Abenach greets him and gives him food in her tent.

In the course of the programme two distinct narrative lines develop. First, we see Bruce develop a relationship with Abenach, who explains the Dasenach way of life and treats him like a son. Second, Bruce befriends the fishermen, known as the 'das', who have a lowly place within the tribe because they do not own livestock. They hunt crocodile in the lake and he accompanies them on their night hunting trips, helping to catch a crocodile and bring it back to the village to eat.

We see the tribe through Bruce's experiences as part of the community. The programme is interesting for many reasons, one of which is that throughout we are made aware that a television programme is being made. Bruce refers to his guides and his crew a number of times. On the crocodile hunt he explains to us that because of the small boats he will film the incidents himself with an infra-red camera, radioing in the proper cameraman only when they have caught a crocodile. On the first trip he describes how he discovered a crocodile but failed to film it, or call in his colleagues in time. On the second excursion we move from the infra-red image to full-colour camerawork as the crocodile is caught.

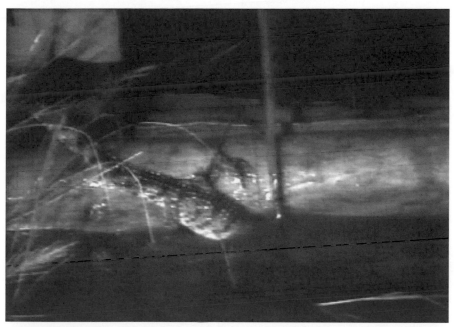

Infra-red image of the crocodile hunt

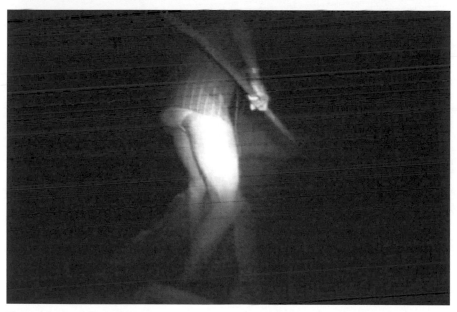

The next shot is a full camera image

The use of interpreters is also key to the construction of the text. While we only see them fleetingly, all the conversations of the tribe are subtitled on screen, commenting on Bruce's actions. We presume that he was not aware of what they

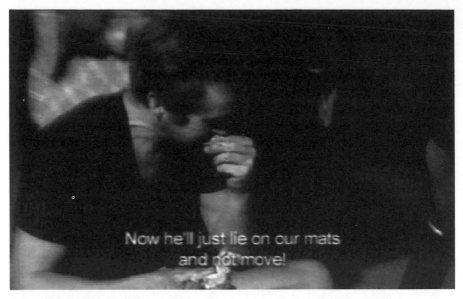

Now he'll just lie on our mats
and not move!

The subtitles offer a different perspective on the action

were saying at the time, so it draws us into complicity with the Dasenach and allows a more objective voice on Bruce and the action. As it happens, although there is some teasing, much of it is quite flattering, as Bruce is quite practical and competent. As they eat the crocodile after the hunt we see titles saying 'He's just like us – he won't go back to his country, he'll just lie on our mats and not move!' and 'We thought he didn't know anything – but he can eat crocodile!'.

Much is made of the bond with Abenach: at the beginning of the programme, before we meet her, he mentions that she is an amazing woman, full of humour. In a number of scenes she compares him to a son, worries when he is away and affectionately mocks him for his snoring. At the end of the programme there is an emotional parting where Bruce lavishes her with gratitude and praise. In subtitled dialogue we hear her say through the interpreters 'I think he is saying he won't forget me.'

How are we positioned as viewers of *Tribe*? We are certainly aligned to Bruce, who frequently speaks directly to us through the camera and his voiceover is added in post-production. There is a direct dialogue between him and us, both about his experiences and about their context, as he gives information about the way of life, history and problems of the Dasenach. However, other devices, such as the openness about the production process and the use of subtitled speech, give us room to make up our own minds much of the time.

There are a couple of dangers in programmes like this where we are viewing a culture very different from our own. The first is that it can be extremely patronising, painting the tribes people as primitive or as quaint oddities for the amusement of

I think he's saying he won't forget me.

Bruce says goodbye to Abenach

wealthy westerners. Many anthropological programmes have been criticised for this approach and in a post-colonial world (that is, a world in which the former imperial powers of Europe no longer directly rule developing nations but are still thought to have undue influence), it is often assumed that they are trying to underline the superiority of western culture. On the other hand it is also possible to be patronising in another sense – to paint the tribal life as some sort of simple paradise and their culture as somehow more 'real' or 'pure' than our own. It could be argued that this is equally offensive.

I would suggest that Parry, despite his army background and apparent colonial air, largely avoids these traps. He underlines his respect for the Dasenach way of life without being patronising, stressing their endurance of hardship and placing it in some kind of political context. Equally he does not resort to cultural relativism, excusing actions because they are specific to that culture. There are a couple of scenes about the universal practice in the tribe of female circumcision. The tribes people (including Abenach) are given a voice in their support of the practice and time to explain why they think it is important. We are allowed to make up our own minds on this basis but Bruce, in voiceover, does give his own view, saying that 'it is one custom I would be happy to see go'. It does not remain unchallenged just on the basis that it is part of their culture.

Channel 4 announced a riposte to *Tribe* in 2006 with *Meet the Natives* (Keo/C4, 2007) in which a group of indigenous tribespeople from Tanna (an island of Vanuatu) came to Britain to give their views on our lifestyle. Simon Dickson of the channel said:

For years we have been looking at remote indigenous people from strange cultures and almost laughing at them and thinking they are strange. But their communities have been forged over centuries and they have as much to say about us as we do about them. (*Broadcast*, 18 August 2006)

However, Bruce Parry attempts to be part of the tribe, and although this is a limited exercise, it does try to show the importance and realities of that kind of life, and respects the skills needed to survive the difficult situations these people endure. As with *Planet Earth*, the BBC produced a promotional trailer about the series, showing Bruce in action. It came with the strapline 'Sometimes to make a documentary, you have to be the documentary. This is what we do.' Bruce's efforts to be part of the tribe and his dialogue with both the viewer at home and the people he lives with, stress the similarities as well as the differences between people. The Dasenach people are treated with respect and as individuals. British television is in any case not short of anthropological studies of its own society, and it could be argued that these are frequently made with considerably less respect than *Tribe*.

'Expert'

Another long-established mode of presentation of fact on TV is mediation through an expert. An on-screen guide talks us through events as they see them, typically appearing in a number of locations as they make a case about what the truth may be. The programmes hinge around the presenter, and their relationship with the material and the viewer. We need to feel that we are in the presence of someone who knows more about this subject than we ever could and is offering us an easy route into learning. The pleasures are in feeling we have been taught something we did not know before, or in reaching an understanding of why events happened or how things work. The expert brings themselves to the text, lending their reputations and education to the medium and making it a respectable source of information. History, science and fine art are favourite topics of this kind of programme, as they offer a set of universally acknowledged and verifiable facts that act as a base on which the expert's interpretation can begin. We have recognisable signposts of general knowledge there to guide us as they suggest why particular leaders may have fallen, machines were invented or paintings created.

In the late 1960s and early 1970s these programmes became very important to television, bestowing some prestige on a medium regarded by many intellectuals as irrevocably vulgar and ephemeral. Kenneth Clark's *Civilisation* (BBC 1969), looking at the great works of classical art, and Jacob Bronowski's chronicle of the advance of scientific evolution *The Ascent of Man* (BBC 1973) were followed by other academics and intellectuals who advanced their careers by appearing on TV. Needless to say TV experts need to be knowledgeable and charismatic to make us want to engage with complex and occasionally difficult concepts. The best example of this is David Attenborough, who has had parallel careers as a natural history presenter and as a TV executive (as Controller of BBC2 he commissioned Clark and Bronowski). In his series, like *Life on Earth* and *The Blue Planet* (BBC 2001), he continues his as expert, imparting knowledge, explaining phenomena and suggesting theories, with an ability to put himself in our shoes and be our representative when confronting the beautiful or the mysterious.

There are numerous current examples of presenter-led 'expert' programming, although they tend to divide into two distinct types. The first could be called the 'enthusiastic amateur', where the alignment is more clearly with the viewer as the presenter discovers amazing facts or experiences sensations on our behalf. Adam Hart-Davis (*What the Victorians Did for Us*, BBC 2001, and other historical science shows) and Dan Cruickshank (*The Lost World of Mitchell and Kenyon*, BBC/BFI 2005, and *Around the World in Eighty Treasures*, BBC 2005) are good examples of this. The second is the acknowledged authority, proven through an academic career or relevant labour. This covers figures as diverse as historian Simon Schama and the late steeplejack-cum-industrial archaeology expert Fred Dibnah. Within this group, though, there are some, like Dibnah, who are there to show us objects or places and tell us stories about them, and those like Schama who, in his *History of Britain* (BBC 2000–2) series, tries to explain their significance, showing them to be part of a bigger picture: revealing them to be emblematic of the underlying forces that shaped the British Empire, for example.

Some experts build on this approach to attempt to retell stories, offering alternative readings of what might have happened and suggesting a different big picture to the received wisdom. Historian Niall Ferguson has done just this in his programmes *Empire* (2003), *Colossus* (2004) and *The War of the World* (2006) (all Blakeway Productions/C4). Each hinges on a theory that goes against conventional thinking: respectively that the British Empire was a benign force, America has always been an imperial power and that the 20th century was one long race war. Ferguson makes his points using the traditional weapons in the TV expert's armoury. He appears on screen at the locations specific to the stories he is telling; where possible there is use of archive footage accompanied by his voiceover explaining its relevance to the argument; and his key points are constantly reiterated. In programmes like Ferguson's (and Schama's) no other people are interviewed and we do not hear dissenting voices to his line of thought. What we are watching is a televisual essay, very similar in structure to those that you write (if with a bigger research budget), and hopefully compelling and thought-provoking. The authority of the expert makes their arguments credible and tends to present them as some sort of truth. As active viewers we assess these claims on the evidence that is presented and decide whether or not we are convinced.

In some ways the expert takes on a similar role to the news reporter. Indeed the aesthetics of the text, the presenter on screen at the site of action – mimic our experiences of news bulletins. The difference is in their analytical intent – their

News theory
The implied objectivity of news bulletins has long troubled scholars, because this supposed objectivity masks the influence of political and social structures. News has widely been held as the propaganda of the ruling powers, used to present a favourable picture of their actions and to ignore opposing arguments. The Glasgow University Media Group's study *Really Bad News* (1982) analysed several news bulletins on industrial disputes and ascertained that workers were allowed considerably less voice than employers. Pierre Bourdieu (1988: 336) suggested that the news agenda deliberately made their focus 'those things which are apt to arouse curiosity but require no analysis, especially in the political sphere'.

Bourdieu also situated the problem with the economic structures of television (in this case in France), arguing that the presence of ratings and advertising made it impossible for the viewer to find the truth. In a broader sense this is the argument of Edward Herman and Noam Chomsky in their study of news media, *Manufacturing Consent* (1988). The structures of ownership (which they call the 'propaganda model') mean it is in the establishment's interest to ignore a news agenda other than their own.

desire to make us see the bigger picture and understand the links between events and their significance. In this way they perform the same function as the experts who are drafted into news bulletins to help clarify the context of the story. Instead of being at the scene, however, these experts sit in the studio next to the news anchor, who then acts as a proxy viewer while the academic, general or doctor explains the importance of this occurrence.

News

The kind of factual texts that we encounter most often in our TV viewing, however, purport to give us not entertainment, not authored or expert opinion, but just 'the facts'. At several points in the schedule we are confronted by what is presented as the truth, and particularly the truth about what is happening now. News, either as bulletins at certain times of the day or as dedicated news channels, is the most obvious example of this but there are others, such as news analysis programmes (for example, *Newsnight*) or investigative documentaries and current affairs shows that have ostensibly objective elements, although these will often be mixed with a variety of selective viewpoints and analysis. Here we will examine these texts, look at their agendas and the way in which what is going on is presented to us and ask how they influence our responses.

The supposed objectivity of this kind of factual programming has always been contested. As probably the most directly influential discourse of what is happening in the world and society, news has long been considered a tool of the establishment.

CASE STUDY: ONE DAY'S NEWS – 18 OCTOBER 2006

Television news remains one of the most powerful sources of information for people, complemented by or competing with other providers such as the Internet or newspapers. One of the best ways to see how news works, and how the presentation of events can vary widely in different factual texts, is to look in detail at the news for one particular day. The day we will look at is Wednesday 18 October 2006. I picked this day at random, though I avoided Friday and the weekend when bulletins are shorter and less prominent in the schedule. This is interesting in itself: things still happen at the weekend but because the formal processes of government are not operating, there is assumed to be less of an agenda and it is possible that viewers feel less inclined to watch news on leisure days. As it happens it proved a useful day to assess, with lots of very different stories competing for attention and new items emerging throughout the day. I saw a wide cross-section of British TV news that day and made detailed notes about it. This included every terrestrial bulletin and representative segments from BBC News 24 and Sky News. Below are listings of the running order for each bulletin, with some explanation of context. After that we will look in closer detail across bulletins to see how particular types of story were covered, and how the same information was presented to us in different ways.

News items

ITV1 Morning News 5.30am (produced by ITN)
1. Petition protesting against post-office closures: a petition containing 4 million signatures (the largest in UK history) is due to be presented at Downing Street.
2. False abuse allegation: in Wales a family's children are returned from care after a court rules that medical claims they were abused were mistaken.
3. Leaks of the Baker Report for the US Congress on Iraq policy: the report is expected to call for an exit strategy but will not be published until after the midterm elections.
4. Medical treatment for injured military personnel: Tony Blair suggests the policy on treating veterans in NHS hospitals may change. As part of ITN's week of reports entitled 'Betrayed? An Investigation' on the treatment of veterans, there is a report from a military rehabilitation centre.
5. Madonna's adoption of a baby boy from Malawi.
6. Report on the markets.
7. Review of newspaper front pages.
8. Rivalry between the two emerging HD DVD formats.
9. Sport: football news and round-up of previous night's results.
10. West-End opening of the Monty Python musical *Spamalot*.

Five News 11.30am (produced by Sky News)
1. Exclusive on a woman's civil case for indecent assault as a girl by child killer Ian Huntley, accompanied by an interview with the woman.
2. Post-office closures petition.
3. Policewoman injured in a shooting in Bradford, in which another WPC, Sharon Beshenivsky, was killed, gives evidence in court at the trial of those accused of the crime.
4. Madonna adoption: she submits an open letter to the media.
5. Hollywood star Wesley Snipes is on the run from US tax authorities.
6. A New York art dealer accidentally puts his elbow through a Picasso masterpiece.
7. Care problems for children: calls for councils to make more facilities accessible to disabled children.

8. Ryanair criticised by the Office of Fair Trading for their lack of customer care.

9. World Health Organisation battles leprosy: extended report from the Philippines.

10. Welsh male-voice choir picked up by a record company with the prospect of a film being made about their story: includes studio interview with choir members.

11. Video of Wayne Rooney larking around at a promotional shoot appears on YouTube.

Channel 4 News at Noon (produced by ITN)
1. Post-office closures petition.
2. Policewoman's testimony in court case.
3. Conservative Party claims the Home Office misled them about escaped prisoners on control orders.
4. An inspector's report criticises the standards of care in old people's homes.
5. A report claims that screening programmes for breast cancer are leading to unnecessary treatment.
6. Wesley Snipes on the run.
7. Picasso picture accident.
8. Economic statistics show a rise in unemployment.
9. Ryanair criticised by Office of Fair Trading.
10. Follow-up report on problems with broadband service providers, particularly in switching ISPs: features viewers' complaints.
11. The markets.
12. Octogenarian former miner and dancer Geoffrey Davidson has a gallery show of his tapestry work. Details of his life story.
13. Breaking news story. At Prime Minister's Question Time, Conservative leader David Cameron challenges Tony Blair about a general's comments on the Iraq situation.

BBC1 1.00pm News (produced by the BBC)
1. Post-office closures petition.
2. Police-shooting court case.
3. Newspaper allegations that in their divorce case Heather Mills has alleged she was physically ill-treated by Paul McCartney.
4. Government encourages faith schools to engage with the wider community.
5. Unemployment figures.
6. Sports car-makers TVR close their Blackpool factory.
7. The US Army reports ten troop deaths in twenty-four hours in Iraq.
8. Breast-cancer screening fears.
9. Report on elderly care services: interviews with carers, clients and managers.
10. Staffordshire arson and murder-trial court report.

11. *Spamalot* premiere report.
12. YouTube video shows a police dog chased by pigs.

ITV1 Lunchtime News 1.30pm (produced by ITN)
1. Police-shooting court case.
2. Post-office closures petition.
3. Blair versus Cameron at Prime Minister's Question Time.
4. Disney ends its association with junk food by drawing up healthy-eating guidelines at its theme parks.
5. Mills/McCartney divorce leaks.
6. Preview of the Children's Champions awards (ITN one of the sponsors.)
7. Madonna's statement on her adoption of a Malawian baby.

News 24 4.15–4.30pm (produced by the BBC)
1. Headline round-up leading with the police shooting and the breast-cancer screening report.
2. Blair versus Cameron at Prime Minister's Question Time.
3. Report on elderly care provision.
4. A businessman involved in London's 2012 Olympic plans quits his position.
5. Effects of India's ban on child labour last year: extended report.
6. Weather.
7. Repeat of headlines.

Five News 5.30 pm (produced by Sky News)
1. Mills/McCartney divorce leaks.
2. Police-shooting trial report.
3. Huntley victim's civil action: slightly extended version of lunchtime report.
4. Murder trial of the killer of London teenager Kiyan Prince.
5. Tissues used in bone grafts in the UK traced to stolen body parts from America.
6. Unemployment figures.
7. Ryanair and the Office of Fair Trading.
8. Post-office closures petition.
9. Sports news, including mention of the Rooney YouTube footage.
10. Persecution of Christians in China: extended report.

BBC1 6.00pm
1. Police-shooting trial report.
2. Post-office closures petition.
3. Mills/McCartney divorce leaks.
4. Details of a Conservative Party policy group's report on taxation suggesting a range of tax cuts. Report accidentally put on the Internet a day before publication date.

5. American troop deaths in Iraq.
6. Breast-cancer screening report.
7. TVR factory closure.
8. First in a series of reports on growth in broadband take-up in the UK. Reports from webcams show how consumers use the technology.
9. Calls for change in IVF procedures to prevent multiple births.
10. Sports news.

ITV News 6.30 pm
1. Police-shooting court report.
2. Post-office closures petition.
3. Conservative Party tax report.
4. Treatment of British soldiers with psychological problems: part of the 'Betrayed? An Investigation' series. Features a bad-tempered interview between the anchor and a government minister.
5. The Queen's tour of the Baltic states.
6. TVR factory closure.
7. Control-order controversy.
8. Mills/McCartney divorce leaks.

Channel 4 News 7.00pm
1. Tory tax report: extended feature.
2. Suicide attacks by the Tamil Tigers in Sri Lanka.
3. Police-shooting court report.
4. Sectarian attacks between Shia and Sunni in Iraq.
5. Control-order controversy.
6. An MP calls for Prince Charles to cancel his forthcoming tour of Pakistan because a British citizen is due to be executed there.
7. Report on care provision.
8. Post-office closures petition.
9. Exclusive investigation of the use of physical restraint on children with medical behavioural problems in mainstream schools, citing a case in Bedfordshire as an example.
10. Mills/McCartney divorce leaks: a rebuttal statement by McCartney over the allegations has now been released.
11. Staffordshire arson and murder trial.
12. Art dealer accidentally damages Picasso masterpiece.
13. Ryanair and Office of Fair Trading.
14. TVR closure.
15. IVF.

BBC1 10.00pm
  1. Tory tax report.
  2. US troop deaths in Iraq and the effects on American public opinion.
  3. Police shooting trial report.
  4. Mills/McCartney divorce leaks.
  5. Post-office closures petition.
  6. Breast-cancer screening report.
  7. Grafts from body parts stolen from American funeral homes.
  8. TVR closure.
  9. Sport: report on that night's European matches.
 10. Accidental damage to Picasso picture.
 11. Discovery of a new archaeological find: an ancient Roman burial ground in the Vatican.

BBC Newsnight 10.30pm
  1. Tory tax report: extended analysis with film report and interviews.
  2. US troops in Iraq: mixes stills taken by a photographer from the *Guardian*, who is with troops from the US airborne division, with moving footage of the soldiers' missions and routines.
  3. Tamil Tiger actions in Sri Lanka.
  4. Other headlines and tomorrow's front pages.

ITV News 10.30pm
  1. Tory tax report.
  2. Police-shooting court report.
  3. Treatment of veterans: edited version of the 'Betrayed? An Investigation' report screened earlier in the day.
  4. US troop deaths in Iraq: leaks of the Baker Report.
  5. Post-office closures petition.
  6. Queen's visit to the Baltic states.
  7. YouTube: uses the Rooney footage screened earlier in the day as the basis for a discussion on whether such sites have been taken over by viral advertisers and corporate interests: extended report.
  8. Sport reports.
  9. Markets.
 10. Mills/McCartney divorce leaks.

Sky News – 24-hour news service 11.50pm – 12.10am
Discussion in the studio with two Fleet Street journalists (Kevin O'Sullivan and Jo-Anne Nadler) about the *Daily Star*'s decision to drop their spoof Daily Fatwa feature after opposition from the National Union of Journalists. The same guests

then discuss a university research report that claims to have created a formula to find the most exciting sporting moments ever.

Midnight bulletin
1. Police-shooting trial report.
2. Mills/McCartney divorce leaks.
3. Tory tax report.
4. Condoleeza Rice's statements on North Korea's nuclear threat.

The news agenda

What do the news agendas on this day tell us about television's relationships with the viewer? News programmes are under pressure to get ratings, both relative to other channel's bulletins but also against other programmes scheduled at the same time. They construct their agendas according to their perceptions of what audiences will find interesting and also try to present stories in a way that will engage and retain viewers. Thus, television news has a difficult task – not just reporting and analysing events that have occurred that day, or analysing general political, social or economic trends, but also making these events relevant to viewers' lives. Presentation is, then, also very important and there are a number of aesthetic as well as content decisions made in news programmes to try and draw the viewers into the text.

> **Think about ...**
> Examine the day's news agenda from these lists. Think about why items may have been included and the reasons for their order. Consider why news editors thought that the public would be interested in these particular stories.

Constructing the agenda

We need to consider why particular items come up on the news agenda at specific times and this information for 18 October enables us to do this. It is an interesting day in that no one story predominates – there was no major disaster or earth-shattering event that was indisputably the main story of the day. In fact not a great deal happened, and certainly very little that was unexpected. Instead producers had to construct a news agenda by picking up some items and speculating around the story, or examining their implications by relating them to the circumstances of individuals.

Many stories arose from prescribed events – the publishing of official reports or policy initiatives suggesting critiques of a current situation and considering ways forward. In different ways this is true of the items on the breast-cancer screening programme, the care provision for the elderly, the lobby for facilities for disabled children and the accidentally launched Conservative Party tax report. It is also true of the lead item in most of the earlier bulletins: the petition against post-office closures. This was due to be presented at Downing Street in the morning, followed by a rally of sub-postmasters in London. As a planned event it could be anticipated and reports prepared analysing the relevant issues. As nothing cataclysmic occurred overnight it was the lead story in the early morning bulletins and first or second on the lunchtime news shows. The three news providers dutifully dispatched reporters to rural areas to stand outside small post offices, interviewing their owners and the customers, especially the elderly.

Equally the police-shooting trial, one of the day's other big stories, was known about well in advance. The crime had been committed nearly a year earlier and today was set aside to hear the testimony of the chief witness, PC Teresa Milburn, who was injured when her colleague was killed. The trial was held in Newcastle, but the crime occurred in Bradford – by the evening bulletins, the pictures on screen had largely shifted from the courthouse to the crime scene.

'Infotainment'

In other cases the agenda was set by leaks or other media sources. The allegations surrounding Heather Mills and Paul McCartney are interesting in this regard. The story arose when the Press Association and the *Daily Mail* were anonymously faxed divorce paper legal documents. The *Mail* ran the story in the morning, reporting that Mills had alleged physical ill-treatment by McCartney. The TV bulletins, possibly on legal advice, showed some initial reticence in getting involved, and it was absent from ITN and Sky's daytime bulletins. The BBC, interestingly, was the provider that covered the item on TV news first on their lunchtime bulletin. This may be because, coincidentally, Mills had appeared on the BBC's *Children's Hospital* programme in the morning, so they had exclusive footage to show.

This coverage is interesting in other respects. It signals the importance of celebrity culture to news programmes today – a world that was considered very separate to the news agenda at one time. The move towards more celebrity, lifestyle and 'light' stories has been dubbed 'infotainment' (Hartley, 2001: 118–20). This represents a shift in thinking away from news based on what we need to know to what we (supposedly) want to know.

The importance of the divorce case and its appearance on the agenda rely on a decision that we would find this domestic detail interesting. The only reason for this is of our knowledge and views of the people involved. Paul McCartney's status in public life as a rock star and former member of the Beatles certainly creates this interest but so does the involvement of former model and disability campaigner Heather Mills. Mills's fraught relationship with the press ups the stakes and is thought to stimulate our interest – it is assumed that people will have a view on Heather Mills and it is also assumed that it is probably a negative one. The way the story – which is, after all, unsupported and based on documents that should not have been in the public domain – is presented to the viewer is telling. No one comments officially until a short statement refuting the allegations is made late in the day by McCartney's lawyers. At no point does either of the participants speak to the camera, so there are no pictures to support the story. Instead divorce lawyers are interested to put their spin on events and reporters appear outside the couple's homes (which are empty). This leads to a reliance on graphics – the text of the allegations is shown on screen on a pictorial representation of divorce papers (a rather unconvincing piece of A4 with a ribbon tied round it). With little verifiable fact to go on, the reports rely on speculation and gossip: there is mention a number of times of how dirty the battle has become and how sad this is, while little reticence is shown in reporting the events or commenting on the supposed strategy behind it.

Prior to the 'infotainment' debate a long-standing feature of television news has been the insertion of lighter items (often known as 'And finally . . .' pieces after ITN's habit of using them to finish the bulletin to offset the inevitable misery and carnage that has gone before). As well as regular pieces, like sports news, the bulletins on the 18th (somewhat desperately) attempted to liven themselves up with special-interest or 'funny' stories. *BBC News at Ten O'Clock* had a long closing piece on a new archaeological find in Rome and there were other arts or popular culture stories, such as the West-End premiere of the musical *Spamalot*. All the bulletins agreed on one amusing story: a New York art collector's accidental destruction of his own Picasso masterpiece with his elbow – showing that funny can often mean laughing at some people's misfortunes.

The political agenda

As one lead story (on the post-office petition) faded throughout the day, so another built up, with the accidental announcement of Tory tax plans in the afternoon. The news organisations have extensive teams dealing with domestic parliamentary politics, and political and economic correspondents were wheeled out to explain the significance of both the leak and the plans. Universally the report was represented as an embarrassment for new Conservative leader David Cameron, because its calls for extensive tax cuts were seen as being in opposition to his attempts to make the Conservatives seem trustworthy on maintaining public spending. The story is interesting as an example of the symbiosis between the media and the political machine – not so much in terms of bias but because the media need material and the politicians want to put their own case. As the accidental uploading put the report out a day earlier than planned, the Conservatives were unprepared and the Labour Party exploited this mistake mercilessly. Treasury Minister Ed Balls appeared on all the news services claiming the proposals proved that the Conservatives were fiscally irresponsible – so that the government were setting the agenda on the story.

World news

While domestic politics are covered in detail and there are a number of forums in which politicians can make statements or debate policy, it has long been argued by some that news from abroad is not covered sufficiently. While not nearly as acute as the situation in the US, studies have suggested that the coverage of foreign affairs, particularly in the developing world, has fallen dramatically in recent years.

The news bulletins on 18 October were light on foreign news events, but there were still some significant reports from abroad. In relative terms it was a lighter day than usual for Iraq coverage, although there was the announcement that ten US troops had died in combat. Many reports on this concentrated on the impact on US public opinion, but *Channel 4 News* looked at the sectarian struggles between Sunni and Shia, and *Newsnight* carried an interestingly stylised report mixing still photographs with footage of US troops' daily routine. Both the more serious and analytical programmes, *Channel 4 News* and *Newsnight*, also featured reports on the latest actions by the Tamil Tigers in Sri Lanka.

> Learning about the world
> A study called 'The World on the Box' by 3WE in summer 2004 claimed that documentaries on the developing world had halved over the last fifteen years. News coverage had increased in the last year but this was almost entirely down to the war in Iraq.

Creating the agenda

If there is little newsworthy action, then the news programmes have to stimulate discussion and provoke reactions. The primary ways of doing this are through investigations and the use of exclusives. Investigations take an underlying social issue and illuminate the problem by focusing on specific situations. They are the main focus of many current affairs programmes (*Panorama*, BBC 1953–, *Tonight with Trevor McDonald*, Granada/ITV 1999–, and *Dispatches*, C4 1982–, are the regular slots on British television) and rely on some particular generic forms. These include constructing a story by establishing situation and character, and using techniques like undercover filming to obtain proof of allegations and to create tension and excitement in the viewer. Increasingly this is becoming part of news programmes too, although unlike current affairs programmes they have much less time to develop the case. On occasion news and current affairs work together, a news bulletin showing clips and promoting the longer version of the investigation. Sometimes the facts revealed in the investigation prove to be part of the news agenda so that the bulletin will carry the findings as a story, and include official reaction and comment. The nature of producing investigations means that they are frequently exclusives, although there are also other types of exclusive such as interviews.

On the 18 October investigations played a key role in the news agenda. ITN carried a major investigation that was running all week on ITV, 'Betrayed? An Investigation'. This alleged the official neglect of veterans of the Iraq conflict when they returned from the campaign. Earlier bulletins on this day focused on an army rehabilitation centre and suggested that some wounded soldiers were not receiving any compensation beyond their pension. The 6.30 bulletin (and the 10.30 bulletin in an edited form) featured interviews with soldiers with psychological problems, including post-traumatic stress disorder. After the report the news anchor, Katie Derham, conducted an interview with a government defence minister, Derek Twigg. This proved compelling, as it quickly became extremely acrimonious. What Twigg did was to try and undermine the status of ITN's investigation by drawing attention to the way in which it was constructed, particularly the programme's decision not to screen an interview they had conducted with an army psychiatrist. Derham reacted angrily to this, as she felt the integrity of the reports was being questioned and berated Twigg for not answering her questions or acknowledging that veterans required specific treatment. The whole investigation proved controversial, with the Ministry of Defence withdrawing co-operation with ITN for a time because of the way it felt the interviews and investigations had been handled. Investigations can, then, become the news agenda in themselves, intensifying debates rapidly.

Another kind of exclusive was used by Sky in early editions of Five News. This was an interview with a victim of notorious child killer Ian Huntley. This victim had been assaulted by Huntley as a child and ten years later brought a civil case against him, with the court ruling in her favour. True crime reports are also an important part of the news agenda and exclusive interviews can be included in this, although there may be legal ramifications. In this case the victim would have had to give up her right to anonymity to appear on the programme.

News and the viewer

An interesting feature of bulletins on the 18 October was a focus on content from other sources, like the website Youtube. The BBC lunchtime news featured a piece of footage showing a number of pigs chasing a police dog. If this inclusion seemed bizarre, more predictable was Youtube footage of Wayne Rooney clowning around at a promotional shoot. ITN's 10.30 bulletin used this as the key to a consumer item suggesting that the Rooney footage was essentially a piece of corporate advertising, indicative of the way in which business hijacks forums that have been previously led by the public – ITN suggested that it was now 'YouTube not YourTube'.

This piece indicates one major change in the way news programmes are constructed in recent years – the tone and address of news bulletins are now very aware of the active viewer and try to include them in the stories and presentation. A major issue in news broadcasting at the moment is 'user-generated content' – that is, material supplied by viewers. These viewers are often referred to now as 'citizen journalists' and open up the possibility of a whole new type of mediation through information derived from diverse, non-professional sources. The material they provide might be on-the-scene footage by passers-by at an event or something constructed as comment. It is also, of course, interaction in the programme itself, not just through the 'red button' services provided by the broadcaster but by expressing views via email.

A feature of many bulletins now is the call for reaction by the anchor, asking for contributions from the public and giving email contacts and phone numbers. At points emails might be read out that express opinions on parts of the programme and a debate on the issues commences. On Sky News the 'ticker' of headlines that constantly runs along the bottom of the page keeps reminding viewers of points of contact. Now production technology is so much more accessible, viewers can be producers too. An interesting example occurred on the BBC's 6pm bulletin in an item on how Britain has embraced the possibilities of broadband, which included three reports by consumers (respectively a man who communicated with family members via a webcam, a young rock band and a small businessman on a Scottish island) who told us via weblinks how the Internet had transformed their lives.

Less direct attempts to engage with the audience at all times rather than just informing them of events can be detected in the use of language. 'We' and 'our' or 'us' are frequently employed to relate the story to our own circumstances – the web story referred to above reports that there is 'research into how we are using broadband'. In the stories about Ryanair we are told by Five News that 'most of us have flown with a budget airline ...' . This mode of address is now commonplace, but think about how this attempt to be inclusive may positively exclude others – does it just lead to news for the majority?

> **Citizen journalism**
> In the rolling news coverage that occupied Pressied most channels on the day of the 7/7 bombings In London, a lot of information supplied by the public was reported on air. Some of this proved misleading, however – many more bombs were reported than actually occurred (often blasts counted twice from different ends of the tunnels), as members of the public were not in a position to assess the bigger picture. It was also a seminal TV news event through the use of mobile phone camera footage to provide pictures of the scene. What do you think are the pros and cons of the public contributing to news reports?

News aesthetics

The look of television news has evolved and is now very carefully formulated to draw us into the bulletin and keep us engaged (Caldwell, 1995). We are now a long way from a static camera focused on a seated presenter intoning into the lens. The new convention seems to be the anchor (or more usually two anchors, one man and one woman) standing together in the middle of the studio set as they deliver the main headlines. Behind the anchor will be a graphically constructed set including logos, images of the world, and a mixture of image and text (Lury, 2005: 161–5). Later in the bulletin links may be delivered by seated anchors or by one anchor standing by a graphic image.

The use of text is becoming more and more widespread. This is especially the case with the twenty-four-hour bulletins and is spreading to other news as its conventions become an embedded part of the form. Twenty-four-hour news is based around two different forms of viewing:

- Because it is repetitive, with headlines every fifteen minutes and filmed reports recurring every hour or so, it is assumed that viewers will be watching in short segments. There is, then, a need for clarity, so that viewers know what is happening and stay with the broadcast for a time. The easiest way to do this is to emblazon a sentence summarising events on screen – supplementary news stories are then highlighted on the moving ticker at the bottom of the screen in the hope of encouraging the viewer to wait for more details.
- Twenty-four-hour news channels are also often found in public places like railway stations, airports or office buildings. They are normally played with the sound down, so displaying text becomes the primary mode of communication.

Other formal conventions are also employed as well as purely visual ones. An increasingly popular style is the use of the 'two-way', in which the anchor interviews the correspondent to analyse events. Sometimes this happens in the studio (on *Newsnight* specialist correspondents will frequently chat at the desk with Jeremy Paxman or Kirsty Wark) but it is also also the convention with correspondents in the field. Frequently a filmed report is shown and then the reporter is asked for a live update, as with Matt Frei in Washington on the BBC's *Ten O'Clock News*.

The increasing use of videophones is another aesthetic change. The ability to use this light equipment to file live reports from the heart of a battle or disaster area liberates reporters from most of the logistical problems that beset news crews, much in the same way as the rise of electronic news-gathering equipment in the 1970s meant that reports could reach bulletins much faster than previously. A *Newsnight* report on Sri Lanka featured a videophone link so the reporter could give an immediate summary of events that day. The immediacy and access achievable outweigh the much poorer picture quality – perhaps producers assume that the widespread use of video on domestic mobile phones means consumers are accustomed to low-resolution images.

Evaluating news

So how do we evaluate news programmes? We need to be aware of how information is being presented to us, and that while it may contain some truth, it is not necessarily the whole truth. The news bulletins on 18 October are reporting events or examining situations in contemporary society, but in doing this they are attempting to influence our responses in particular ways, making certain assumptions and putting an emphasis on certain aspects of the story. For example, in the reports on the shooting of the policewoman in Bradford, it was repeatedly emphasised that PC Milburn broke down and cried during her testimony. In earlier reports it was stated that she remained calm for most of the time but finally broke down, while in later reports her earlier calmness was not mentioned. In the ITV Lunchtime News the court reporter mentions her clear, calm testimony only to be prompted by the anchor in a two-way to mention that she became emotional. The stress on her emotional response to events could be read in a number of ways. It could be

- An emphasis on the trauma endured by the policewoman as proof of the wickedness of her attackers;
- A rather patronising attempt to stress her vulnerability over her professionalism;
- A determination to engage the viewer on an emotional level, stressing the human-interest angle to maintain our interest rather than risk losing our attention by simply repeating what was said in court;

Or, indeed, it could be elements of all three potential readings.

News programmes are rich texts because of the amount of complex information in them and the codes of reference that pass between text and viewer. The roles of the anchor, the reporter, the set, the use of graphics and archive footage, as well as the material filmed directly at events, all play a part in presenting 'fact'. However, this fact is mediated and we always need to interrogate both the selection of material and the manner in which it is relayed to us. Claims of 'objectivity' should always be questioned.

The arrival of Fox News, a Rupert Murdoch station that, despite its motto of 'fair and balanced', takes a partisan approach to much of the political agenda, has generated renewed debate about the nature of impartiality. Fox News, and lead anchor Bill O'Reilly in particular, make it clear that they are 'reading' the news from a particular ideological perspective – in this case Republican neo-conservatism.

Both the claims of impartiality that news has traditionally assumed, and presumably also the rise of stations of like Fox, have led critics like Bourdieu and Chomsky to present TV news as inevitably compromised. However, it could be argued that, for all its limitations, TV

> Think about . . .
> Look at a news story across several bulletins. What assumptions do you think are being made about viewers' responses? Do the bulletins adopt different approaches?

news can still be of enormous benefit to viewers. It at least provides us with an awareness of what is happening that can make us want to find out more and analyse the reasons for events. TV may not provide answers for, say, the crisis in Darfur, but it does at least tell us that there is one and equips us to ask questions, including how it is covered by the media. There are many occasions in which the presentation of situations in the news or other factual programmes has provoked a mass response to try to stop them happening (US news coverage of Vietnam, John Pilger's documentaries on the Khmer Rouge, 1979, 1980, and Michael Buerk's news reports in 1984 on the famine in Ethiopia, for example). It is hard to conceive of other media having such a dramatic impact.

Current affairs

The kind of fact we are assumed to be interested in has changed considerably in recent years. Current affairs programmes are good examples of this: the prime aim now is maintaining an audience, and certain formula like undercover filming or making a compelling narrative to elicit an emotional reaction are seen as ways to achieve this. There have always been elements of this, of course, and important work illuminating people and situations that may have been overlooked does still occur (for example, the insight into police bigotry in *The Secret Policeman*, BBC 2003). One thing that has changed, though, is the news agenda for these programmes – the emphasis now is on the domestic and on issues that affect the majority, like consumer-led stories on banks or motoring. For instance, we can compare the agendas of ITV's main current affairs shows, shown in the same primetime slot, at different periods of time.

In November 1981 *World in Action* (Granada ITV 1963–98), a weekly programme, covered the following stories:

- Political murders in El Salvador
- Poverty in the UK
- Asbestos-related diseases in South African workers
- Profiles of Northern Irish Protestant leader Ian Paisley and the then Taisoch of the Republic of Ireland Garrett Fitzgerald
- Civil war in Uganda.

In October 2006 the current twice-weekly primetime current affairs show *Tonight with Trevor McDonald* (also Granada) ran the following stories:

- Babies affected by binge drinking
- Eco-friendly lifestyles
- Soft sentencing of criminals
- Boy racers – dangerous driving by young men
- Mortgage debts
- The crisis in midwife provision
- Coleen McLoughlin (the girlfriend of football star Wayne Rooney) and her campaign for more funding for children's hospices
- Uninsured drivers
- 'Lifting the Veil?' Saira Khan (a participant in the 2005 series of *The Apprentice*) on the veil and Muslim women in the UK.

I am not trying to suggest that one is necessarily better than the other but the contrasts are striking. The current-affairs agenda now is closer to debates in the press and is predominately based around personal experience. Rather than offering an objective analysis of a situation (and you could, of course, argue that this is impossible), it relies on the testimony of individuals and on subjects likely to be familiar to the viewer. It is evident that celebrity culture is seen as a way into stories; a well-known face is used to grab the attention of the viewer.

The personal agenda

The tendencies we see in *Tonight with Trevor McDonald* – the concentration on the local and especially the primacy of the personal – also dominate other parts of factual TV.

Think about . . .
What are your thoughts on the differences between the two programmes and the two periods? What kind of current-affairs approach makes you think? Consider an example of such a programme and analyse why it had that effect on you.

Real people's stories are the basis of the daytime talk shows that have become such an integral part of British culture: *Trisha Goddard* (Town House/Five 2005–), *The Jeremy Kyle Show* (Granada/ITV 2005–) and previously *Kilroy* (BBC 1987–2003), *The Time . . . The Place* (Anglia/ITV 1987–98), *Vanessa* (Anglia/ITV 1994–8) and the British version of *Jerry Springer* (Granada 2004–). People and their feelings, opinions and reactions are now our main measure of fact, and these programmes have become one of the dominant modes of address.

They are also problematic, because although real people and their problems are their focus, we are often not aligned with them but position ourselves as very different to them, even as superior, because of the extremity of their situations or the way they behave on screen. As many have noted, there is an element of the circus here: sometimes we are gawping at events in fascinated horror rather than responding to them with empathy or analysing the problem rationally (Dovey, 2000: 118); indeed it's hard not to when faced with 'Did my Mum have sex with my man – lie detector results!' (*Trisha Goddard* 20 June 2006). These are factual shows but rather than provide information, they merely elicit a response of disbelief. Evaluative processes are used to choose sides between the warring participants instead.

In this situation it would be useful to know more about the motivations of those involved in the shows – how did the participants get involved and what do they think their appearance will achieve? Do they think their problems will be resolved or are they just seeking to humiliate someone else in public and taking the chance that they might end up the target of the booing? On the producers' part, how do they view the people who appear on the programme? Are they interested in their problems or do they see the programme purely in terms of how it will play with the audience?

Performance in factual TV

Texts like *Trisha Goddard* are intensely performative: we expect people to act in a particular way and view the rows on screen as a performance, an entertainment, although as far as we are aware it is genuinely felt and really happening. Chapter 3 looked at performance in TV fiction. However, while character and acting in creative, imagined work are something that we are familiar with, we need to acknowledge that performance is a big part of factual television too.

TV personalities

This can work in a couple of ways. As discussed, there is the performance of participants – the contestants in *Big Brother* or *The Apprentice*, the mum and the man on *Trisha Goddard*, or even the author film-makers like Jon Ronson or Bruce Parry. However, the 'television personality' is also an important figure in our understanding of television and its texts. Television personalities dominate factual broadcasting. They are familiar faces that strike a chord with the public in particular programmes and can then be inserted into other texts and situations. Most importantly they bring something to the texts – the audience's knowledge of them and assessment of their character. This may, of course, be nothing like their real self – we do not really know them – but a persona is constructed that leads us to certain assumptions about them. Ultimately we are imposing an identity on them, projecting what we want to see. Once this is established, this persona can be reinforced, duplicated or occasionally undermined.

Often TV personalities come to the screen because of a particular skill or area of knowledge: Alan Titchmarsh is a gardener, David Dickinson an antique dealer, Jeremy Clarkson knows about cars. We got to know them in these guises but they have also become well-known personalities way beyond this sphere of interest. Titchmarsh has a wry and intimate way with the audience, his Yorkshire background communicates a kind of down-to-earth common sense and he is able to impart information with a relaxed good humour. He is perceived to be particularly popular with older women and has been used in other kinds of programme without his trowel and wellies, from *A Natural History of Britain* (BBC 2005) to presenter of the Proms.

Clarkson, by contrast, has built a reputation as an affable, funny, if rather reactionary and splenetic voice of menopausal middle-aged men. His motoring programmes (notably *Top Gear*) built up this constituency, to the extent that collections of his newspaper columns are at the top of the book bestseller lists and his TV appearances have ranged from documentaries on Victorian engineer Brunel to programmes following him round Europe. His fans clearly see something of themselves in him. At the same time this is sufficiently complex, and his TV presence engaging and funny enough, to pull in other audiences too and occasionally confound expectations – his European series *Jeremy Clarkson Meets the Neighbours* (BBC 2002) was notably less xenophobic than some might have expected.

Television personalities use real people and real traits but are essentially constructions we make ourselves. We respond to what we see on screen, we see what we want to see. This can be seen sometimes in the reactions to the deaths of TV personalities. In 2005 the long-standing host of Channel 4's daytime quiz show

Countdown and anchor for Yorkshire's local news, Richard Whiteley, died suddenly and there was a national outpouring of grief. Part of this resulted from the early death of a palpably nice man but there was something else too. Whiteley had a relaxed, modest style, made amiably lame jokes and just seemed to want everyone to be happy. Perhaps viewers saw something they wanted to be or something they wanted in their lives. His departure as a constant reassuring presence upset us because we projected our needs onto him and we expected him always to be there, even if we were not regular viewers of his show. This is what television can do: its immersion in everyday life provides us with a mirror we put up to ourselves and to the world around us.

Think about . . .
Think of a TV personality that you have responded to positively, and another that has created a negative response in you. What is the nature of, respectively, their appeal and your antipathy?

Fact on television is, then, something of a minefield. Fact can be presented as entertainment, analysis and argument or as an objective statement. We also need to differentiate between the content of the programme, its subject, and the programme itself and the way it is constructed. To take *Tribe* as an example: we may have views on Africa and the problems facing tribal societies and we will need to assess the information in the programme. However, we also need to analyse *Tribe* as a text in itself – is it well made? Is it entertaining and gripping regardless of its subject? Has it something to say to us beyond the information it is imparting? John Corner has developed a useful way to consider this problem. He distinguishes between 'thin texts', programmes or news items that are primarily concerned with giving us information and have little to offer besides, and 'thick texts', which can be analysed on a number of levels (2001: 125).

TV fact can help us get nearer some kind of truth, but we need to understand the processes of mediation that it adopts and the assumptions and motivations behind the text. We must ask how our responses are being formulated, and perhaps manipulated, and use the text to think for ourselves.

Conclusion

In conclusion I would like to summarise some of the points made and the questions raised in this book, and consider where they have taken us.

First, we need to think about the distinctiveness of television as a medium. Key points to remember here include:

- The importance of the domestic and the everyday to television – TV comes to us in the home and becomes part of our environment. This involves a different relationship between text and viewer than both cinema or theatre.
- TV's history as a mass medium reaching vast audiences. While this may be changing, it is important to recognise that the medium is informed by this past.
- When they are broadcast, television texts exist as part of a 'flow' of material and the nature of the text is affected by other material in this flow.

Then we need to consider the context of the text. Questions to ask include:

- What kinds of institutions have created the text? Who has produced it? What channel is it on? Is it being broadcast at all or are we consuming it in some other way?
- What is the political and economic situation both within these institutions and in the wider culture at the moment of production? To what extent is the text the product of its time?
- How is the text scheduled? Who is the intended audience and what kind of reaction does it stimulate?

It's also very important to think about what viewers, including, of course, ourselves, are bringing to the text. This includes:

- Cultural identity
- Previous experience of the text
- Experience of other television texts
- Mood while we watch
- Personal history and values

All of these questions need to be asked if we want to really understand the text. If we are truly 'active viewers', we need to interrogate it on all these levels. However, much of our viewing is inherently 'active' – we have a dynamic relationship with the text, and as it is attempting to engage us, we are trying to engage with it. It is this process that creates meaning, for meaning is not something that can be found purely within the text. It is not an inert property that we can separate and define, proclaiming that we have discovered what it all means. Texts may well *suggest* certain readings but meaning is something that we make through our consumption of it. Our emotional responses, evaluations and intellectual deductions create an understanding of the text that may be different in some respects to that of other viewers.

John Ellis says that 'television provides routes towards understanding ... perspectives rather than answers. That is why it is important' (2004). The extraordinarily varied forms that make up the medium contribute to this, as well as the relationship between text and viewer. Television programmes offer a range of perspectives through forming a collective 'flow', but we should also recognise that individually they can allow various responses. TV texts can be open enough to do this and they can also be very sophisticated, or 'rich'. We can read a lot into them because there is a lot there, made up of three different elements that work together with us as we create meaning (adapted from Ellis, 2004):

- Aesthetics – TV programmes convey meaning through the way they look, their visual style.
- Emotional expression – how does the text make us feel?
- Social document – what is the text telling us about the society in which it is made?

Television studies has had something of a crisis of confidence, because television has experienced that crisis too, despite, or even because of, its status as a mass medium. It easy to underestimate or devalue TV, because it is so familiar – it is just there, something we watch every day and probably always have done. When we come home from college or work, there it is in the corner of the room. Yet its place at the heart of our experience makes it all the more important. As the dominant entertainment form of the last fifty years, it is inevitable that some of the best works of art have been on television.

Hopefully this book will have made you feel even more strongly than you did before that that is the case. As such, studying television is not only justified, I would argue that it is necessary. It is necessary not just because it is a sociological phenomenon, not just for its effects on its viewers (and its viewers' effects on the medium), but because its texts demand to be studied.

It is likely that the nature of television will change very dramatically over the next few years. The process of that change is already well under way and the television industry of today would have been unthinkable as recently as ten years ago. The relationship between viewer and text is, I believe, dynamic enough to withstand change; while the delivery systems and industrial contexts might be different, there will still be television texts that we want to watch and we want to understand.

Bibliography

Abercrombie, Nicholas and Brian Longhurst (1998) *Audiences: A Sociological Theory of Performance and Imagination* (London: Sage)

Adorno, Theodor and Max Horkheimer (2001) 'The Culture Industry' in Durham, Gigi Meenakshi and Douglas. M. Kellner (eds), *Media and Cultural Studies: Keyworks* (Oxford: Blackwell)

Althusser, Louis (2001), 'Ideology and the Ideological State Apparatus' (first published in Meenakshi Gigi Durham and Douglas. M. Kellner (eds), *Media and Cultural Studies: Keyworks* (Oxford: Blackwell)

Ang, Ien (1985) *Watching Dallas: Soap Opera and the Melodramatic Imagination* (London: Methuen)

Aufderheide, Patricia (2004) 'Public Television' in Horace Newcomb (ed.), *Encyclopedia of Television* (4 vols) (Chicago, IL: Fitzroy Dearborn)

Barker, Martin and Julian Petley (2001) *Ill Effects: The Media/Violence Debate* (London: Routledge)

Barthes, Roland (1972) *Mythologies* (first published in France in 1957) (London: Jonathan Cape)

Barthes, Roland (1977) (first published in France in 1968) 'The Death of the Author' in *Image, Music, Text* (London: Fontana)

Bellamy, Robert V. (2004) 'Remote Control Device' in Horace Newcomb (ed.), *The Encyclopedia of Television* (4 vols) (Chicago, IL: Fitzroy Dearborn)

Biressi, Anita and Heather Nunn (2005) *Reality TV: Realism and Revelation* (London: Wallflower Press)

Bonner, Paul and Lesley Aston (2003) *Independent Television in Britain: Volume 6: New Developments in Independent Television, 1981–92: Channel 4, TV-am, Cable and Satellite* (Basingstoke: Palgrave Macmillan)

Bourdieu, Pierre (1998) *On Television and Journalism* (London: Pluto Press)

Bordwell, David and Kristin Thompson (1979) *Film Art* (McGraw-Hill)

Brandt, George (1981) *British Television Drama* (Cambridge: Cambridge University Press)

Brunsdon, Charlotte (1990) 'Problems with Quality', *Screen* 31:1, Spring

Brunsdon, Charlotte (2000) *The Feminist, the Housewife and Soap Opera* (Oxford: Oxford University Press)

Brunsdon, Charlotte (2004) 'Television Studies' in Horace Newcomb (ed.), *The Encyclopedia of Television* (4 vols) (Chicago, IL: Fitzroy Dearborn)

Caldwell, John T. (1995) *Televisuality: Style, Crisis and Authority in American Television* (New Brunswick, NJ: Rutgers University Press)

Caldwell, John T. (2002) 'New Media/Old Augmentation: Television, Internet and Interactivity' in Ann Jerslev (ed.), *Realism and Reality in Film and Media* (Copenhagen: Northern Lights)

Cardwell, Sarah (2006) 'Television Aesthetics' in *Critical Studies in Television* vol. 1 no. 1

Caughie, John (2000) *Television Drama: Realism, Modernism, and British Culture* (Oxford: Oxford University Press)

Caughie, John (2005) 'Telephilia, Distraction and the Author', paper delivered at the *Cultures of British TV Drama* conference, September, University of Reading

Cooke, Lez (2003) *British Television Drama: A History* (London: BFI)

Corner, John (ed.) (1991) *Popular Television in Britain* (London: BFI)

Corner, John (2001) 'Studying Documentary' in Glen Creeber (ed.), *The Television Genre Book* (London: BFI)

Corner, John (2002) 'Documentary Values' in Ann Jerslev (ed.), *Realism and Reality in Film and Media* (Copenhagen: Northern Lights)

Creeber, Glen (ed.) (2006) *The Television Genre Book* (London: BFI)

Creeber, Glen (ed.) (2006) *Tele-Visions* (London: BFI)

Creeber, Glen (2006) 'The Joy of Text? Television and Textual Analysis' in *Critical Studies in Television* vol. 1 no. 1

Crisell, Andrew (1997) *An Introductory History of British Broadcasting* (London: Routledge)

Dovey, Jon (2000) *Freakshow: First Person Media and Factual TV* (London: Pluto Press)

Durham, Meenakshi Gigi and Douglas. M. Kellner (eds) (2001) *Media and Cultural Studies: Keyworks* (Oxford: Blackwell)

Ellis, John (1982) *Visible Fictions: Cinema, Television, Video* (London: Routledge)

Ellis, John (2000) *Seeing Things: Television in the Age of Uncertainty* (London: I. B. Tauris)

Ellis, John (2004) 'The Past as Television. Are Television Programmes More than Nostalgic Ephemera?', paper given at the FIAT conference

Fiske, John (1987) *Television Culture* (London: Methuen)

Gauntlett, David and Annette Hill (1999) *TV Living: TV, Culture and Everyday Life* (London: Routledge)

Glasgow University Media Group (1982) *Really Bad News* (London: Writers and Readers)

Grierson, John (1979) *Grierson on Documentary* (London: Faber and Faber)

Hall, Stuart (1980) 'Encoding/Decoding' In Hall *et al.* (ed.), *Culture, Media, Language* (London: Hutchinson)

Hartley, John (2001) 'The Infotainment Debate' in Glen Creeber (ed.), *The Television Genre Book* (London: BFI)

Herman, Edward and Noam Chomsky (2001) 'Manufacturing Consent – The Propaganda Model' (First published in 1988) in Meenakshi Gigi Durham and Douglas M. Kellner (eds), *Media and Cultural Studies: Keyworks* (Oxford: Blackwell)

Hills, Matt (2006) 'Fandom and Fan Studies' in Glen Creeber (ed.), *Tele-Visions* (London: BFI)

Hilmes, Michele (2003) *The Television History Book* (London: BFI)

Jacobs, Jason (2000) *The Intimate Screen* (Oxford: Oxford University Press)

Jacobs, Jason (2001) 'Issues of Judgment and Value in Television Studies', *International Journal of Cultural Studies* vol. 4 no. 4, December

Jacobs, Jason (2006) 'The Television Archive: Past, Present and Future', *Critical Studies in Television* vol. 1 no. 1

Jacobson, Howard (1997) *Seriously Funny* (London: Channel 4 Books)

Jermyn, Deborah and Su Holmes (2005) *Understanding Reality Television* (London: Routledge)

Jermyn, Deborah and Su Holmes (2006) ' "The Audience is Dead: Long Live the Audience!" Interactivity, "Telephilia" and the Television Audience', *Critical Studies in Television* vol. 1 no. 1

Kelly, Richard (1998) *Alan Clarke* (London: Faber)

Kilborn, Richard (2000) *The Docusoap: A Critical Assessment* (Luton: University of Luton Press)

Lavery, David (2006) *Reading The Sopranos* (London: I. B. Tauris)

Lawson, Mark (2006) 'Why Newspapers Should Stop Publishing TV Reviews', *Critical Studies in Television* vol. 1 no. 1

Lewis, Justin (2001) 'Studying Television News' in Glen Creeber (ed.), *The Television Genre Book* (London: BFI)

Lury, Karen (2005) *Interpreting Television* (London: Hodder Arnold)

Lury, Karen (2006) 'The Ghost Concerns Us: Remembering Public Service Television', paper delivered at the *Screen* conference, June

Mast, Gerald (1973) *The Comic Mind* (New York: Bobbs-Merrill)

Miller, Toby (ed.) (2002) *Television Studies* (London: BFI)

Mills, Brett (2005) *Television Sitcom* (London: BFI)

Morley, David (1980) *The 'Nationwide' Audience: Structure and Decoding* (London: BFI)

Morley, David (1992) *Television, Audiences and Cultural Studies* (London: Routledge)

Neale, Steve and Frank Krutnik (1990) *Popular Film and Television Comedy* (London: Routledge)

Neale, Steve (2001) 'Genre and Television' in Glen Creeber (ed.), *The Television Genre Book* (London: BFI)

Nelson, Robin (1997) *Television Drama in Transition: Forms, Values and Cultural Change* (London: Macmillan)

Nelson, Robin (1997) 'Studying Television Drama' in Glen Creeber (ed.), *The Television Genre Book* (London: BFI)

Nelson, Robin (2006) 'Quality TV', *Critical Studies in Television* vol. 1 no. 1

Newcomb, Horace (ed.) (2004) *The Encyclopedia of Television* (4 vols) (Chicago, IL: Fitzroy Dearborn)

Nicholas, Kyle (2006) 'Post TV?: The Future of Television' in Glen Creeber (ed.), *Tele-Visions* (London: BFI)

Palmer, Gareth (2005) 'Class and Reality TV' in Deborah Jermyn and Su Holmes (eds), *Understanding Reality Television* (London: Routledge)

Prys, Catrin (2006) 'Issues in Television Authorship' in Glen Creeber (ed.), *Tele-Visions* (London: BFI)

Rolinson, Dave (2005) *Alan Clarke* (Manchester: Manchester University Press)

Sandbrook, Dominic (2005) *Never Had It So Good: Britain from Suez to the Beatles* (London: Jonathan Cape)

Sandbrook, Dominic (2006) *White Heat: Britain in the Swinging Sixties* (London: Jonathan Cape)

Shubik, Irene (2000) *Play for Today: The Evolution of Television Drama* (2nd ed) (Manchester: MUP)

Steemers, Jeanette (2003) *Selling Television* (London: BFI)

Tulloch, John (1990) *Television Drama: Agency, Audience and Myth* (London: Routledge)

Turner, Graeme, (1998/2006) *Film as Social Practice* (London: Routledge)

Williams, Raymond (1974) *Television: Technology and Cultural Form* (London: Routledge)

Winston, Brian (2000) *Lies, Damn Lies and Documentaries* (London: BFI)

Useful websites include:

www.bfi.org.uk

www.screenonline.org.uk

www.criticalstudiesintelevision.com

www.offthetelly.com

www.classic-tv.com

http://tv.cream.org

www.imdb.com

www.whirligig-tv.co.uk

www.televisionheaven.co.uk

www.museum.tv/archives/etv/index.html

www.kaleidoscope.org.uk

www.tvhistory.tv

www.birth-of-tv.org

Index

Numbers in bold refer to references in the grey boxes